THE FIRST DICTIONARY

H. Höfer
L. Gressmann
G. W. Smith

English-German

Drawings by *ems*

R. OLDENBOURG VERLAG
MÜNCHEN

THE FIRST DICTIONARY

Verfasser
Hanns Höfer
Ludwig Gressmann

Mitarbeit
Cedric Sherratt
Cornelia Haselberger
Rosemary Jackson

Illustrationen
G.W. Smith ('Gus')

© 1982 R. Oldenbourg Verlag GmbH, München

1. Auflage 1982   4 3 2 1   86 85 84 83

Gesamtherstellung: R. Oldenbourg, Graph. Betriebe GmbH, München

ISBN 3-486-10841-7

CONTENTS

1. Vocabulary English–German 5
2. Abbreviations 106
3. Homophones 108
4. Homonyms 109
5. Synonyms 110
6. Opposites 117
7. Prefixes and Suffixes 122
8. List of "A" words 123

Vorwort für den Lernenden

Das FIRST DICTIONARY dient gleichzeitig zum Nachschlagen und hilft beim Lernen der englischen Wörter. Wenn ein Wort nicht aufgeführt ist, kommt es im Lehrbuch wahrscheinlich nur vereinzelt vor und gehört deshalb meist nicht zu dem wichtigen „Lernwortschatz", der in Tests und in Abschlußprüfungen erfahrungsgemäß verlangt wird. Da aber alles, namentlich auch dieses Wörterbuch, unvollkommen ist, wurde auf jeder Seite ein breiter Rand gelassen für eigene Einträge des Benützers. Es ist zweckmäßig, die neuen Wörter so einzutragen, wie dies in den handgeschriebenen Beispielen geschehen ist. Innerhalb der Seite kommt es dabei nicht mehr auf die alphabetische Reihenfolge an.

Dies ist ein erstes Wörterbuch, und die Wörter sind in Spalten angeordnet wie in den Verzeichnissen im Englischbuch. Diese Anordnung ermöglicht es weiterhin, die deutsche Spalte abzudecken, um die Wortschatzkenntnisse sehr gezielt zu überprüfen. Freilich genügen diese englisch–deutschen Wortgleichungen nur für eine erste Orientierung. Die angegebene Übertragung ins Deutsche erfaßt nicht immer scharf genug die Bedeutung, die das Wort im englischen Sprachgebrauch besitzt. Aber das weiß man ja vom Unterricht her, wo man die Sprache im Zusammenhang anhand von Texten und in Situationen lernt.

Besonders wichtig sind die „A"-Wörter. Sie kommen gesprochen und geschrieben immer wieder vor, und es wird erwartet, daß man sie in eigenen sprachlichen Leistungen, wie bei der Beantwortung von Fragen, in Gesprächen, Briefen usw., richtig verwenden kann. Also mehr, als lediglich die Bedeutung erraten! Für Wiederholungs- und Übungszwecke sind diese Grundwörter am Ende des Wörterbuchs in einer eigenen Liste zusammengestellt. Zu diesem Grundwortschatz gehören auch die unerläßlichen Funktionswörter, wie Zahlwörter, Fürwörter, Verhältniswörter usw.

Natürlich ist die Einteilung der Wörter in A, B, C letztlich willkürlich und kann nur von den schulischen Anforderungen her „expedient" sein. Mit einiger Sicherheit läßt sich aber sagen, daß nach sechs Lernjahren, also in der 10. Klasse, ein Wortschatz vorausgesetzt wird, der so ziemlich alle „A"- und „B"-Wörter umfaßt. Dazu noch eine Anzahl „C"-Wörter, vor allem wenn sie im Unterricht vorgekommen sind. Wohl auch mal ein Wort, das, vom Lehrer vorgegeben oder als Eigenfund, in handschriftlicher Form ins DICTIONARY gelangt ist! Einige wenige Wörter sind mit „W" gekennzeichnet. Vor allem Schüler der Wirtschaftsschulen werden sich dafür interessieren.

Je länger man die Sprache lernt, desto umfangreicher wird selbstverständlich der aktive oder „produktive" Wortschatz, über den man sicher und nicht nur passiv oder „rezeptiv" verfügt. Die Zusätze A, B, C sind somit Orientierungshilfen für die ersten Englischjahre. Ein Lernender in der Oberstufe wird sehr wohl über einen produktiven Wortschatz verfügen, der mehr oder weniger sämtliche Wörter dieses ersten Wörterbuchs einschließt.

Neben der "List of "A" Words" (S. 122) können auch die Übersichten über Abkürzungen, gleichlautende Wörter sowie Wörter mit ähnlicher und gegensätzlicher Bedeutung von Nutzen sein. Hingegen gibt dieses Wörterbuch keine Definitionen oder Beispielsätze. Dies macht in der Regel das Lehrbuch und ist die Aufgabe des einsprachigen Wörterbuchs.

Sollte die eine oder andere Zeichnung hilfreich sein oder ein Schmunzeln hervorrufen, so ist dies ganz im Sinne des englischen Karikaturisten GUS.

H. H.   L. G.

A

a	eɪ	A	a
a, an	ə, ən	A	ein(e); pro, je
abandon	ə'bændən	B	verlassen, aufgeben
abbey	'æbɪ	C	Abtei
abbreviate	ə'bri:vɪeɪt	C	abkürzen
abbreviation	əbri:vɪ'eɪʃn	C	Abkürzung
able	eɪbl	A	fähig, imstande
be able to		A	können
ability	ə'bɪlətɪ	B	Fähigkeit
aboard	ə'bɔ:d	B	an Bord
abolish	ə'bɒlɪʃ	B	abschaffen
abolition	æbə'lɪʃn	C	Abschaffung
aboriginal = aborigine	æbə'rɪdʒɪnəl æbə'rɪdʒɪni:	C	(austr.) Ureinwohner
about	ə'baʊt	A	über; ungefähr; herum
be about to		A	im Begriff sein zu
what about …?		A	was ist mit …?
how about …?		A	wie wär's mit …?
above	ə'bʌv	A	über, oberhalb
above all	ə'bʌv ˌɔ:l	A	vor allem
abroad	ə'brɔ:d	A	im (ins) Ausland
from abroad		A	aus dem Ausland
absent	'æbsənt	A	abwesend
be absent		A	fehlen
absent-minded	'æbsənt'maɪndɪd	C	zerstreut
absence	'æbsəns	B	Abwesenheit
absolute(ly)	'æbsəlu:t	B	völlig, ganz
absorb	əb'sɔ:b	C	aufnehmen
absorbed (in)		C	vertieft (in)
abstract	'æbstrækt	B	abstrakt
abundant	ə'bʌndənt	C	reichlich
abuse	ə'bju:z	C	mißbrauchen
abuse	ə'bju:s	C	Mißbrauch
academic	ækə'demɪk	C	akademisch
accelerate	ək'seləreɪt	C	beschleunigen, Gas geben
accelerator	ək'seləreɪtə	C	Gaspedal
accent	'æksənt	B	Akzent; Betonung
accept	ək'sept	A	annehmen
acceptable	ək'septəbl	B	annehmbar
acceptance	ək'septəns	C	Annahme
access	'ækses	C	Zugang, Zugriff
accident	'æksɪdənt	A	Unfall
by accident		C	zufällig
accidental	æksɪ'dentl	C	zufällig
accommodate	ə'kɒmədeɪt	C	aufnehmen, unterbringen
accommodation	əkɒmə'deɪʃn	B	Unterkunft
accompany	ə'kʌmpənɪ	A	begleiten
accomplish	ə'kʌmplɪʃ	C	vollbringen
accordance	ə'kɔ:dəns	C	Übereinstimmung
in accordance with		C	in ~ mit
according to	ə'kɔ:dɪŋ tə	B	gemäß, nach
accordingly	ə'kɔ:dɪŋlɪ	C	(dem)entsprechend
account	ə'kaʊnt	B	Konto; Bericht
on account of		B	aufgrund
account for		C	s. erklären
take into account		C	berücksichtigen
accuracy	'ækjərəsɪ	C	Genauigkeit
accurate	'ækjərət	B	genau
accuse (of)	ə'kju:z	B	beschuldigen
accusation	ækju'zeɪʃn	C	Beschuldigung
accustomed to	ə'kʌstəmd	B	gewöhnt an
get accustomed to		B	s. gewöhnen an
ache	eɪk	A	Schmerz; weh tun
achieve	ə'tʃi:v	B	erringen, leisten
achievement	ə'tʃi:vmənt	B	Leistung

A remarkable achievement

acknowledge	ək'nɒlɪdʒ	C	bestätigen, anerkennen
acknowledg(e)ment	ək'nɒlɪdʒmənt	C	Bestätigung
acquaintance	ə'kweɪntəns	A	Bekannte(r), Bekanntschaft
acquainted (with)	ə'kweɪntɪd	B	bekannt (mit)
acquire	ə'kwaɪə	B	erwerben
acquisition	ækwɪ'zɪʃn	C	Erwerb(ung)
across	ə'krɒs	A	(quer) über; auf der anderen Seite
act	ækt	A	Handlung; handeln
Act of Parliament		C	Parlamentsakte, Gesetz
action	ækʃn	A	Tat, Vorgang
active	'æktɪv	B	aktiv, tätig
activity	æk'tɪvətɪ	B	Tätigkeit
actor; actress	æktə, -rɪs	A	Schauspieler(in)
actual(ly)	'æktʃʊəl	B	eigentlich
A.D. (= anno domini)		C	n. Chr.

A.D.

<u>absolutely</u>
|-----|
ja, unbedingt

<u>absurd</u>
absurd, albern

<u>accountancy</u>
Rechnungs-
wesen

<u>accountant</u>
Bilanz-
buchhalter

<u>acre</u>
(Flächenmaß
4047 m²)

adapt

adapt	əˈdæpt	C	anpassen; bearbeiten
adaptation	ˌædəpˈteɪʃn	C	Anpassung, Bearbeitung
add (to)	æd	A	hinzufügen
addict	ˈædɪkt	C	Süchtige(r)
addition	əˈdɪʃn	B	Addition, Hinzufügung
in addition		B	außerdem
in addition to		B	außer, zusätzlich zu
additional	əˈdɪʃənəl	B	zusätzlich
address	əˈdres	A	Adresse; anreden C
adequate	ˈædɪkwət	C	angemessen
adjective	ˈædʒɪktɪv	B	Adjektiv
adjust	əˈdʒʌst	C	einstellen; anpassen

To adjust

aggressive
aggressiv,
feindselig

administration	ˌədmɪnɪˈstreɪʃn	B	Verwaltung
admiral	ˈædmərəl	C	Admiral
admire	ədˈmaɪə	A	bewundern
admiration	ˌædməˈreɪʃn	B	Bewunderung
admirable	ˈædmərəbl	C	bewundernswert
admission	ədˈmɪʃn	C	Einlaß, Eintritt
admit	ədˈmɪt	A	zugeben
adolescent	ˌædəˈlesnt	C	Heranwachsende(r)
adopt	əˈdɒpt	B	übernehmen; adoptieren
adore	əˈdɔː	C	anbeten, verehren
adult	ˈædʌlt	B	Erwachsene(r)
advance	ədˈvɑːns	B	Fortschritt; vorrücken
in advance		B	im voraus
advanced	ədˈvɑːnst	B	fortgeschritten
advantage	ədˈvɑːntɪdʒ	A	Vorteil
adventure	ədˈventʃə	A	Abenteuer
adventurous	ədˈventʃərəs	C	abenteuerlich
adverb	ˈædvɜːb	B	Adverb
advertise	ˈædvətaɪz	B	Reklame machen für
advertising	ˈædvətaɪzɪŋ	C	Werbung, Reklame
advertisement	ədˈvɜːtɪsmənt / US: ˌædvəˈtaɪzmənt	B	Anzeige, Annonce
(= advert, ad)			

advice	ədˈvaɪs	B	Rat
advise	ədˈvaɪz	A	(be)raten
adviser	ədˈvaɪzə	C	Berater
advisable	ədˈvaɪzəbl	C	ratsam
aerial	ˈeərɪəl	C	Antenne
aeroplane	ˈeərəpleɪn	A	Flugzeug
affair	əˈfeə	B	Angelegenheit
affect	əˈfekt	C	berühren; betreffen
affection	əˈfekʃn	C	Zuneigung
affectionate	əˈfekʃənət	C	zugetan, herzlich
afford	əˈfɔːd	B	s. leisten
afraid	əˈfreɪd	A	ängstlich
be afraid (of)		A	s. fürchten (vor)
I'm afraid (that)...		B	leider...
Africa	ˈæfrɪkə	B	Afrika
African	ˈæfrɪkən	B	afrikanisch
after	ˈɑːftə	A	nach
after all		A	schließlich, doch noch
after that		A	(und) dann
afternoon	ˌɑːftəˈnuːn	A	Nachmittag
afterwards	ˈɑːftəwədz	A	nachher
again	əˈgeɪn, əˈgen	A	wieder
again and again		A	immer wieder
against	əˈgeɪnst, əˈgenst	A	gegen
age	eɪdʒ	A	Alter; Epoche B
what's her age?		A	wie alt ist sie?
aged (thirty)	eɪdʒd	B	(30 Jahre) alt
for ages		B	ewig, seit langem
agency	ˈeɪdʒənsɪ	A	Vertretung, Agentur
agent	ˈeɪdʒənt	A	Vertreter, Händler
ago	əˈgəʊ	A	vor (zeitl.)
long ago		A	vor langer Zeit
agree (with, to)	əˈgriː	A	zustimmen, einverstanden sein
as agreed (on, upon)		C	wie vereinbart
agreeable	əˈgriːəbl	C	angenehm, freundlich
agreement	əˈgriːmənt	B	Übereinstimmung, Vertrag
agriculture	ˈægrɪkʌltʃə	B	Landwirtschaft
agricultural	ˌægrɪˈkʌltʃərəl	B	landwirtschaftlich
ahead	əˈhed	B	voran
be ahead (of)		B	voraus sein
go ahead (with)		B	anfangen mit
aid	eɪd	B	Hilfe; helfen C
first aid		B	Erste Hilfe
aim	eɪm	A	Ziel, Zweck; zielen
aimless		B	ziellos
ain't	eɪnt	C	(Vulgärform für am/are/is/have/has + not)
air	eə	A	Luft
by air		A	per Flugzeug, mit Luftpost
in the open air		A	im Freien
be on the air		C	senden (Radio)

airbed	ˈeəbed	C	Luftmatratze
air-conditioning	ˌkəndɪʃənɪŋ	C	Klimaanlage
air-conditioned	ˌkəndɪʃənd	C	klimatisiert
aircraft	ˈeəkrɑːft	B	Flugzeug(e)
aircraft carrier	ˌ..kærɪə	C	Flugzeugträger
Air Force	ˈeəfɔːs	C	Luftwaffe
air-freight	ˈeəfreɪt	W	Luftfracht
air-hostess	ˈeəhəʊstɪs	B	Stewardeß
airline	ˈeəlaɪn	A	Fluglinie
airliner	ˈeəlaɪnə	C	Linienflugzeug
airmail	ˈeəmeɪl	A	Luftpost
airport	ˈeəpɔːt	A	Flughafen
air terminal	ˈeəˌtɜːmɪnəl	C	Flugabfertigung
alarm-clock	əˈlɑːmklɒk	A	Wecker
alarmed	əˈlɑːmd	C	bestürzt
album	ˈælbəm	C	Album
alcohol	ˈælkəhɒl	C	Alkohol
alcoholic	ˌælkəˈhɒlɪk	C	alkoholisch, Alkoholiker
ale	eɪl	B	Bier
A-levels	ˈeɪlevlz	C	(etwa:) Abitur
alien	ˈeɪljən	C	Fremder; fremd
alike	əˈlaɪk	C	gleich; ebenso
alive	əˈlaɪv	A	lebendig; am Leben
all	ɔːl	A	all(e, es); ganz
at all	əˈtɔːl	A	überhaupt
all day		A	den ganzen Tag
all right		A	in Ordnung
it's all right with me		B	ich bin einverstanden
allow	əˈlaʊ	A	erlauben
be allowed to		A	dürfen
allowance	əˈlaʊəns	B	Zuwendung; (US:) Taschengeld
almighty	ɔːlˈmaɪtɪ	C	allmächtig
almost	ˈɔːlməʊst	A	fast, beinahe
alone	əˈləʊn	A	allein
along	əˈlɒŋ	A	längs, entlang
aloud	əˈlaʊd	B	laut
alphabet	ˈælfəbet	B	Alphabet, Abc
alphabetical	ˌælfəˈbetɪkl	C	alphabetisch

To alter

the Alps	ælps	B	die Alpen
already	ɔːlˈredɪ	A	schon, bereits
also	ˈɔːlsəʊ	A	auch; außerdem
altar	ˈɔːltə	C	Altar
alter	ˈɔːltə	C	(s.) (ver)ändern
alteration	ˌɔːltəˈreɪʃn	C	(Ver-)Änderung
alternative	ɔːlˈtɜːnətɪv	C	Alternative, Wahl
although	ɔːlˈðəʊ	A	obwohl
altitude	ˈæltɪtjuːd	C	Höhe
altogether	ˌɔːltəˈgeðə	B	ganz; im ganzen
aluminium		C	Aluminium
	ˌæljʊˈmɪnjəm		
(US) aluminum	əˈluːmɪnəm		
always	ˈɔːlweɪz, -əz	A	immer
a.m.	ˈeɪem	A	früh, vormittags
amateur	ˈæmətə	C	Amateur
amaze	əˈmeɪz	B	erstaunen
amazement	əˈmeɪzmənt	B	Erstaunen
amazing	əˈmeɪzɪŋ	B	erstaunlich
ambassador	æmˈbæsədə	B	Botschafter
ambition	æmˈbɪʃn	B	Ehrgeiz
ambitious	æmˈbɪʃəs	B	ehrgeizig
ambulance	ˈæmbjʊləns	A	Krankenwagen
America	əˈmerɪkə	A	Amerika, USA
American	əˈmerɪkən	A	amerikanisch, Amerikaner(in)
amid(st)	əˈmɪd(st)	C	inmitten
amnesty	ˈæmnəstɪ	C	Amnestie
among(st)	əˈmʌŋ(st)	A	unter (mehreren)
be among		B	zählen zu, gehören
among other things		B	unter anderem
amount	əˈmaʊnt	A	Betrag, Menge
amount to		A	s. belaufen auf, betragen
ample	æmpl	C	reichlich
amplifier	ˈæmplɪfaɪə	C	Verstärker
amuse	əˈmjuːz	A	unterhalten, belustigen
amusement		B	Unterhaltung
amusing	əˈmjuːzɪŋ	B	unterhaltsam
analyse(-yze)	ˈænəlaɪz	C	analysieren
ancestor	ˈænsestə	B	Vorfahre
anchor	ˈæŋkə	C	Anker
ancient	ˈeɪnʃənt	B	alt, ehemalig
and	ænd, ənd	A	und
and so on	əndˌˈsəʊˌɒn	A	und so weiter
anecdote	ˈænɪkdəʊt	C	Anekdote
angel	ˈeɪndʒəl	C	Engel
anger	ˈæŋgə	B	Ärger, Zorn
angry	ˈæŋgrɪ	A	ärgerlich, zornig
angling	ˈæŋglɪŋ	C	angeln
Anglo-...	ˈæŋgləʊ	C	Anglo-
Anglo-Saxon		C	angelsächsisch
	ˌæŋgləʊˈsæksən		
animal	ˈænɪməl	A	Tier
ankle	æŋkl	B	Knöchel

ankle

*alcoholism
Alkoholismus,
Trunksucht*

anniversary

antenna
Antenne

anniversary	æniˈvɜːsəri	C	Geburts-, Jahrestag
announce	əˈnaʊns	B	ankündigen
announcement	əˈnaʊnsmənt	B	Ankündigung, Ansage
annoy	əˈnɔɪ	B	(ver)ärgern
annoyed	əˈnɔɪd	B	verärgert
annoying	əˈnɔɪɪŋ	B	ärgerlich
annual	ˈænjʊəl	B	jährlich
anorak	ˈænəræk	C	Anorak
another	əˈnʌðə	A	ein(e) andere(r), noch eine(r)
one another		A	einander, sich
answer	ˈɑːnsə	A	Antwort; antworten
ant	ænt	C	Ameise
anthem	ˈænθəm	C	Hymne
anti-...	ˈænti	C	anti-, ...feindlich
anticipate	ænˈtɪsɪpeɪt	C	voraussehen
antique	ænˈtiːk	B	antik, alt
antiques	ænˈtiːks	C	Antiquitäten
anxious	ˈæŋkʃəs	B	besorgt
be anxious to		C	bestrebt sein
anxiety	æŋˈzaɪəti	C	Angst, Besorgnis
any	ˈeni	A	(irgend)ein(e); jede(r) (beliebige)
not any		A	kein(e)
anybody	ˈenibɒdi	A	(irgend)jemand; jeder (beliebige)
anyhow	ˈenihaʊ	B	irgendwie; jedenfalls
anyone	ˈeniwʌn	A	(irgend)jemand; jeder (beliebige)
anything	ˈeniθɪŋ	A	(irgend)etwas; alles
anyway	ˈeniweɪ	A	ohnehin, sowieso
anywhere	ˈeniweə	A	irgendwo(hin)
apart	əˈpɑːt	A	auseinander, extra
apart from		A	abgesehen von, außer
apartment	əˈpɑːtmənt	A	Appartement, Wohnung
ape	eɪp	C	(Menschen-)Affe
apologise(-ize) for		A	(s.) entschuldigen (wegen)
	əˈpɒlədʒaɪz		
apology	əˈpɒlədʒi	B	Entschuldigung

apartheid
(Rassentrennung in Südafrika)

apostrophe	əˈpɒstrəfi	C	Apostroph
appalling	əˈpɔːlɪŋ	C	erschreckend, entsetzlich
appalled	əˈpɔːld	C	entsetzt
apparent	əˈpærənt	C	offenbar
appeal to	əˈpiːl	C	zusagen, gefallen
appear	əˈpɪə	A	erscheinen
appearance	əˈpɪərəns	B	Erscheinung
appendix	əˈpendɪks	C	Blinddarm; Anhang
appendicitis	əpendɪˈsaɪtɪs	C	Blinddarmentzündung
appetite	ˈæpɪtaɪt	B	Appetit
applaud	əˈplɔːd	B	applaudieren
applause	əˈplɔːz	B	Beifall
apple	æpl	A	Apfel
appliance	əˈplaɪəns	C	Gerät
applicant	ˈæplɪkənt	C	Bewerber(in)
application	æplɪˈkeɪʃn	B	Bewerbung; Anwendung C
apply (to)	əˈplaɪ	C	anwenden, gelten
apply (for, to)		A	s. bewerben (um, bei)

To apply for a job

appoint	əˈpɔɪnt	C	ernennen
appointment	əˈpɔɪntmənt	A	Verabredung, Termin; Ernennung C
appreciate	əˈpriːʃieɪt	B	schätzen, danken für
appreciation	əpriːʃiˈeɪʃn	C	Würdigung, Dank
apprentice	əˈprentɪs	B	Lehrling
apprenticeship	əˈprentɪsʃɪp	B	Lehre, Lehrzeit
approach	əˈprəʊtʃ	B	s. nähern; ansprechen; Herannahen; Methode
appropriate	əˈprəʊpriət	C	angemessen, passend
approve	əˈpruːv	C	billigen
approval	əˈpruːvl	C	Zustimmung
approximate(ly)	əˈprɒksɪmət(li)	B	annähernd; ungefähr

To apologise

apricot	'eɪprɪkɒt C	Aprikose	
April	'eɪprəl A	April	
apt	æpt C	treffend, passend	
be apt to		C	dazu neigen
aptitude	'æptɪtjuːd C	Fähigkeit, Talent	
aquarium	ə'kweərɪəm B	Aquarium	
Arab	'ærəb C	Araber, arabisch	
Arabic	'ærəbɪk C	arabisch (Sprache)	
arch	aːtʃ C	Bogen	
archaeology	aːkɪ'ɒlədʒɪ C	Archäologie	
archaeologist	aːkɪ'ɒlədʒɪst	C	Archäologe
archbishop	aːtʃ'bɪʃəp B	Erzbischof	
architect	'aːkɪtekt C	Architekt	
architecture	'aːkɪtektʃə C	Architektur	
arctic	'aːktɪk C	arktisch, Polar-	
area	'eərɪə A	Fläche, Gebiet	
argue	'aːgjuː A	streiten, einwenden	
argument	'aːgjʊmənt B	Argument; Streit	
arise	ə'raɪz B	aufsteigen,	
arose	ə'rəʊz		s. erheben
arisen	ə'rɪzn		
arithmetic	ə'rɪθmətɪk B	Rechnen	
arm	aːm A	Arm; Waffe, bewaffnen C	
armchair	'aːmtʃeə A	Lehnstuhl	
army	'aːmɪ B	Heer, Armee	
around	ə'raʊnd A	um... herum	
arrange	ə'reɪndʒ A	vereinbaren, veranlassen	
arrangement	ə'reɪndʒmənt B	Anordnung; Abmachung	
arrest	ə'rest A	verhaften	
arrive	ə'raɪv A	ankommen	
arrival	ə'raɪvl A	Ankunft	
arrow	'ærəʊ C	Pfeil	
art	aːt A	Kunst	
arts	aːts C	Geisteswissenschaften	
article	'aːtɪkl A	Artikel	
artificial	aːtɪ'fɪʃl B	künstlich	
artist	'aːtɪst A	Künstler	
as	æz, əz A	als; da; während	
as ... as	əz...əz A	ebenso ... wie	
as far as	əz faːr əz A	bis (örtl.)	
as if (= though)	əz ɪf A	als ob	
as to	æz tə C	bezüglich	
as well	əz wel A	auch, ebenso	
as well as	əz wel əz A	sowie	
as yet	əz jet C	bis jetzt	
ash(es)	'æʃɪz B	Asche	
Ash Wednesday		C	Aschermittwoch
ashamed	ə'ʃeɪmd B	beschämt	
be ashamed of		B	s. schämen (wegen)
ashtray	'æʃtreɪ C	Aschenbecher	
Asia	'eɪʃə B	Asien	
Asian	'eɪʃn B	asiatisch; Asiate	
aside	ə'saɪd B	beiseite, seitwärts	
aside from (US)		C	abgesehen von, neben
ask (for)	aːsk A	fragen (nach); bitten (um)	
ask the way		A	nach dem Weg fragen
be asleep	ə'sliːp A	schlafen	
fall asleep		A	einschlafen
aspect	'æspekt C	Aspekt, Seite	
assassinate	ə'sæsɪneɪt C	ermorden	
assemble	ə'sembl B	versammeln; montieren	
assembly	ə'semblɪ B	Versammlung; Montage C	
assembly line		C	Fließband
assert	ə'sɜːt C	behaupten	
assist	ə'sɪst B	unterstützen, helfen	
assistance	ə'sɪstəns C	Unterstützung, Hilfe	
assistant	ə'sɪstənt A	Assistent	
associate (with)		C	verbinden
	ə'səʊʃɪeɪt		
association	əsəʊsɪ'eɪʃn C	Verbindung, Verband	
assume	ə'sjuːm C	übernehmen; annehmen	
assumption	ə'sʌmpʃn C	Annahme, Vermutung	
assure	ə'ʃʊə B	versichern, zusichern	
asterisk	'æstərɪsk C	Sternchen (*)	
astonish	ə'stɒnɪʃ A	erstaunen, wundern	
astonishing	ə'stɒnɪʃɪŋ A	erstaunlich	
astonished	ə'stɒnɪʃt B	erstaunt	
astonishment		B	Erstaunen
astronaut	'æstrənɔːt A	Astronaut	
at	æt, ət A	an, in, um	
at all	ət ɔːl A	überhaupt	
at best	ət best C	höchstens	
at first	ət fɜːst A	zuerst, anfangs	
at last	ət laːst A	zuletzt, endlich	
at least	ət liːst A	wenigstens	
at most	ət məʊst C	höchstens	
at once	ət wʌns A	sofort, gleichzeitig C	
athletics	æθ'letɪks C	Leichtathletik	
Atlantic (Ocean)		C	Atlantik
	ət'læntɪk		
atlas	'ætləs C	Atlas	
atmosphere	'ætməsfɪə B	Atmosphäre	
atom	'ætəm A	Atom	
atomic	ə'tɒmɪk A	Atom-, atomar	
attach	ə'tætʃ B	befestigen; beilegen	
attack	ə'tæk A	angreifen; Angriff	
attempt	ə'temt B	versuchen; Versuch	
attend	ə'tend A	besuchen (Schule)	
attend (to)		C	bedienen, erledigen

attend

ashore
an Land

athlete
/'æθliːt/
Athlet

attendance

attendance	əˈtendəns	C	Anwesenheit
attendant	əˈtendənt	C	Aufseher(in), Wärter(in)
attention	əˈtenʃn	A	Aufmerksamkeit
pay attention (to)		A	aufpassen (auf)
attentive	əˈtentɪv	C	aufmerksam
attic	ˈætɪk	C	Dachgeschoß, Speicher
attitude	ˈætɪtjuːd	B	Haltung, Einstellung
attract	əˈtrækt	B	anziehen, fesseln
attraction	əˈtrækʃn	B	Anziehung(skraft); Reiz
attractive	əˈtræktɪv	A	anziehend, reizvoll
auction (sale)	ˈɔːkʃən	C	Versteigerung
audience	ˈɔːdɪəns	C	Zuhörer, Publikum
August	ˈɔːgəst	A	August
aunt	ɑːnt	A	Tante
au pair (girl)	əʊˈpeə	B	Au-pair(-Mädchen)
Australia	ɒˈstreɪljə	A	Australien
Australian	ɒˈstreɪljən	A	australisch; Australier(in)
Austria	ˈɒstrɪə	A	Österreich
Austrian	ˈɒstrɪən	A	österreichisch; Österreicher(in)
authentic	ɔːˈθentɪk	C	authentisch, echt
author	ˈɔːθə	B	Autor, Verfasser
authorise(-ize)	ˈɔːθəraɪz	C	ermächtigen
authority	ɔːˈθɒrɪtɪ	B	Autorität, Behörde
autograph	ˈɔːtəgrɑːf	C	Autogramm
automatic	ɔːtəˈmætɪk	A	automatisch

aviation	eɪvɪˈeɪʃn	C	Luftfahrt
avoid	əˈvɔɪd	A	vermeiden
await	əˈweɪt	C	erwarten
awake	əˈweɪk	B	wecken; aufwachen
awoke	əˈwəʊk		
awoken	əˈwəʊkən		
be awake		A	wach, munter sein
award	əˈwɔːd	C	zuerkennen, verleihen

To be aware

aware	əˈweə	C	gewahr
be aware (of)		C	s. ... bewußt sein
away	əˈweɪ	A	weg, fort
awful	ˈɔːfʊl	A	furchtbar
awkward	ˈɔːkwəd	C	komisch, sonderbar
axe	æks	C	Axt, Beil

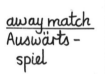

*away match
Auswärts-
spiel*

It opens automatically

automation	ɔːtəˈmeɪʃn	C	Automation
automobile	ˈɔːtəməbiːl	C	Auto(mobil)
autumn	ˈɔːtəm	A	Herbst
auxiliary	ɔːgˈzɪljərɪ	C	Hilfszeitwort
available	əˈveɪləbl	B	verfügbar, erhältlich
avalanche	ˈævəlɑːntʃ	C	Lawine
avenue	ˈævənjuː	C	Straße, Allee
average	ˈævərɪdʒ	B	Durchschnitt, durchschnittlich
on (an) average		C	im Durchschnitt

B

b	biː	A	b
baby	ˈbeɪbɪ	A	Baby
babysitter	ˈbeɪbɪsɪtə	C	Babysitter
bachelor	ˈbætʃələ	B	Junggeselle
Bachelor of Arts (B.A.)		C	1. akad. Grad (Geistesw.)
Bachelor of Science (=B.S., B.Sc.)		C	1. akad. Grad (Naturw.)
back	bæk	A	zurück, Rücken; unterstützen C
background	ˈbækgraʊnd	A	Hintergrund
backwards	ˈbækwədz	A	rückwärts, zurück
bacon	ˈbeɪkən	A	(Schinken-)Speck
bad	bæd	A	schlecht, schlimm, böse
worse	wɜːs		
worst	wɜːst		
badly off	ˈbædlɪ ˈɒf	C	arm
badge	bædʒ	C	Abzeichen
badminton	ˈbædmɪntən	C	Federball

bag	bæg	A	Tasche, Tüte
bagpipes	'bægpaɪps	B	Dudelsack
baggage	'bægɪdʒ	B	(US) Gepäck
bake	beɪk	A	backen
baker	'beɪkə	A	Bäcker
balance	'bæləns	C	Gleichgewicht
balance of payments		W	Zahlungsbilanz
balance sheet	'..ʃi:t	W	Bilanz
balcony	'bælkənɪ	C	Balkon
bald	bɔ:ld	C	kahl
ball	bɔ:l	A	Ball
ballpoint(pen) 'bɔ:lpɔɪnt		B	Kugelschreiber
ballad	'bæləd	C	Ballade
ballet	'bæleɪ	B	Ballett
balloon	bə'lu:n	C	(Luft-)Ballon, Sprechblase
ballot	'bælət	C	Stimmzettel; ausgezählte Stimme
ban	bæn	C	verbieten
banana	bə'na:nə	A	Banane
band	bænd	A	Band
bandage	'bændɪdʒ	B	Verband
bang	bæŋ	C	Knall; klopfen
bank	bæŋk	A	Ufer; Bank
bank account 'bæŋk əkaʊnt		B	Bankkonto
bank draft 'bæŋk drɑ:ft		W	Bankscheck
bank holiday		C	(GB) öffentl. Feiertag
banking	'bæŋkɪŋ	W	Bankwesen
bank-note	'bæŋknəʊt	A	Banknote
bankrupt	'bæŋkrʌpt	C	bankrott
bankruptcy 'bæŋkrʌptsɪ		C	Bankrott
banner	'bænə	C	Transparent
baptise(-ize)	bæp'taɪz	C	taufen
bar	bɑ:	A	Stange; Bar
bar of chocolate		C	eine Tafel Schokolade
barber	'bɑ:bə	C	Barbier, Friseur
bare	beə	B	bloß
barely	'beəlɪ	B	kaum
bargain	'bɑ:gən	C	Sonderangebot, Gelegenheitskauf
bark	bɑ:k	B	bellen; Rinde C
barley	'bɑ:lɪ	C	Gerste
barman	'bɑ:mən	C	Barkellner
barn	bɑ:n	C	Scheune
baron	'bærən	C	Baron
baroque	bə'rɒk	C	Barock
barrel	'bærəl	B	Faß, Barrel
barrier	'bærɪə	B	Schranke, Hindernis
base	beɪs	C	Basis
baseball	'beɪsbɔ:l	B	Baseball
basement	'beɪsmənt	B	Keller
basic	'beɪsɪk	C	grundlegend
basis	'beɪsɪs	B	Grundlage
basin	beɪsn	C	Becken
basket	'bɑ:skɪt	A	Korb
basketball		B	Basketball
bat	bæt	C	Kricketschläger; Fledermaus

Bats

bath	bɑ:θ	A	Bad; Badewanne
bath	bɑ:θ	C	(das Baby) baden
bathroom	'bɑ:θrʊm	A	Bad
bathe	beɪð	C	baden
bathing costume		B	Badeanzug
baths	bɑ:ðz	C	Schwimmbad
battery	'bætərɪ	C	Batterie
battle	bætl	B	Schlacht, Kampf
Bavaria	bə'veərɪə	A	Bayern
Bavarian	bə'veərɪən	A	bayerisch
bay	beɪ	C	Bucht
B.C. (= before Christ)		C	v. Chr.
be	bi	A	sein; werden
was, were			
been	bi:n, bɪn		
be to		A	sollen
beach	bi:tʃ	A	Strand
beak	bi:k	C	Schnabel
beam	bi:m	C	Balken; Strahl; strahlen
bean	bi:n	A	Bohne
bear	beə	B	Bär
bear	beə	B	tragen, ertragen
bore	bɔ:		
borne	bɔ:n		
bear in mind		C	beachten, s. merken
beard	bɪəd	A	Bart
beast	bi:st	B	Tier
beastly	'bi:stlɪ	C	scheußlich
beat	bi:t	A	schlagen; Takt
beat	bi:t		
beaten	bi:tn		
beautiful	'bju:təfʊl	A	schön
beauty	'bju:tɪ	C	Schönheit
because	bɪ'kɒz	A	weil, da
because of		A	wegen

because of

barbecue /'bɑ:bɪkju:/ Grillparty

English	Pronunciation	Cat.	German
become	bɪˈkʌm	A	werden (zu)
became	bɪˈkeɪm		
become	bɪˈkʌm		
bed	bed	A	Bett
bed and breakfast place		C	Frühstückspension
bedroom	ˈbedrʊm	A	Schlafzimmer
bee	biː	C	Biene
beef	biːf	A	Rindfleisch
beefeater	ˈbiːfiːtə	C	Wächter (Tower)
beer	bɪə	A	Bier
beetle	ˈbiːtl	C	Käfer
before	bɪˈfɔː	A	vor(her), bevor, ehe
before long		B	in Kürze
beg	beg	C	betteln, bitten
I beg your pardon?		A	wie bitte?
	pɑːdn		
I (do) beg your pardon!		B	ich bitte um Entschuldigung
beggar	ˈbegə	C	Bettler
begin	bɪˈgɪn	A	anfangen
began	bɪˈgæn		
begun	bɪˈgʌn		
to begin with, ...		C	zunächst
beginning	bɪˈgɪnɪŋ	A	Anfang
on behalf of	bɪˈhɑːf	C	im Namen (von)
behave	bɪˈheɪv	A	s. (gut) benehmen
behaviour	bɪˈheɪvjə	B	Benehmen, Verhalten
behead	bɪˈhed	C	enthaupten
behind	bɪˈhaɪnd	A	hinter
beige	beɪʒ	B	beige
being	ˈbiːɪŋ	C	Wesen
Belgian	ˈbeldʒən	C	Belgier(in), belgisch
Belgium	ˈbeldʒəm	C	Belgien
belief (in)	bɪˈliːf	B	Glaube (an)
believe (in)	bɪˈliːv	A	glauben (an)
bell	bel	A	Glocke, Klingel
belly	ˈbelɪ	C	Bauch
belong (to)	bɪˈlɒŋ	A	gehören
below	bɪˈləʊ	A	unter(halb)
belt	belt	A	Gürtel
bench	bentʃ	C	Sitzbank
bend	bend	B	biegen; s. beugen
bent	bent		
bent			
beneath	bɪˈniːθ	B	unterhalb; unten
benefit	ˈbenɪfɪt	C	Gewinn; profitieren
beret	ˈbereɪ	C	Baskenmütze
berry	ˈberɪ	B	Beere
beside	bɪˈsaɪd	A	neben
besides	bɪˈsaɪdz	A	außerdem; außer
best seller	bestˈselə	B	Bestseller
best wishes	ˈwɪʃɪz	B	viele Grüße
bet	bet	C	wetten; Wette
bet, betted			
bet, betted			
betray	bɪˈtreɪ	C	verraten
better, best	ˈbetə, best	A	besser, am besten
had better		A	sollte lieber
between	bɪˈtwiːn	A	zwischen, unter
beyond	bɪˈjɒnd	B	jenseits
biased	ˈbaɪəst	C	voreingenommen
Bible	baɪbl	B	Bibel
bicycle	ˈbaɪsɪkl	A	Fahrrad
bid	bɪd	C	(an)bieten, entbieten
bade, bid	bæd, bɪd		
bidden	bɪdn		
big	bɪg	A	groß, dick
bike	baɪk	A	Fahrrad
bilingual	baɪˈlɪŋgwəl	C	zweisprachig
bill	bɪl	A	Rechnung; Gesetzesvorlage C
bill of exchange		W	Wechsel
	ˌɪksˈtʃeɪndʒ		
billion	ˈbɪljən	C	Billion; (US) Milliarde
billionaire	bɪljəˈneə	C	Multimillionär
bind	baɪnd	B	(an)binden
bound	baʊnd		
bound			
binding	ˈbaɪndɪŋ	C	(Ski-)Bindung
binoculars	bɪˈnɒkjʊləz	C	Fernglas
biography	baɪˈɒgrəfɪ	B	Lebensbeschreibung
biology	baɪˈɒlədʒɪ	A	Biologie
biological	baɪəˈlɒdʒɪkl	C	biologisch
bird	bɜːd	A	Vogel
birth	bɜːθ	B	Geburt
birthday	ˈbɜːθdeɪ	A	Geburtstag

The birthday cake

English	Pronunciation	Cat.	German
biscuit	ˈbɪskɪt	B	Keks
bishop	ˈbɪʃəp	C	Bischof
bit	bɪt	A	kl. Stück, kl. Menge
a (little) bit		A	ein (klein)wenig
bite	baɪt	A	beißen; kl. Imbiß
bit	bɪt		
bitten	bɪtn		
bitter	ˈbɪtə	B	bitter, Bitter(bier)
black	blæk	A	schwarz
blackbird	ˈblækbɜːd	C	Amsel

blackboard	'blækbɔ:d A	(Wand-)Tafel	
blackcurrants	C	schwarze	
	blæk'kʌrənts	Johannisbeeren	
blackmail	'blækmeɪl C	Erpressung; erpressen	
blacksmith	'blæksmɪθ C	Schmied	
blame	bleɪm B	tadeln; Tadel	
I am to blame	C	ich bin schuld daran	
blank	blæŋk C	leere Stelle, Lücke	
blanket	'blæŋkɪt B	Wolldecke	
blazer	'bleɪzə B	Blazer	
bleed	bli:d B	bluten	
bled	bled		
bled			
bless	bles C	segnen	
blind	blaɪnd A	blind	
blizzard	'blɪzəd C	Schneesturm	
block of flats	B	Wohnblock	
bloke	bləʊk C	Kerl, Mensch	
blond	blɒnd C	blond	
blonde	blɒnd C	Blondine	
blood	blʌd B	Blut	
bloody	'blʌdɪ B	blutig; verdammt	
bloom	blu:m C	Blüte; blühen	
blossom	'blɒsəm C	Blüte; aufblühen	
blouse	blaʊz A	Bluse	
blow	bləʊ B	Schlag; wehen,	
blew	blu:	blasen	
blown	bləʊn		
blow up	C	sprengen; vergrößern	
blue	blu: A	blau	
blunt	blʌnt B	stumpf	
blush	blʌʃ B	erröten	
board	bɔ:d A	Brett, (Wand-)Tafel; einsteigen C	
full board	C	Vollpension	
on board	A	an Bord	
boarding card	B	Bordkarte	
boarding house	B	Pension	
boarding school	B	Internat(sschule)	
boast	bəʊst C	prahlen	

The Boat Race

boat	bəʊt A	Boot, Schiff	
bobsleigh	'bɒbsleɪ C	Bob(schlitten)	
body	'bɒdɪ A	Körper; -schaft	
bodily	'bɒdɪlɪ C	körperlich	
boil	bɔɪl A	kochen, sieden	
bold	bəʊld C	kühn, dreist	
boldness	'bəʊldnɪs C	Kühnheit	
bolt	bəʊlt C	Bolzen, Schraube	
bomb	bɒm B	Bombe; bombardieren	
bonanza	bə'nænzə C	Glückssträhne, Goldgrube	
bone	bəʊn B	Knochen, Gräte	
bonfire	'bɒnfaɪə C	Feuer (im Freien)	
bonnet	'bɒnɪt C	Motorhaube, Haube	
book	bʊk A	Buch, Heft; buchen	
bookcase	'bʊkkeɪs B	Bücherschrank	
booking-office	A	Schalter, Kasse	
bookkeeper	'bʊkki:pə B	Buchhalter	
bookkeeping	'bʊkki:pɪŋ B	Buchführung	
booklet	'bʊklɪt C	Broschüre	
bookseller	'bʊkselə C	Buchhändler	
bookshelf	'bʊkʃelf A	Bücherbrett	
bookshelves	A	Bücherregal	
bookshop	'bʊkʃɒp A	Buchhandlung	
bookstall	'bʊkstɔ:l C	Zeitschriftenkiosk	
boom	bu:m C	(Hoch-)Konjunktur	
boomerang	'bu:məræŋ C	Bumerang	
boot	bu:t A	Stiefel; Kofferraum C	
booth,s	bu:ð,ðz C	Kabine	
border	'bɔ:də B	Grenze	
bore	bɔ: B	langweilen	
boredom	'bɔ:dəm C	Langeweile	
boring	'bɔ:rɪŋ A	langweilig	
born (on ...)	bɔ:n A	geboren (am ...)	
borrow	'bɒrəʊ A	borgen, entleihen	
boss	bɒs B	Chef, Boß	
both	bəʊθ A	beide(s)	
both... and	A	sowohl... als auch	
bother	'bɒðə A	belästigen, s. bemühen	
bottle	bɒtl A	Flasche	
bottom	'bɒtəm A	Boden, Grund	
at the bottom	A	unten	
be bound to	baʊnd B	wird bestimmt, müssen	
bound for ...	C	mit Reiseziel ...	
boutique	bʊ'ti:k C	Boutique	
bow	baʊ C	s. verneigen; (Schiffs-)Bug	
bow	bəʊ C	Bogen	
bow-wow	baʊ'waʊ C	wau-wau	
bowl	bəʊl B	Schale, Schüssel; Kegelkugel C	
bowler (hat)	'bəʊlə C	Melone	

bowler

borough /'bʌrə/ Stadtteil

It was bound to happen

bowls, bowling	bəʊlz,-ɪŋ	C	Kegelspiel
box	bɒks	A	Schachtel, Kiste; boxen
Boxing Day		C	Stephanitag (26.12.)
boy	bɔɪ	A	Bub, Junge
boyfriend		B	(fester) Freund
boy scout	ˈbɔɪskaʊt	B	Pfadfinder
bra	brɑː	C	Büstenhalter
bracelet	ˈbreɪslɪt	C	Armband
bracket	ˈbrækɪt	C	Klammer
brag	bræg	C	prahlen
brain	breɪn	B	Gehirn; Verstand
brake	breɪk	A	Bremse; bremsen
branch	brɑːntʃ	A	Ast, Zweig; Filiale C
branch off		C	abzweigen
brand	brænd	C	Marke
brand-new	ˌˈnjuː	C	nagelneu
brandy	ˈbrændɪ	C	Branntwein
brass	brɑːs	C	Messing
brave	breɪv	B	tapfer, mutig
bread	bred	A	Brot
bread-and-butter		C	bestrichenes Brot
breadth	bredθ	B	Breite, Weite
break	breɪk	A	brechen; Pause B
broke	brəʊk		
broken	ˈbrəʊkən		
break down		A	kaputtgehen
breakdown	ˈbreɪkdaʊn	B	Panne
break in		C	einbrechen
break out		C	ausbrechen
break up		C	zerbrechen
breakfast	ˈbrekfəst	A	Frühstück
have breakfast		A	frühstücken
breast	brest	B	Brust
breath	breθ		Atem
breathe	briːð	C	atmen
breathless	ˈbreθlɪs	C	atemlos
breed	briːd	C	züchten
bred	bred		
bred			
breeze	briːz	C	Brise
brevity	ˈbrevətɪ	C	Kürze
brew	bruː	C	brauen
brewery	ˈbruːərɪ	C	Brauerei
bribe	braɪb	C	bestechen
brick	brɪk	B	Ziegelstein
bricklayer	ˈbrɪkleɪə	C	Maurer
bride	braɪd	B	Braut
bridegroom	ˈbraɪdgruːm	B	Bräutigam
bridge	brɪdʒ	A	Brücke
brief	briːf	B	kurz, bündig
briefcase	ˈbriːfkeɪs	A	Aktenmappe, -tasche
bright	braɪt	B	glänzend; gescheit
brilliant	ˈbrɪljənt	C	brilliant
bring	brɪŋ	A	bringen
brought	brɔːt		
brought			
bring about		B	zustande bringen
bring up		B	erwähnen; erziehen
brisk	brɪsk	C	frisch, flott
Britain	brɪtn	A	Großbritannien
British	ˈbrɪtɪʃ	A	britisch
Briton	brɪtn	B	Brite, -in
broad	brɔːd	A	breit, weit
broaden	brɔːdn	C	(s.) verbreitern
broadcast	ˈbrɔːdkɑːst	B	senden; Sendung
broadcast			
broadcast			
broccoli	ˈbrɒkəlɪ	C	Broccoli
brochure	ˈbrəʊʃə	C	Broschüre, Prospekt
broke	brəʊk	C	pleite
broker	ˈbrəʊkə	C	Makler
brook	brʊk	C	Bach
broom	bruːm	C	Besen
brother	ˈbrʌðə	A	Bruder
brother-in-law		B	Schwager
brow	braʊ	B	Augenbraue
brown	braʊn	A	braun
brown bread		C	Schwarzbrot
brush	brʌʃ	A	bürsten; Bürste
bucket	ˈbʌkɪt	C	Eimer, Kübel
bud	bʌd	C	Knospe
budgerigar	ˈbʌdʒərɪgɑː	C	Wellensittich
(= budgie)			
budget	ˈbʌdʒɪt	C	Haushalt, Budget
buffalo	ˈbʌfələʊ	C	Büffel
bug	bʌg	C	Wanze; Abhörgerät
build	bɪld	A	bauen
built	bɪlt		
built			
build up		B	aufbauen, entwickeln
built-in		C	Einbau-
building	ˈbɪldɪŋ	A	Gebäude
bulb	bʌlb	C	Knolle; Glühbirne

brooch /brəʊtʃ/ Brosche

The bull

bull	bʊl	B	Bulle, Stier
bullfinch	'bʊlfɪntʃ	C	Dompfaff
bump	bʌmp	C	stoßen; Stoß
bumper	'bʌmpə	C	Stoßstange
bunch	bʌntʃ	B	Bund, Strauß
bundle	'bʌndl	C	Bündel; bündeln
bungalow	'bʌŋgələʊ	B	Bungalow
burden	'bɜːdən	C	Last, Bürde
burglar	'bɜːglə	C	Einbrecher
burn	bɜːn	A	(ver)brennen
burnt (=ed)	bɜːnt		
burnt (=ed)			
burst	bɜːst	B	bersten, platzen
burst			
burst			
bury	'berɪ	B	begraben
burial	'berɪəl	C	Begräbnis
bus	bʌs	A	Bus
bus stop	'bʌsstɒp	A	Bushaltestelle
bush	bʊʃ	B	Busch, Strauch
business	'bɪznɪs	A	Geschäft
do business with		B	Geschäfte tätigen (mit)
on business		C	geschäftlich
business letter		B	Geschäftsbrief
businessman		A	Geschäftsmann
busy	'bɪzɪ	A	beschäftigt; belebt
be busy		A	zu tun haben
but	bʌt	A	aber, sondern
all but		C	alle(s) außer
nothing but		B	nichts als, nur
butcher	'bʊtʃə	A	Metzger
butter	'bʌtə	A	Butter
butterfly	'bʌtəflaɪ	B	Schmetterling
button	bʌtn	A	Knopf; zuknöpfen
buy	baɪ	A	kaufen
bought	bɔːt		
bought			
buyer	'baɪə	C	Käufer(in)
buzzer	'bʌzə	C	Summer
by	baɪ	A	durch; von; neben; bis (Termin)
by bus		A	mit dem Bus

by + ing form		A	dadurch, daß; indem...
by now		C	inzwischen
by the way		A	übrigens
bye, bye-bye	'baɪ'baɪ	A	Wiedersehen!
by-election	'baɪɪˌlekʃn	C	Nachwahl

C

c	siː	A	c
cab	kæb	B	Taxi
cabbage	'kæbɪdʒ	B	Kohl
cabin	'kæbɪn	B	Kabine, Hütte
cabinet	'kæbɪnɪt	C	Kabinett
cable	keɪbl	C	Kabel; Telegramm
café	'kæfeɪ	A	Café
cafeteria	kæfɪ'tɪərɪə	B	Selbstbedienungs- lokal
cage	keɪdʒ	B	Käfig
cake	keɪk	A	Kuchen
calculate	'kælkjʊleɪt	B	(be)rechnen
calculation		C	Berechnung
	kælkjʊ'leɪʃn		
calculator	'kælkjʊleɪtə	A	Taschenrechner
calendar	'kælɪndə	B	Kalender
calf, ves	kɑːf, kɑːvz	B	Kalb; Wade C
call	kɔːl	A	rufen, nennen; anrufen, Anruf
call for		C	verlangen
call off		C	absagen
call on sb		B	jd. besuchen
call on sb to		C	auffordern
callbox	'kɔːlbɒks	B	Telefonzelle
be called		A	heißen
calm	kɑːm	A	ruhig; beruhigen B
calm down		C	(s.) beruhigen
calmness	'kɑːmnɪs	B	Ruhe
calorie	'kælərɪ	B	Kalorie
camel	'kæməl	C	Kamel
camera	'kæmərə	A	Fotoapparat, Kamera
camp	kæmp	A	Lager; kampieren
camper	'kæmpə	C	(US)Campingbus
camping	'kæmpɪŋ	A	Zelten
camp-site	'kæmpsaɪt	B	Campingplatz
campaign	kæm'peɪn	B	Kampagne, Feldzug; kämpfen (für)
can	kæn, kən, kn	A	kann
could	kʊd	A	konnte, könnte
can	kæn	B	Kanne; Konserve
Canada	'kænədə	A	Kanada
Canadian	kə'neɪdjən	B	kanadisch
canal	kə'næl	B	(künstl.) Kanal
cancel	kænsl	A	absagen, streichen
cancellation		C	Streichung
	kænsə'leɪʃn		

cancellation

bunnie
/'bʌnɪ/
Häschen

to buzz
summen

candidate

candidate	'kændɪdət	C	Kandidat, Bewerber
candle	kændl	B	Kerze
candy (US)	'kændɪ	C	Bonbon(s)
canoe	kə'nu:	C	Kanu
canteen	kæn'ti:n	B	Kantine
canvas	'kænvəs	C	Leinwand; Segeltuch
(go) canvassing	'kænvəsɪŋ	C	Wählerbesuche machen
cap	kæp	A	Mütze, Kappe
capable (of)	'keɪpəbl	B	fähig (zu)
capability	keɪpə'bɪlɪtɪ	C	Fähigkeit
capacity	kə'pæsətɪ	C	Kapazität; Fähigkeit
cape	keɪp	C	Kap; Umhang
capital	'kæpɪtl	A	Hauptstadt; Kapital W
capital letter		B	Großbuchstabe
Capitol	'kæpɪtl	C	Kapitol
captain	'kæptɪn	B	Kapitän; Hauptmann
caption	kæpʃn	C	Bildunterschrift
capture	'kæptʃə	C	fangen, erbeuten
car	kɑ:	A	Auto, Wagen
carbon (paper)	'kɑ:bən	C	Kohlepapier
car park		A	Parkplatz
caravan	'kærəvæn	C	Wohnwagen
card	kɑ:d	A	Karte
cardigan	'kɑ:dɪgən	B	Strickjacke
cardinal	'kɑ:dɪnəl	C	Kardinal
cardinal number		C	Grundzahl
care	keə	A	Sorge, Sorgfalt; interessiert sein
care for sb		A	jd. mögen
I couldn't care less		C	es ist mir wurscht
take care		B	s. Mühe geben; aufpassen
take care of		A	s. kümmern um
careful	'keəfʊl	A	sorgfältig; vorsichtig
careless	'keəlɪs	A	sorglos; unvorsichtig
carelessness		B	Unachtsamkeit
career	kə'rɪə	A	Laufbahn, Beruf
caretaker	'keəteɪkə	C	Hausmeister
cargo, es	'kɑ:gəʊ	W	Fracht
carnation	kɑ:'neɪʃn	C	Nelke
carnival	'kɑ:nɪvəl	C	Fasching
carol	'kærəl	C	Adventslied
carpenter	'kɑ:pɪntə	B	Zimmermann
carpet	'kɑ:pɪt	A	Teppich
carriage	'kærɪdʒ	B	Wagen
carrier bag	'kærɪəbæg	C	Tragtasche
carrot	'kærət	B	Gelbe Rübe, Karotte
carry	'kærɪ	A	tragen, befördern
carry on		A	weitermachen, -gehen
carry out		B	ausführen
cart	kɑ:t	C	Karren, Wagen
carton	kɑ:tn	C	Karton, Schachtel
cartoon	kɑ:'tu:n	B	Karikatur

A cartoon

cartoon film		C	Zeichentrickfilm
cartoonist	kɑ:'tu:nɪst	C	Karikaturist
cartridge	'kɑ:trɪdʒ	C	Patrone
carve	kɑ:v	B	schnitzen, meißeln; tranchieren
case	keɪs	A	Kiste; Fall, Sache
in case		A	falls
in any case		A	jedenfalls
in this case		A	in diesem Fall
cash	kæʃ	C	Kasse; Bargeld; (Scheck) einlösen
cashier	kæ'ʃɪə	B	Kassierer(in)
cast	kɑ:st	C	werfen; Ensemble
cast	kɑ:st		
cast			
cassette	kə'set	A	Cassette
cassette radio		A	Cassettenradio
cassette recorder		A	Cassettenrecorder
castle	kɑ:sl	A	Schloß, Burg
casual	'kæʒʊəl	C	lässig
cat	kæt	A	Katze
catalogue	'kætəlɒg	B	Katalog
catastrophe	kə'tæstrəfɪ	C	Katastrophe
catch	kætʃ	A	fangen; erwischen
caught	kɔ:t		
caught			
catch hold of		C	ergreifen
catch sight of		C	erblicken
catch up		C	ein-, aufholen
catch a cold		A	s. erkälten
get caught		B	erwischt werden
cathedral	kə'θi:drəl	A	Dom, Kathedrale
Catholic	'kæθəlɪk	C	katholisch
cattle	kætl	A	Rinder, Vieh
cauliflower	'kɒlɪflaʊə	C	Blumenkohl
cause	kɔ:z	B	Grund; verursachen
caution	kɔ:ʃn	C	Vorsicht
cautious	'kɔ:ʃəs	C	vorsichtig

cave	keɪv	B	Höhle
cease	siːs	B	einstellen, beenden
ceiling	ˈsiːlɪŋ	A	Zimmerdecke
celebrate	ˈselɪbreɪt	A	feiern
celebration	selɪˈbreɪʃn	B	Feier
cell	sel	C	Zelle
cellar	ˈselə	A	Keller
cello,s	ˈtʃeləʊ	C	Cello
Celtic	ˈkeltɪk	C	keltisch
Celtic	ˈseltɪk	C	Celtic (Fußballclub)
cemetery	ˈsemɪtrɪ	C	Friedhof
cent	sent	A	Cent
per cent	pəˈsent	A	Prozent
centigrade	ˈsentɪgreɪd	C	Grad (Celsius)
centimetre	ˈsentɪmiːtə	C	Zentimeter
central	ˈsentrəl	A	zentral
central heating		B	Zentralheizung
	ˈhiːtɪŋ		
centre	ˈsentə	A	Zentrum, Mittelpunkt
centre forward		C	Mittelstürmer
century	ˈsentʃərɪ	A	Jahrhundert
cereal	ˈsɪərɪəl	C	Kornfrucht
ceremony	ˈserɪmənɪ	B	Zeremonie
certain	sɜːtn	A	sicher
certainly	ˈsɜːtnlɪ	A	sicher(lich)
certainty	ˈsɜːtntɪ	C	Sicherheit
certificate	səˈtɪfɪkət	A	Zeugnis
chain	tʃeɪn	B	Kette; anketten
chain store	ˈtʃeɪnstɔː	C	Ladenkette
chair	tʃeə	A	Stuhl
chairman	ˈtʃeəmən	C	Vorsitzender
chalk	tʃɔːk	B	Kreide
challenge	ˈtʃælɪndʒ	B	Herausforderung; herausfordern
chamber	ˈtʃeɪmbə	C	Kammer
chamber music		C	Kammermusik
chamber of commerce		W	Handelskammer
champagne	ʃæmˈpeɪn	B	Champagner, Sekt
champion	ˈtʃæmpjən	B	Sieger, Meister
championship		B	Meisterschaft
chance	tʃɑːns	A	Möglichkeit; Gelegenheit

Changeable

by chance		A	zufällig
chancellor	ˈtʃɑːnsələ	C	Kanzler
change	tʃeɪndʒ	A	(ver)ändern; s. umkleiden; umsteigen; (Ver-)Änderung; Wechselgeld
for a change		C	zur Abwechslung
changeable	ˈtʃeɪndʒəbl	B	veränderlich, wechselhaft
channel	tʃænl	B	Kanal
the English Channel		B	der Ärmelkanal
chapel	tʃæpl	B	Kapelle; Messe
chapter	ˈtʃæptə	B	Kapitel
character	ˈkærəktə	B	Charakter
characteristic (of)	kærəktəˈrɪstɪk	B	kennzeichnend (für)
charge	tʃɑːdʒ	A	(be)laden; berechnen
be in charge (of)		C	zuständig sein, die Leitung haben
free of charge		B	kostenlos, gratis
charges	ˈtʃɑːdʒɪz	C	Kosten, Ausgaben
charity	ˈtʃærətɪ	C	Nächstenliebe; Spende
charm	tʃɑːm	B C	Charme; bezaubern
charming	ˈtʃɑːmɪŋ	A	bezaubernd, reizend
charter flight	ˈtʃɑːtə	B	Charterflug
chat	tʃæt	B	plaudern; Gespräch
chatter	ˈtʃætə	C	plappern, ratschen
cheap	tʃiːp	A	billig
cheat	tʃiːt	A	(an)schwindeln
check	tʃek	A	überprüfen; Karo; (US) Scheck C; (US) Rechnung C

To check

check in		A	zur Abfertigung gehen
check-in (desk)		B	(Flug)Abfertigung
cheek	tʃiːk	C	Backe, Wange
cheeky	ˈtʃiːkɪ	C	frech
cheer	tʃɪə	C	jubeln

to charge with — *beschuldigen*

the charts — *die Hitliste*

Cheddar (englische Käsesorte)

cheer up	C	aufmuntern; nicht traurig sein		church	tʃɜ:tʃ	A	Kirche; Gottesdienst
cheerful	'tʃɪəfəl	B	heiter, fröhlich	churchyard	'tʃɜ:tʃjɑ:d	B	Friedhof
cheers!	tʃɪəz	A	Prost!	chute	ʃu:t	C	Rutsche
cheerio	tʃɪərɪ'əʊ	A	Servus	cigar	sɪ'gɑ:	A	Zigarre
cheese	tʃi:z	A	Käse	cigarette	sɪgə'ret	A	Zigarette
cheeseburger 'tʃi:zbɜ:gə		B	Cheeseburger	cine (camera)	'sɪnɪ	C	Filmkamera
				cinema	'sɪnəmə	A	Kino
chemical	'kemɪkl	B	chemisch; Chemikalie	circle	sɜ:kl	B	Kreis; kreisen
chemist	'kemɪst	A	Apotheker; Chemiker	circular	'sɜ:kjʊlə	C	kreisförmig; Rundschreiben
chemistry	'kemɪstrɪ	B	Chemie	circulation	sɜ:kjʊ'leɪʃn	C	Umlauf; Auflagenhöhe
cheque	tʃek	A	Scheck	circumstances 'sɜ:kəmstənsɪz		B	Verhältnisse, Lage
cheque book		C	Scheckheft				
cheque card		C	Scheckkarte	under these circumstances		B	unter diesen Umständen
cherry	'tʃerɪ	A	Kirsche				
chess	tʃes	C	Schach	circus	'sɜ:kəs	C	Zirkus; Platz
chest	tʃest	B	Kasten; Brust(kasten)	citizen	'sɪtɪzn	B	(Staats-)Bürger
				city	'sɪtɪ	A	Stadt, Großstadt
chest of drawers	drɔ:z	C	Kommode	the City		B	Londoner Innenstadt
chestnut	'tʃesnʌt	B	Kastanie				
chew	tʃu:	B	kauen	civil	sɪvl	B	bürgerlich; höflich
chewing gum 'tʃu:ɪŋ gʌm		B	Kaugummi	civil (=public) servant		C	Beamter
				civil (=public) service		C	öffentlicher Dienst
chicken	'tʃɪkɪn	A	Hühnchen; Küken	civil war		C	Bürgerkrieg
chief	tʃi:f	B	Anführer, Haupt-	civilised(-z-)	'sɪvɪlaɪzd	C	zivilisiert, gesittet
child, children	tʃaɪld,-ɪ	A	Kind	civilisation(-z-)		B	Zivilisation, Kultur
childhood	'tʃaɪldhʊd	B	Kindheit		sɪvɪlaɪ'zeɪʃn		
childish	'tʃaɪldɪʃ	B	kindisch	claim	kleɪm	C	beanspruchen; behaupten; Anspruch
childlike	'tʃaɪldlaɪk	C	kindlich				
chilly	'tʃɪlɪ	B	frostig, eisig				
chimney	'tʃɪmnɪ	B	Kamin	clan	klæn	B	Sippe
chimney-sweep 'tʃɪmnɪswi:p		C	Kaminkehrer	clarinet	klærɪ'net	C	Klarinette
				class	klɑ:s	A	Klasse
chimpanzee 'tʃɪmpən'zi:		C	Schimpanse	classify	'klæsɪfaɪ	C	klassifizieren
chin	tʃɪn	B	Kinn	classmate	'klɑ:smeɪt	B	Klassenkamerad
china	'tʃaɪnə	B	Porzellan	first-class		B	erstklassig
China	'tʃaɪnə	C	China	classical	'klæsɪkl	B	klassisch
Chinese	tʃaɪ'ni:z	C	chinesisch	classroom	'klɑ:srʊm	A	Schulzimmer
chip	tʃɪp	C	Computerelement	clause	klɔ:z	B	Nebensatz
chips	tʃɪps	A	Pommes frites	clay	kleɪ	C	Ton, Erde
chivalrous	'ʃɪvəlrəs	C	ritterlich	clean	kli:n	A	rein, sauber; reinigen
chocolate	'tʃɒkələt	A	Schokolade				
chocolates	'tʃɒkələts	A	Pralinen	clean up		B	aufräumen
choice	tʃɔɪs	B	(Aus-)Wahl	clear	'klɪə	A	klar, deutlich; räumen
choir	'kwaɪə	C	Chor				
choose	tʃu:z	A	(aus)wählen	clear up		B	aufräumen
chose	tʃəʊz			clerihew	'klerɪhju:	C	lustiger Vierzeiler
chosen	tʃəʊzn			clerk	klɑ:k	C	Büroangestellte(r)
chop	tʃɒp	C	(zer)hauen; Kotelett	clever	'klevə	A	klug, geschickt
Christ	kraɪst	C	Christus	cleverness	'klevənɪs	B	Klugheit
christen	krɪsn	C	taufen	client	'klaɪənt	C	Kunde, -in
Christian	'krɪstʃən	B	christlich, Christ	cliff	klɪf	B	Klippe, Steilküste
Christian name (=first name)		A	Vorname	climate	'klaɪmət	B	Klima
				climax	'klaɪmæks	C	Höhepunkt
Christmas	'krɪsməs	A	Weihnachten	climb	klaɪm	A	klettern, (be)steigen
Christmas Eve	..ˌi:v	C	Heiliger Abend				

cling (to)	klɪŋ	C	s. klammern (an)
clung	klʌŋ		
clung			
clip	klɪp	C	zuschneiden; Klammer
cloak	kləʊk	C	Umhang
cloakroom	'kləʊkrʊm	B	Garderobe; Toilette
clock	klɒk	A	(Wand-)Uhr
eight o' clock		A	acht Uhr
round the clock		C	rund um die Uhr
close (to, by)	kləʊs	A	nahe (bei)
close-up	'kləʊs ˌʌp	C	Nahaufnahme
close	kləʊz	A	schließen; Schluß
closet	'klɒzɪt	C	(US) Kleiderschrank
closing time		C	Ladenschluß
cloth,s	klɒθ,θs	B	Tuch; Stoff
clothing	'kləʊðɪŋ	B	Kleidung
clothes	kləʊðz	A	Kleider, Kleidung

Clothes

cloud	klaʊd	A	Wolke
cloudy	'klaʊdɪ	B	wolkig
clover	'kləʊvə	C	Klee
clown	klaʊn	C	Clown
club	klʌb	A	Klub; Keule C
clue	klu:	C	Anhaltspunkt, Ahnung
clumsy	'klʌmzɪ	C	unbeholfen
clutch	klʌtʃ	C	Kupplung
coach	kəʊtʃ	A	Kutsche, Reisebus, Eisenbahnwaggon; Trainer C
coal	kəʊl	B	Kohle
coalmine	'kəʊlmaɪn	C	Kohlenbergwerk, Zeche
coast	kəʊst	A	Küste
coat	kəʊt	A	Mantel; Schicht C
(coat)hanger	'kəʊthæŋə	C	Kleiderbügel
cock	kɒk	C	Hahn
Cockney	'kɒknɪ	C	Londoner Dialekt
cockpit	'kɒkpɪt	C	Pilotenkanzel
cocktail	'kɒkteɪl	C	Cocktail
cocoa	'kəʊkəʊ	C	Kakao
cod	kɒd	C	Kabeljau
code	kəʊd	B	Code, Schlüssel
coffee	'kɒfɪ	A	Kaffee
coffee bar	'..ˌbɑ:	C	Café
coin	kɔɪn	B	Münze
coke	kəʊk	C	Cola; Koks
cold	kəʊld	A	kalt; Kälte; Erkältung
catch (a) cold		A	s. erkälten
collar	'kɒlə	B	Kragen
colleague	'kɒli:g	C	Kollege, -in
collect	kə'lekt	A	sammeln; abholen
collection	kə'lekʃn	A	Sammlung
college	'kɒlɪdʒ	A	College, Hochschule
collide	kə'laɪd	C	zusammenstoßen
colloquial	kə'ləʊkwɪəl	B	umgangssprachlich
colon	'kəʊlən	B	Doppelpunkt
colonial	kə'ləʊnjəl	C	Kolonial-, kolonial
colonise(-ize)	'kɒlənaɪz	B	kolonisieren
colonisation (-iz-)		B	Kolonisierung
colonist	'kɒlənɪst	C	Siedler
colony	'kɒlənɪ	A	Kolonie, Siedlung
colour	'kʌlə	A	Farbe
what colour is it?		A	welche Farbe hat es?
coloured	'kʌləd	B	farbig
colourful	'kʌləfʊl	C	bunt
column	'kɒləm	C	Säule; Spalte
comb	kəʊm	A	Kamm; kämmen
combine	kɒm'baɪn	B	verbinden, vereinen
combination	kɒmbɪ'neɪʃn	C	Verbindung
combustion engine	kəm'bʌstʃn	C	Verbrennungsmotor
come	kʌm	A	kommen
came	keɪm		
come	kʌm		
come about		C	zustandekommen
come across		B	zufällig finden (begegnen)
come along		A	mitkommen

come along

<u>collective noun</u>
<u>Sammelbegriff</u>

Comfortable

come and see

come and see		A	besuchen
come in		A	hereinkommen
come on!		A	komm; ach was!
come round		B	vorbeischauen
comeback	'kʌmbæk	C	Comeback
coming	'kʌmɪŋ	B	kommend, folgend
comedy	'kɒmədɪ	B	Komödie
comic	'kɒmɪk	B	Comic(sheft)
comfort	'kʌmfət	B	Behaglichkeit; trösten, Trost
comfortable	'kʌmf(ə)t(ə)bl	A	bequem
are you comfortable?		C	fühlen Sie sich gut?
comma	'kɒmə	B	Komma
command	kə'mɑːnd	C	befehlen; Befehl
commander (-in-chief)	kə'mɑːndə	C	(Ober-)Befehlshaber
commemorate	kə'meməreɪt	C	erinnern an, gedenken
comment	'kɒment	B	Kommentar; kommentieren
no comment!	nəʊ'kɒment	B	kein Kommentar!
commentary	'kɒməntərɪ	C	Kommentar
commentator	'kɒmənteɪtə	C	Kommentator
commerce	'kɒmɜːs	B	Handel
commercial	kə'mɜːʃl	B	kaufmännisch; Werbespot
commercial school		B	Wirtschaftsschule
commission	kə'mɪʃn	W	Provision
commit	kə'mɪt	B	begehen (Verbrechen)
committee	kə'mɪtɪ:	B	Komitee, Ausschuß
commodity	kə'mɒdətɪ	W	Ware
common	'kɒmən	B	gemeinsam; üblich
common sense	..'sens	C	gesunder Menschenverstand
Common Market		B	Gemeinsamer Markt
have in common		C	gemeinsam haben
House of Commons		A	Unterhaus
Commonwealth	'kɒmənwelθ	B	Staatenbund, Commonwealth
communicate	kə'mjuːnɪkeɪt	B	s. verständigen
communication	kəmjuːnɪ'keɪʃn	B	Kommunikation
Communism	'kɒmjʊnɪzm	C	Kommunismus
Communist	'kɒmjʊnɪst	C	Kommunist(in)
community	kə'mjuːnɪtɪ	B	Gemeinschaft; Gemeinde
commuter	kə'mjuːtə	C	(Berufs-)Pendler
companion	kəm'pænjən	C	Begleiter(in)
company	'kʌmpənɪ	B	Gesellschaft; Firma
comparable	'kɒmpərəbl	C	vergleichbar
comparative	kəm'pærətɪv	C	Komparativ
comparatively	kəm'pærətɪvlɪ	C	vergleichsweise
compare	kəm'peə	A	vergleichen
comparison	kəm'pærɪsn	B	Vergleich; Steigerung
compartment	kəm'pɑːtmənt	A	Abteil
compel	kəm'pel	C	zwingen
be compelled to		B	müssen
compensate	'kɒmpənseɪt	C	ausgleichen
compete	kəm'piːt	C	wetteifern
competent	'kɒmpɪtənt	B	fähig, tüchtig
competition	kɒmpɪ'tɪʃn	B	Wettstreit, Konkurrenz
competitor	kəm'petɪtə	B	Konkurrent(in)
complain	kəm'pleɪn	A	s. beschweren
complaint	kəm'pleɪnt	B	Beschwerde
complete	kəm'pliːt	A	vollständig; vollenden
completely	kəm'pliːtlɪ	A	völlig, ganz
complicated	'kɒmplɪkeɪtɪd	C	kompliziert, schwierig
compliment	'kɒmplɪmənt	B	Kompliment; beglückwünschen
component	kəm'pəʊnənt	C	Bauteil
compose	kəm'pəʊz	B	zusammensetzen; komponieren
be composed of		C	bestehen aus
composer	kəm'pəʊzə	B	Komponist
composition	kɒmpə'zɪʃn	B	Komposition
compound	'kɒmpaʊnd	C	(chem.) Verbindung
compound word	'..ˌ.	C	zusammengesetztes Wort
comprehension	kɒmprɪ'henʃn	B	Verständnis, Verstehen

To have in common

comprehensive	ˌkɒmprɪˈhensɪv	C	umfassend
comprehensive school		A	Gesamtschule
comprise	kəmˈpraɪz	C	umfassen, bestehen aus
compromise	ˈkɒmprəmaɪz	B	Kompromiß
compulsory	kəmˈpʌlsəri	C	obligatorisch; Pflicht-
computer	kəmˈpjuːtə	A	Computer, Rechner
conceited	kənˈsiːtɪd	C	eingebildet
concentrate (on)	ˈkɒnsəntreɪt	C	s. konzentrieren
concentration	ˌkɒnsənˈtreɪʃn	C	Konzentration
concern	kənˈsɜːn	C	Betroffenheit; Konzern; betreffen
concerned about	kənˈsɜːnd	C	besorgt (wegen)
concerned with		C	befaßt (mit)
concerning	kənˈsɜːnɪŋ	A	betreffend
as far as ... is concerned		C	was... betrifft
concert	ˈkɒnsət	A	Konzert
concerthall		C	Konzertsaal
concise	kənˈsaɪs	C	knapp, präzis
conclude	kənˈkluːd	C	beenden; folgern
conclusion	kənˈkluːʒn	B	Schluß(folgerung)
concrete	ˈkɒnkriːt	C	konkret; Beton
condemn	kənˈdem	C	verurteilen
condition	kənˈdɪʃn	A	Bedingung; Zustand
on condition (that)		B	unter der Bedingung, (daß)
conduct	ˈkɒndʌkt	B	Benehmen, Führung
conduct	kənˈdʌkt	C	führen, dirigieren
conductor	kənˈdʌktə	B	Schaffner; Dirigent C
conference	ˈkɒnfərəns	B	Konferenz, Besprechung
confess	kənˈfes	C	gestehen, beichten
confession	kənˈfeʃn	C	Geständnis, Beichte
confidence	ˈkɒnfɪdəns	B	Vertrauen, Zuversicht
confident (of)	ˈkɒnfɪdənt	C	zuversichtlich
confidential	ˌkɒnfɪˈdenʃl	C	vertraulich
confirm	kənˈfɜːm	C	bestätigen
confirmation	ˌkɒnfəˈmeɪʃn	C	Bestätigung
conflict	ˈkɒnflɪkt	B	Kampf, Konflikt
confuse	kənˈfjuːz	C	verwirren; verwechseln
confusion	kənˈfjuːʒn	C	Verwirrung; Verwechslung
congratulate (on)	kənˈgrætjʊleɪt	A	beglückwünschen (zu)
congratulation(s)	kənˌgrætjʊˈleɪʃn(z)	A	Glückwunsch
congress	ˈkɒŋgres	B	Kongreß
Congress		C	am. Parlament
Congressman	ˈkɒŋgresmən	C	Kongreßabgeordneter
conjunction	kənˈdʒʌŋkʃn	C	Bindewort
in conjunction with		C	in Verbindung mit
connect (to)	kəˈnekt	B	verbinden (mit)
connection (= connexion)	kəˈnekʃn	B	Verbindung
conquer	ˈkɒŋkə	B	erobern, besiegen
conqueror	ˈkɒŋkərə	B	Eroberer
conquest	ˈkɒŋkwest	C	Eroberung
conscience	ˈkɒnʃəns	B	Gewissen
conscious (of)	ˈkɒnʃəs	C	bewußt
consent	kənˈsent	C	einwilligen; Einwilligung
consequence	ˈkɒnsɪkwəns	B	Folge
in consequence of		B	als Folge
consequently	ˈkɒnsɪkwəntli	C	folglich
conservative	kənˈsɜːvətɪv	A	konservativ
Conservative Party		A	(GB)Konservative Partei
consider	kənˈsɪdə	B	erwägen; berücksichtigen; betrachten (als)
considerable	kənˈsɪd(ə)rəbl	B	beträchtlich
considerate	kənˈsɪdrət	C	rücksichtsvoll
consideration	ˌkənsɪdəˈreɪʃn	B	Überlegung; Rücksicht
considering...	kənˈsɪdərɪŋ	C	in Anbetracht...
consignment	kənˈsaɪnmənt	W	Sendung, Lieferung
consignment note		W	Frachtbrief
consist (of)	kənˈsɪst	A	bestehen (aus)
consolation	ˌkɒnsəˈleɪʃn	C	Trost
consonant	ˈkɒnsənənt	B	Konsonant

consonant

The conductor

Conspicuous

conspicuous	kənˈspɪkjʊəs	C	auffällig
constable	ˈkʌnstəbl	B	Wachtmeister
constant	ˈkɒnstənt	B	beständig
constituency	kənˈstɪtjʊənsɪ	C	Stimmkreis
constitute	ˈkɒnstɪtjuːt	C	darstellen
constitution		B	Verfassung
constitutional	kɒnstɪˈtjuːʃənl	C	verfassungsmäßig
construct	kənˈstrʌkt	B	bauen, errichten; konstruieren
construction	kənˈstrʌkʃn	B	Bau; Konstruktion
consul	ˈkɒnsl	C	Konsul
consulate	ˈkɒnsjʊlət	C	Konsulat
consult	kənˈsʌlt	C	nachschlagen, konsultieren
consultation	kɒnsəlˈteɪʃn	C	Beratung; Arztbesuch
consume	kənˈsjuːm	C	verbrauchen
consumer	kənˈsjuːmə	B	Verbraucher
consumer goods		C	Verbrauchsgüter
consumption	kənˈsʌm(p)ʃn	C	Verbrauch
contact	ˈkɒntækt	A	Kontakt; Verbindung aufnehmen
contact lenses	ˈ..lenzɪz	C	Kontaktlinsen
contagious	kənˈteɪdʒəs	C	ansteckend
contain	kənˈteɪn	A	enthalten
container	kənˈteɪnə	C	Behälter, Container
contemporary	kənˈtemprərɪ	C	Zeitgenosse; zeitgenössisch
contempt	kənˈtem(p)t	C	Verachtung
content	kənˈtent	C	zufrieden
contented	kənˈtentɪd	C	zufrieden
contentment		C	Zufriedenheit
content(s)	ˈkɒntent	B	Inhalt
contest	ˈkɒntest	B	Wettbewerb
context	ˈkɒntekst	B	Zusammenhang
continent	ˈkɒntɪnənt	A	Festland, Kontinent
continental	kɒntɪˈnentl	A	kontinental
continue	kənˈtɪnjuː	A	fortsetzen
continue to		A	weiterhin (tun)
continual	kənˈtɪnjʊəl	C	unaufhörlich
continuation	kəntɪnjʊˈeɪʃn	C	Fortsetzung
continuous	kənˈtɪnjʊəs	B	fortlaufend
continuous form		B	Verlaufsform
contract	ˈkɒntrækt	C	Vertrag
contracted form	kənˈtræktɪd	C	Kurzform
contradict	kɒntrəˈdɪkt	C	widersprechen
contrary	ˈkɒntrərɪ	C	Gegenteil
on the contrary		B	im Gegenteil
contrast	ˈkɒntrɑːst	C	Gegensatz
in contrast to		C	im Gegensatz
contribute	kənˈtrɪbjuːt	C	beitragen
contribution	kɒntrɪˈbjuːʃn	C	Beitrag
control	kənˈtrəʊl	A	Aufsicht; Leitung; leiten
convenient	kənˈviːnjənt	C	passend, bequem
convention	kənˈvenʃn	C	Kongreß
conventional	kənˈvenʃənəl	C	herkömmlich
conversation	kɒnvəˈseɪʃn	B	Unterhaltung, Gespräch
conversational	kɒnvəˈseɪʃənəl	C	Unterhaltungs-
conveyor belt	kənˈveɪə	C	Förderband

The conveyor belt

conviction	kənˈvɪkʃn	B	Überzeugung
convince	kənˈvɪns	A	überzeugen
convinced	kənˈvɪnst	B	überzeugt
convincing	kənˈvɪnsɪŋ	C	überzeugend
cook	kʊk	A	kochen; Koch, Köchin
cooker	ˈkʊkə	B	Herd
cookie(US)	ˈkʊkɪ	C	Keks
cool	kuːl	A	kühl; s. abkühlen
coolness	ˈkuːlnəs	C	Kühle
co-operate	kəʊˈɒpəreɪt	B	zusammenarbeiten
co-operation	kəʊɒpəˈreɪʃn	C	Zusammenarbeit

cope (with)	kəʊp B	zurechtkommen (mit)	
copper	'kɒpə B	Kupfer	
copy	'kɒpɪ B	Abschrift, Kopie; Exemplar; abschreiben; kopieren	
cord	kɔ:d C	Schnur, Strick	
cordial	'kɔ:dɪəl C	herzlich	
core	kɔ: C	Kern	
cork	kɔ:k C	Kork(en)	
corkscrew	'kɔ:kskru: C	Korkenzieher	
corn	kɔ:n B	Korn; Getreide; Mais	
cornflakes	'kɔ:nfleɪks B	Kornflakes	
corner	'kɔ:nə A	Ecke	
Cornwall	'kɔ:nwəl B	Cornwall	
Cornish	'kɔ:nɪʃ C	kornisch	
coronation	kɒrə'neɪʃn C	Krönung	
corporation	kɔ:pə'reɪʃn W	(US) Firma	
correct	kə'rekt A	richtig; verbessern	
correction	kə'rekʃn C	Korrektur	
correspond	kɒrɪs'pɒnd B	Briefwechsel führen; entsprechen	
correspondence kɒrɪs'pɒndəns	B	Briefwechsel	
correspondent kɒrɪs'pɒndənt	C	Korrespondent	
corridor	'kɒrɪdɔ: B	Flur, Gang	
cosmetics	kɒz'metɪks C	Kosmetik	
cost	kɒst A	kosten; Kosten C	
cost			
cost			
cost of living	B	Lebenshaltungskosten	
costume	'kɒstju:m B	Kostüm	
cosy	'kəʊzɪ C	warm, behaglich	
cottage	'kɒtɪdʒ B	Häuschen	
cotton	'kɒt(ə)n B	Baumwolle	
cotton wool	kɒtn 'wʊl B	Watte	
couch	kaʊtʃ B	Couch, Liege(bett)	
cough	kɒf A	husten; Husten	
could	kʊd, kəd A	konnte, könnte	
council	kaʊnsl B	Rat(sversammlung)	
count	kaʊnt A	zählen; Graf	
count on	B	rechnen mit	
countable	'kaʊntəbl C	zählbar	
countdown	'kaʊntdaʊn C	Countdown	
countless	'kaʊntləs C	zahllos	
country	'kʌntrɪ A	Land	
countryside	'kʌntrɪsaɪd B	Landschaft	
county	'kaʊntɪ B	Grafschaft	
couple	kʌpl B	Paar	
a couple of	B	ein paar	
courage	'kʌrɪdʒ B	Mut	
courageous	kə'reɪdʒəs B	mutig	
course	kɔ:s A	Lauf; Lehrgang; Gang (Essen)	
of course	əv 'kɔ:s A	natürlich	cross-country
in the course of	B	im Laufe	
court	kɔ:t B	Hof, Gerichts-, Königshof	
courteous	'kɜ:tjəs C	höflich	
courtesy	'kɜ:tɪsɪ C	Höflichkeit	
courtier	'kɔ:tjə C	Höfling	
courtyard	'kɔ:tjɑ:d B	Hof	
cousin	kʌzn A	Vetter; Base	
cover	'kʌvə B	(be)decken; umfassen; Decke, Hülle	
cow	kaʊ A	Kuh	
cowboy	'kaʊbɔɪ B	Rinderhirt	*country and western (amerik. Volksmusik)*
cowshed	'kaʊʃed C	Kuhstall	
coward	'kaʊəd B	Feigling	
cowardly	'kaʊədlɪ C	feig	
crack	kræk C	Riß, Sprung	
cracker	'krækə C	Knallbonbon; Keks	
cradle	'kreɪdl C	Wiege	
craftsman	'krɑ:ftsmən B	Handwerker	
cram	kræm C	pauken, büffeln	
crane	kreɪn C	Kran; Kranich	
crash	kræʃ A	krachen; zerschmettern; Krach, Absturz	
crash helmet	'helmɪt C	Sturzhelm	
crate	kreɪt C	Lattenkiste; Träger	
crawl	krɔ:l B	kriechen; kraulen	
crazy	'kreɪzɪ A	verrückt	
cream	kri:m A	Rahm; Creme	
create	krɪ'eɪt B	schaffen	
creation	krɪ'eɪʃn C	Schöpfung; Schaffung	*Covent Garden (Lond. Oper)*
creative	krɪ'eɪtɪv C	schöpferisch	
creature	'kri:tʃə B	Geschöpf	
credit	'kredɪt C	Kredit; Haben W	
credit card	W	Kreditkarte	
creep	kri:p B	kriechen, schleichen	
crept	krept		
crept			
crew	kru: A	Besatzung	
cricket	'krɪkɪt B	Kricket(spiel)	
crime	kraɪm B	Verbrechen	
criminal	'krɪmɪnəl A	Verbrecher(in); verbrecherisch	
crisis, crises	'kraɪsɪs,-i:z C	Krise	
critic	'krɪtɪk B	Kritiker(in)	
critical	'krɪtɪkl B	kritisch	
criticise(-ize)	'krɪtɪsaɪz B	kritisieren	
criticism	'krɪtɪsɪzm B	Kritik	
crockery	'krɒkərɪ C	Gebrauchsgeschirr	
crocodile	'krɒkədaɪl C	Krokodil	
crop	krɒp B	Ernte	
cross	krɒs A	Kreuz; kreuzen; überqueren	
cross out	ˌˈ C	durchstreichen	
crossbar	'krɒsbɑ: C	Querstange	
cross-country	ˌˈ C	Geländelauf	

crossing

Crossing the road

crossing	ˈkrɒsɪŋ	B	Kreuzung; Überfahrt
crossroads	ˈkrɒsrəʊdz	A	Kreuzung
crossword	ˈkrɒswɜːd	B	Kreuzworträtsel
crow	krəʊ	C	Krähe
crowd	kraʊd	A	(Menschen-)Menge, Gedränge; s. drängen C
crowded	ˈkraʊdɪd	A	überfüllt
crown	kraʊn	A	Krone; krönen
crucial	kruːʃl	C	entscheidend
cruel	ˈkrʊəl	B	grausam
cruelty	ˈkrʊəltɪ	B	Grausamkeit
cruise	kruːz	C	kreuzen, fahren
crush	krʌʃ	C	zerquetschen, vernichten
cry	kraɪ	A	schreien, weinen; Schrei B
cuckoo	ˈkʊkuː	C	Kuckuck
cucumber	ˈkjuːkʌmbə	C	Gurke
cultivate	ˈkʌltɪveɪt	B	kultivieren, hegen
culture	ˈkʌltʃə	B	Kultur
cultural	ˈkʌltʃərəl	B	kulturell
cultured	ˈkʌltʃəd	C	gepflegt, kultiviert
cup	kʌp	A	Tasse; Pokal
cupboard	ˈkʌbəd	A	Schrank
cure	kjʊə	C	heilen; Kur; Heilmittel
curiosity	kjʊərɪˈɒsɪtɪ	B	Neugierde
curious	ˈkjʊərɪəs	B	komisch; neugierig
curl	kɜːl	C	Locke; s. kräuseln
curly	ˈkɜːlɪ	B	lockig
currants	ˈkʌrənts	C	Rosinen
currency	ˈkʌrənsɪ	B	Währung
current	ˈkʌrənt	C	Strom; Strömung; laufend
current affairs		C	Tagesgeschehen
curriculum vitae kəˈrɪkjʊləmˈviːtaɪ		C	Lebenslauf
curse	kɜːs	C	(ver)fluchen; Fluch
curtain	kɜːtn	A	Vorhang
curve	kɜːv	C	Kurve, Krümmung
cushion	kʊʃn	B	Kissen, Polster; polstern
custard	ˈkʌstəd	C	Vanillesoße
custom	ˈkʌstəm	B	Gewohnheit; Brauch, Sitte
customs	ˈkʌstəmz	A	Zoll
customary	ˈkʌstəmərɪ	C	gewohnt, gebräuchlich
customer	ˈkʌstəmə	A	Kunde
cut	kʌt	A	schneiden; Schnitt
cut			
cut			
cut down	⌣	B	fällen; herabsetzen
cut off	⌣	B	abschneiden
cutlery	ˈkʌtlərɪ	C	Besteck
cycle	saɪkl	A	Zyklus; radfahren B
cyclist	ˈsaɪklɪst	B	Radfahrer
cylinder	ˈsɪlɪndə	C	Zylinder
Czech	tʃek	C	tschechisch, Tscheche(in)
Czechoslovakia tʃekəsləˈvækjə		C	Tschechoslowakei

D

d	diː	A	d
dad(dy)	ˈdæd(ɪ)	A	Vati, Papi
daffodil	ˈdæfədɪl	C	Märzenbecher, Osterglocke
daily	ˈdeɪlɪ	A	täglich
dairy	ˈdeərɪ	C	Molkerei
damage	ˈdæmɪdʒ	A	(be)schädigen; Schaden
damn	dæm	C	verdammen
damp	dæmp	B	feucht; Feuchtigkeit
dance	dɑːns	A	tanzen; Tanz
dancer	ˈdɑːnsə	B	Tänzer(in)
Dane	deɪn	B	Däne,-in
Danish	ˈdeɪnɪʃ	B	dänisch
danger	ˈdeɪndʒə	A	Gefahr
in danger of		C	in Gefahr zu
dangerous	ˈdeɪndʒərəs	A	gefährlich
Danube	ˈdænjuːb	C	Donau
dare	deə	B	wagen
I daresay	aɪˈdeəseɪ	C	wahrscheinlich
daring	ˈdeərɪŋ	C	waghalsig
dark	dɑːk	A	dunkel; Dunkel(heit) B
darken	ˈdɑːkən	C	verdunkeln; dunkel werden
darkness	ˈdɑːknəs	B	Dunkelheit
darling	ˈdɑːlɪŋ	A	Liebling

crude — roh
crude oil — Rohöl
cute — niedlich

darts	dɑːts C	Darts(spiel)	
dash	dæʃ C	eilen, losstürzen; Gedankenstrich	
dashboard	'dæʃbɔːd C	Armaturenbrett	
data processing	'deɪtə ˌprəʊsesɪŋ C	Datenverarbeitung	
date	deɪt A	Datum; Verabredung	
out of date		B veraltet	
up to date		B zeitgemäß, modern	
date (back) from		C datieren von	
daughter	'dɔːtə A	Tochter	
daughter-in-law	'...ˌ..ˌ. C	Schwiegertochter	
dawn	dɔːn C	(Morgen-)Dämmerung	
day	deɪ A	Tag	
daylight	'deɪlaɪt B	Tageslicht	
dead	ded A	tot	
deaf	def B	taub	
deal	diːl B	Geschäft(sabschluß)	
deal in		A handeln mit	
dealt	delt	(Waren)	
dealt			
deal with		A s. befassen mit, behandeln	

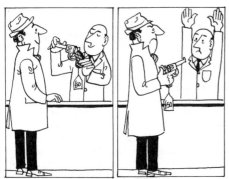

To deal in   *To deal with*

a great deal (of)		B eine Menge; sehr viel(e)	
dealer	'diːlə B	Händler	
dear	dɪə A	lieb; teuer	
dear me!		B ach, du liebe Zeit!	
death	deθ A	Tod	
put to death		B hinrichten	
death warrant	ˌ..ˈwɒrənt C	Todesurteil	
debate	dɪ'beɪt C	Debatte	
debit	'debɪt W	(Konto:) Soll	
debt	det C	Schuld	
decade	'dekeɪd C	Jahrzehnt	
deceive	dɪ'siːv C	täuschen, betrügen	
December	dɪ'sembə A	Dezember	
decent	'diːsnt B	anständig	

decency	'diːsnsɪ C	Anstand	
decide	dɪ'saɪd A	(s.) entscheiden	
decision	dɪ'sɪʒn B	Entscheidung, Entschluß	
decided(ly)	dɪ'saɪdɪd C	entschieden, bestimmt	
decisive	dɪ'saɪsɪv C	entscheidend	
decimal	'desɪməl C	Dezimalzahl	
decimal point	...ˈ. C	Dezimalkomma	
deck	dek C	Deck; Verdeck	
deckchair	'dektʃeə C	Liegestuhl	
declare	dɪ'kleə A	erklären; verzollen	
declaration	dekləˈreɪʃn B	Erklärung	
decline	dɪ'klaɪn C	ablehnen	
decorate	'dekəreɪt B	schmücken; tapezieren	
decoration	dekəˈreɪʃn B	Schmuck, Verzierung	
decorative	'dekərətɪv B	dekorativ, hübsch	
decrease	dɪ'kriːs C	abnehmen, sinken	
	'diːkriːs C	Abnahme	
dedicate	'dedɪkeɪt C	widmen	
deduct	dɪ'dʌkt C	abziehen	
deduction	dɪ'dʌkʃn W	Abzug, Rabatt	
deed	diːd C	Tat	
deep	diːp A	tief	
deepen	'diːpən C	vertiefen	
deep-freeze	'diːpfriːz C	Tiefkühltruhe	
deer	dɪə B	Rotwild; Reh	
defeat	dɪ'fiːt B	Niederlage; besiegen	
defective	dɪ'fektɪv B	fehlerhaft, unvollständig	
defence, (US) defense		B Verteidigung	
defend	dɪ'fend B	verteidigen	
define	dɪ'faɪn B	definieren	
definite	'defɪnɪt A	bestimmt; genau	
definitely	'defɪnɪtlɪ A	unbedingt	
definition	defɪ'nɪʃn A	Definition	
degree	dɪ'griː A	Grad; Stufe	
delay	dɪ'leɪ B	Aufschub, Verzögerung; aufschieben, verzögern	

A slight delay

be delayed				
be delayed		B	Verspätung haben	
without delay		C	unverzüglich	
delegate	'delıgət	C	Abgeordnete(r)	
delegation	delı'geıʃn	B	Abordnung	
deliberate	dı'lıbərət	C	absichtlich	
delicate	'delıkət	B	zart; heikel	
delicious	dı'lıʃəs	A	köstlich	
delight	dı'laıt	B	Vergnügen, Entzücken	
delighted	dı'laıtıd	A	erfreut, entzückt	
delightful	dı'laıtfʊl	B	entzückend, herrlich	
deliver	dı'lıvə	B	liefern	
delivery	dı'lıvərı	B	Lieferung	
demand	dı'mɑ:nd	C	verlangen, fordern; Nachfrage, Bedarf C	
democracy	dı'mɒkrəsı	A	Demokratie	
democrat	'deməkræt	A	Demokrat	
democratic	demə'krætık	A	demokratisch	
demonstrate	'demənstreıt	B	vorführen; demonstrieren	
demonstration	demən'streıʃn	B	Vorführung; Demonstration	
demonstrative pronoun	dı'mɒnstrətıv	C	hinweisendes Fürwort	
Denmark	'denmɑ:k	B	Dänemark	
denim	'denım	B	Denim, Jeansstoff	
dense	dens	B	dick; dicht	
dentist	'dentıst	A	Zahnarzt	
dental	'dent(ə)l	C	zahnärztlich	
deny	dı'naı	B	(ver)leugnen	
denial	dı'naıəl	B	Leugnen; Dementi	
depart	dı'pɑ:t	C	abfahren	
department	dı'pɑ:tmənt	A	Abteilung	
department store	'...˛.	A	Kaufhaus	
departure	dı'pɑ:tʃə	B	Abfahrt	
depend (on)	dı'pend	A	abhängen (von); s. verlassen (auf)	
it (= that) depends		A	das kommt darauf an! je nachdem!	
dependent (on, upon)	dı'pendənt	C	angewiesen (auf)	
to depose	dı'pəʊz	C	absetzen	
deposit	dı'pɒzıt	C	Anzahlung; Ablagerung; hinterlegen	
depression	dı'preʃn	C	Depression, Flaute, Wirtschaftskrise	
depressed	dı'prest	C	deprimiert, niedergeschlagen	
depth	depθ	B	Tiefe	
derive (from)	dı'raıv	C	herleiten (von)	
descend	dı'send	C	her-, hinabsteigen	
be descended from		C	abstammen von	
descendant	dı'sendənt	C	Nachkomme	
describe	dı'skraıb	A	beschreiben	
description	dı'skrıpʃn	B	Beschreibung	
desert	'dezət	C	Wüste	
desert	dı'zɜ:t	C	verlassen	
deserted	dı'zɜ:tıd	C	verlassen, leer	
deserve	dı'zɜ:v	B	verdienen	
design	dı'zaın	A	Muster; Entwurf; entwerfen, konstruieren	
designer	dı'zaınə	C	Gestalter, Konstrukteur	
designation	dezıg'neıʃn	C	Bezeichnung	
desirable	dı'zaıərəbl	C	wünschenswert	
desire	dı'zaıə	C	Wunsch, Verlangen; wünschen	
desk	desk	A	Pult, Schreibtisch	
despair	dı'speə	B	Verzweiflung; verzweifeln	
desperate	'despərət	B	verzweifelt	
despise	dı'spaız	C	verachten	
despite	dı'spaıt	B	trotz	
dessert	dı'zɜ:t	A	Nachtisch	
destination	destı'neıʃn	B	Bestimmungsort	
destiny	'destını	B	Schicksal, Geschick	
destroy	dı'strɔı	A	zerstören, vernichten	
destruction	dı'strʌkʃn	B	Zerstörung	
destructive	dı'strʌktıv	C	zerstörerisch	
detail	'di:teıl	B	Einzelheit, Detail	
detailed	'di:teıld	C	ausführlich	
detective	dı'tektıv	A	Detektiv	
detective story	'...˛.	C	Kriminalroman	
determination	dıtɜ:mı'neıʃn	C	Entschlossenheit; Entschluß	
determine	dı'tɜ:mın	C	bestimmen	
determined	dı'tɜ:mınd	B	entschlossen	
develop	dı'veləp	A	(s.) entwickeln	
developing country		C	Entwicklungsland	
development	dı'veləpmənt	B	Entwicklung	
device	dı'vaıs	C	Vorrichtung, Gerät	
devil	devl	C	Teufel	
devolution	dıvə'l(j)u:ʃn	C	Regionalisierung	
devote	dı'vəʊt	C	widmen, hingeben	
devoted (to)	dı'vəʊtıd	C	ergeben, treu	
diagonal	daı'ægənəl	C	diagonal, quer	
dial	'daıəl	B	Nummernscheibe; wählen (Tel.)	
dialling tone	'...˛.	C	Wählton	
dialect	'daıəlekt	C	Dialekt	
dialogue	'daıəlɒg	B	Zwiegespräch, Dialog	
diamond	'daıəmənd	B	Diamant	
diary	'daıərı	A	Tagebuch; Terminkalender	
dictate	dık'teıt	B	diktieren	
dictation	dık'teıʃn	B	Diktat	
dictator	dık'teıtə	C	Diktator	

to demolish — abreißen

depressing — deprimierend

To dictate

dictatorship	dɪkˈteɪtəʃɪp	C	Diktatur
dictionary	ˈdɪkʃənrɪ	A	Wörterbuch
die (from, of)	daɪ	A	sterben (an)
diet	ˈdaɪət	C	Kost; Diät
be on a diet		C	Diät halten
differ (from)	ˈdɪfə	C	s. unterscheiden; abweichen
difference	ˈdɪfrəns	A	Unterschied; Verschiedenheit
different (from)	ˈdɪfrənt	A	verschieden (von), anders (als)
differing	ˈdɪfərɪŋ	C	unterschiedlich
difficult	ˈdɪfɪkəlt	A	schwierig
difficulty	ˈdɪfɪkəltɪ	A	Schwierigkeit
dig	dɪg	B	graben
dug	dʌg		
dug			
digestion	daɪˈdʒestʃn	B	Verdauung
dignity	ˈdɪgnətɪ	C	Würde
dime	daɪm	C	(US)10-Cent-Münze
dim	dɪm	C	trübe, dunkel
diminish	dɪˈmɪnɪʃ	C	verringern, abnehmen
dining-room	ˈdaɪnɪŋˌrʊm	A	Eßzimmer
dinner	ˈdɪnə	A	Hauptmahlzeit, Abendessen
dip	dɪp	C	eintauchen
diploma	dɪˈpləʊmə	C	Diplom
diplomatic	dɪpləˈmætɪk	C	diplomatisch
direct	daɪˈrekt	C	leiten; direkt
directly	daɪˈrektlɪ	C	gerade(wegs); sofort
direction	daɪˈrekʃn	A	Richtung
director	daɪˈrektə	B	Direktor; Regisseur
directory	daɪˈrektərɪ	C	Telephonbuch
dirndl	dɜːndl	C	Dirndl(kleid)
dirt	dɜːt	C	Schmutz
dirty	ˈdɜːtɪ	A	schmutzig
disadvantage	dɪsədˈvɑːntɪdʒ	A	Nachteil
disagree	dɪsəˈgriː	A	nicht übereinstimmen
disagreeable	dɪsəˈgriːəbl	C	unangenehm
disappear	dɪsəˈpɪə	B	verschwinden
disappearance	dɪsəˈpɪərəns	C	Verschwinden
disappoint	dɪsəˈpɔɪnt	A	enttäuschen
disappointment		B	Enttäuschung
disapprove	dɪsəˈpruːv	C	mißbilligen
disapproval	dɪsəˈpruːvl	C	Mißbilligung
disarm	dɪsˈɑːm	C	entwaffnen; abrüsten
disarmament	dɪsˈɑːməmənt	C	Abrüstung
disaster	dɪˈzɑːstə	C	Unglück(sfall); Katastrophe
disastrous	dɪˈzɑːstrəs	C	katastrophal
disc (US: disk)	dɪsk	B	Scheibe; Schallplatte
disc jockey	ˈdɪskˌdʒɒkɪ	C	Diskjockey
to discharge	dɪsˈtʃɑːdʒ	C	entladen
discipline	ˈdɪsɪplɪn	A	Disziplin
discotheque	ˈdɪskətek	A	Diskothek
disco	ˈdɪskəʊ		
discount	ˈdɪskaʊnt	B	Preisnachlaß, Skonto W
discourage	dɪsˈkʌrɪdʒ	C	entmutigen
discouragement	dɪsˈkʌrɪdʒmənt	C	Entmutigung
discover	dɪsˈkʌvə	A	entdecken

A discovery

discoverer	dɪsˈkʌvərə	B	Entdecker
discovery	dɪsˈkʌvrɪ	B	Entdeckung
discuss	dɪsˈkʌs	A	erörtern, besprechen
discussion	dɪsˈkʌʃn	A	Diskussion, Besprechung
disgrace	dɪsˈgreɪs	C	Schande
disease	dɪˈziːz	C	Krankheit
disguise	dɪsˈgaɪz	C	(s.)verkleiden
disgust	dɪsˈgʌst	C	Abscheu, Ekel
disgusted	dɪsˈgʌstɪd	C	entsetzt

to ask for directions — nach dem Weg fragen

to give directions — den Weg erklären

disabled — behindert

discrimination — Diskriminierung

disgusting

disgusting	dɪsˈgʌstɪŋ	C	widerlich, ekelig
dish	dɪʃ	A	Gericht, Speise; Schüssel
dishes	ˈdɪʃɪz	A	Geschirr
dishwasher	ˈdɪʃwɒʃə	C	Geschirrspülmaschine
disinterested	dɪsˈɪntrɪstɪd	B	uninteressiert; unparteiisch C
dislike	dɪsˈlaɪk	A	nicht mögen; Abneigung
dismiss	dɪsˈmɪs	C	entlassen; abtun
dismissal	dɪsˈmɪsl	C	Entlassung
disobedient	dɪsəˈbiːdjənt	C	ungehorsam
disobey	dɪsəˈbeɪ	C	nicht gehorchen
disorder	dɪsˈɔːdə	C	Unordnung
display	dɪsˈpleɪ	B	Ausstellung, Auslage; ausstellen
be on display		C	ausgestellt sein
displease	dɪsˈpliːz	C	mißfallen
dispose (of)	dɪsˈpəʊz	C	verfügen (über)
disposal	dɪsˈpəʊzl	B	Verfügung
at your disposal		B	zu Ihrer Verfügung
dispute	dɪsˈpjuːt	C	streiten; Streit
to disqualify	dɪsˈkwɒlɪfaɪ	C	disqualifizieren
dissolve	dɪˈzɒlv	C	(s.) auflösen
distance	ˈdɪstəns	B	Entfernung
distant	ˈdɪstənt	C	entfernt
distinct	dɪˈstɪŋkt	C	deutlich; verschieden (von)
distinction	dɪˈstɪŋkʃn	C	Unterschied; Auszeichnung
distinguish	dɪˈstɪŋgwɪʃ	C	unterscheiden; auszeichnen
distinguished	dɪˈstɪŋgwɪʃt	B	ausgezeichnet, vornehm
to distract	dɪˈstrækt	C	ablenken
distress	dɪˈstres	C	Not; bedrängen
distressed	dɪˈstrest	C	bedrängt, bekümmert
distribute	dɪˈstrɪbjuːt	B	aus-, verteilen
distribution	dɪstrɪˈbjuːʃn	C	Verteilung; Verbreitung

To divide

dome
Kuppel

district	ˈdɪstrɪkt	A	Bezirk, Gebiet
distrust	dɪsˈtrʌst	C	mißtrauen
disturb	dɪsˈtɜːb	A	stören
ditch	dɪtʃ	C	Graben
dive	daɪv	C	(unter)tauchen
diving-board		C	Sprungbrett
diver	ˈdaɪvə	C	Taucher
to divert	daɪˈvɜːt	C	umleiten; ablenken
divide	dɪˈvaɪd	A	teilen
divine	dɪˈvaɪn	C	göttlich, himmlisch
division	dɪˈvɪʒn	B	Trennung; Teilung; Abteilung
divorce	dɪˈvɔːs	C	Scheidung
get a divorce		B	s. scheiden lassen
divorced	dɪˈvɔːst	C	geschieden
dizzy	ˈdɪzɪ	C	schwindelig, benommen
do	duː	A	tun, machen
did	dɪd		
done	dʌn		
how do you do		A	Grüß Gott, guten Tag (Vorstellung)
what do you do?		B	was machen Sie beruflich?
do well (at school)		A	s. gut machen
do one's best		A	sein Bestes tun
it's (=has/is) to do with ...		B	es hat mit ... zu tun
that'll do		B	das genügt
docks	dɒks	C	Hafen(anlagen)
doctor	ˈdɒktə	A	Arzt
document	ˈdɒkjʊmənt	B	Urkunde, Beleg
shipping documents		W	Versandpapiere
documentary	dɒkjʊˈmentrɪ	C	Dokumentarfilm
dog	dɒg	A	Hund
doll	dɒl	A	Puppe
dollar	ˈdɒlə	A	Dollar
a dollar bill		B	ein Dollarschein
domestic	dəˈmestɪk	B	heimisch; inländisch
domestic flight	flaɪt	C	Inlandflug
domestic science		C	Hauswirtschaft
dominate	ˈdɒmɪneɪt	C	beherrschen
donkey	ˈdɒŋkɪ	C	Esel
door	dɔː	A	Tür
indoors	ɪnˈdɔːz	C	drinnen
out of doors	ˌaʊtəvˈdɔːz	C	draußen
doorbell	ˈdɔːbel	B	Türglocke
dormitory	ˈdɔːmɪtrɪ	C	Schlafsaal
dot	dɒt	B	Punkt, Fleck
double	ˈdʌbl	B	doppelt; Doppel-; verdoppeln C
double room		B	Doppelzimmer
doubt	daʊt	A	zweifeln; Zweifel
no doubt		A	zweifellos, wohl
doubtful	ˈdaʊtfʊl	B	zweifelhaft
doubtless	ˈdaʊtləs	B	zweifellos

dough	dəʊ	C	Teig
doughnut	ˈdəʊnʌt	C	Krapfen
down	daʊn	A	unten, abwärts
down with ...		C	erkrankt an...; nieder mit...!
downhill (race)		C	Abfahrt(slauf)
downstairs	ˌdaʊnˈsteəz	A	(nach) unten
downtown (US)		C	Stadtmitte
down under		C	'da unten' (in Australien)
downward(s)	ˈdaʊnwəd(z)	B	abwärts
dozen	dʌzn	B	Dutzend
half a dozen		B	ein halbes Dutzend
draft	drɑːft	C	aufsetzen; Entwurf; Tratte W
drag	dræg	C	ziehen, zerren
drama	ˈdrɑːmə	A	Schauspiel
dramatic	drəˈmætɪk	B	dramatisch
dramatist	ˈdræmətɪst	C	Dramatiker
draught	drɑːft	C	Zugluft
draught beer		C	Bier vom Faß
draw	drɔː	A	ziehen, zeichnen
drew	druː		
drawn	drɔːn		
a draw		C	ein Unentschieden
drawback	ˈdrɔːbæk	C	Nachteil
drawer	drɔː	B	Schublade
chest of drawers		C	Kommode
drawing	ˈdrɔːɪŋ	A	Zeichnung
drawing-room		C	Wohnzimmer, Salon
dread	dred	C	fürchten
dreadful	ˈdredfəl	B	fürchterlich
dream	driːm	B	träumen; Traum
dreamt, dreamed	dremt, driːmd		
dreamt, dreamed			
dress	dres	A	Kleid; s. ankleiden
get dressed		B	s. ankleiden
dressing	ˈdresɪŋ	C	Sauce; Verband
dressing-gown	ˌ..gaʊn	C	Morgenrock
dressing-room		C	Ankleideraum
dressmaker	ˈdresmeɪkə	C	Damenschneider(in)
drill	drɪl	C	Bohrer; bohren
drink	drɪŋk	A	trinken; Getränk
drank	dræŋk		
drunk	drʌŋk		
drunk(en)	ˈdrʌŋk(ən)	C	betrunken
drive	draɪv	A	treiben; fahren; Schwung C
drove	drəʊv		
driven	drɪvn		
driver	ˈdraɪvə	A	Fahrer
driving licence	ˌ..laɪsəns	A	Führerschein
(US) driver's license			
driving test	test	C	Fahrprüfung
drizzle	drɪzl	C	nieseln; Sprühregen
drop	drɒp	A	fallen; fallen lassen; Tropfen
drop in		B	(kurz) vorbeikommen
drown	draʊn	B	ertränken; ertrinken
get drowned		B	ertrinken
drug	drʌg	A	Droge, Arznei
drug addict	ˈædɪkt	C	Rauschgiftsüchtige(r)
drugstore (US)	ˈdrʌgstɔː	C	Drugstore, Apotheke
drum	drʌm	B	Trommel
drums	drʌmz	B	Schlagzeug
dry	draɪ	A	trocken; trocknen B
dry up		B	aus-, abtrocknen
duck	dʌk	B	Ente
due	djuː	B	fällig; schuldig
due to		A	infolge
is due to		C	ist auf... zurückzuführen
duel	ˈdjuːəl	C	Duell
duke	djuːk	B	Herzog
duchess	ˈdʌtʃɪs	B	Herzogin
dull	dʌl	A	trübe; langweilig
duly	ˈdjuːlɪ	C	ordnungsgemäß, korrekt
dumb	dʌm	C	stumm; (US)dumm
during	ˈdjʊərɪŋ	A	während (Präp.)
dusk	dʌsk	C	(Abend-)Dämmerung
dust	dʌst	B	Staub; abstauben
dusty	ˈdʌstɪ	B	staubig
dustbin	ˈdʌstbɪn	C	Mülleimer
duster	ˈdʌstə	C	Staublappen
dustman	ˈdʌstmən	C	Müllmann
Dutch	dʌtʃ	B	holländisch
Dutchman	ˈdʌtʃmən	B	Holländer
duty	ˈdjuːtɪ	A	Pflicht; Zoll
duty-free		B	zollfrei
on duty		B	im Dienst
off duty		B	dienstfrei

off duty

A drink

dwarf

On duty   Off duty

dwarf,s (=ves)	dwɔːf	C	Zwerg
dwell	dwel	C	wohnen; verweilen
dwelt	dwelt		
dwelt			
dwelling	ˈdwelɪŋ	C	Wohnung, -sitz
dye	daɪ	C	färben
dynamic	daɪˈnæmɪk	C	dynamisch, schwungvoll
dynamo	ˈdaɪnəməʊ	C	Lichtmaschine
dynasty	ˈdɪnəstɪ	C	Dynastie, Herrschergeschlecht

E

e	iː	A	e
each	iːtʃ	A	jede(r,s)
each other	ˈiːtʃˌʌðə	A	einander, sich
eager (to)	ˈiːgə	B	begierig; eifrig
eagerness	ˈiːgənəs	C	Begierde; Eifer
eagle	ˈiːgl	C	Adler
ear	ɪə	A	Ohr
earphones	ˈɪəfəʊnz	C	Kopfhörer
earl	ɜːl	B	(engl.) Graf
early	ˈɜːlɪ	A	früh, zeitig
earn	ɜːn	A	verdienen (Geld)
earnest	ˈɜːnəst	C	ernst(haft)
earnings	ˈɜːnɪŋz	C	Einkünfte
earth	ɜːθ	A	Erde; Welt
earthquake	ˈɜːθkweɪk	C	Erdbeben
ease	iːz	C	erleichtern
at ease		C	ungezwungen
east	iːst	A	Osten; östlich
Easter	ˈiːstə	A	Ostern
eastern	ˈiːstən	A	östlich
eastward(s)	ˈiːstwəd(z)	C	ostwärts
easy	ˈiːzɪ	A	leicht
easy-going	ˈiːzɪˌgəʊɪŋ	C	unkompliziert
eat	iːt	A	essen
ate	et		
eaten	iːtn		
echo	ˈekəʊ	B	Echo
economic	iːkəˈnɒmɪk	C	wirtschaftlich; Wirtschafts-
economical	iːkəˈnɒmɪkl	C	sparsam; wirtschaftlich
economics	iːkəˈnɒmɪks	C	Wirtschaftslehre
economy	iˈkɒnəmɪ	C	Wirtschaft
edge	edʒ	B	Rand; Schneide; Kante
edition	ɪˈdɪʃn	B	Ausgabe
editor	ˈedɪtə	B	Herausgeber, Schriftleiter
educate	ˈedjʊkeɪt	A	erziehen, ausbilden
educated	ˈedjʊkeɪtɪd	B	gebildet
education	edjʊˈkeɪʃn	A	Erziehung, Bildung
educational	edjʊˈkeɪʃənəl	C	Erziehungs-
effect	ɪˈfekt	A	Wirkung; bewirken
effective	ɪˈfektɪv	B	wirkungsvoll
efficiency	ɪˈfɪʃənsɪ	B	Tüchtigkeit, Leistungsfähigkeit
efficient	ɪˈfɪʃənt	B	tüchtig, wirksam
effort	ˈefət	B	Anstrengung, Mühe
make an effort		B	s. anstrengen
e.g.	fərˌɪgˈzɑːmpl	C	z.B.
egg	eg	A	Ei
Egypt	ˈiːdʒɪpt	C	Ägypten
Egyptian	ɪˈdʒɪpʃn	C	ägyptisch
eight	eɪt	A	acht
eighteen	eɪˈtiːn	A	achtzehn
eighty	ˈeɪtɪ	A	achtzig
eisteddfod	aɪsˈteðvɒd	C	Dichter- u. Sängerwettstreit (Wales)
either	ˈaɪðə	A	eine(r,s) von beiden; beide(s)
(US)	ˈiːðə		
not... either		A	auch nicht
either... or		A	entweder... oder
elbow	ˈelbəʊ	C	Ell(en)bogen
elder, eldest	ˈeldə, ɪst	A	ältere, r (Geschw.)
elderly	ˈeldəlɪ	C	ältere(r,s)
elect	ɪˈlekt	A	wählen
election	ɪˈlekʃn	A	Wahl
General Election		C	(GB)Parlamentswahlen
elector	ɪˈlektə	C	(US) Wahlmann
electric	ɪˈlektrɪk	A	elektrisch
electrical	ɪˈlektrɪkl	B	elektrisch; Elektro-
electrician	ɪlekˈtrɪʃn	C	Elektriker
electricity	ɪlekˈtrɪsɪtɪ	A	Elektrizität
electron	ɪˈlektrɒn	C	Elektron
electronic	ɪlekˈtrɒnɪk	B	elektronisch
electronics	ɪlekˈtrɒnɪks	B	Elektronik
elegant	ˈelɪgənt	A	elegant

element	'elɪmənt	B	Element, Bestandteil
elementary	elɪ'mentərɪ	B	elementar
elementary school		B	(US) Grundschule
elephant	'elɪfənt	B	Elefant
elevator	'elɪveɪtə	C	(US) Aufzug
eleven plus	ɪ'levn‿plʌs	C	elf (Jahre) oder darüber
eliminate	ɪ'lɪmɪneɪt	C	beseitigen
elimination	ɪ'lɪmɪneɪʃn	C	Beseitigung
...else	els	A	sonst
or else	ɔː‿r'els	A	sonst, andernfalls
someone else		B	jemand anderer
something else		B	etwas anderes
somewhere else		B	wo anders, anderswo
elsewhere	els'weə	B	anderswo(hin)
emancipation	ɪmænsɪ'peɪʃn	C	Befreiung, Gleichberechtigung
embarrass	ɪm'bærəs	B	verlegen machen
embarrassment	ɪm'bærəsmənt	C	Verlegenheit
embarrassing	ɪm'bærəsɪŋ	B	peinlich
embassy	'embəsɪ	C	Botschaft
emblem	'embləm	C	Sinnbild, Wahrzeichen
emerge	ɪ'mɜːdʒ	C	auftauchen
emergency	ɪ'mɜːdʒənsɪ	B	Notfall, Notstand

An emergency — *Embarrassing*

emergency call		C	Notruf
emergency landing		C	Notlandung
emigrate	'emɪgreɪt	C	auswandern
emotion	ɪ'məʊʃn	B	Gefühl(sregung)
emotional	ɪ'məʊʃənəl	B	gefühlsbetont, emotionell
emperor	'empərə	B	Kaiser
emphasise(-ize)	'emfəsaɪz	C	betonen
emphasis	'emfəsɪs	C	Betonung
emphatic	ɪm'fætɪk	C	verstärkend, betont
empire	'empaɪə	B	(Welt-)Reich
employ	ɪm'plɔɪ	A	beschäftigen
employee	emplɔɪ'iː em'plɔɪiː	A	Beschäftigte(r), Arbeitnehmer(in)
employer	ɪm'plɔɪə	A	Arbeitgeber
employment	ɪm'plɔɪmənt	B	Beschäftigung; Stelle
empress	'emprəs	C	Kaiserin
empty	'emtɪ	A	leer
emptiness	'emtɪnəs	C	Leere
enable	ɪ'neɪbl	B	befähigen, ermöglichen
enclose	ɪn'kləʊz	W	einschließen; beilegen
enclosure	ɪn'kləʊʒə	W	(Brief:) Anlage
encourage	ɪn'kʌrɪdʒ	B	ermutigen
encouragement	ɪn'kʌrɪdʒmənt	B	Unterstützung, Ermunterung
end	end	A	Ende; Zweck; enden
at the end		A	am Ende
in the end		A	schließlich
(for) hours on end		C	stundenlang
ending	'endɪŋ	B	Endung; Schluß
endless	'endləs	B	endlos
endure	ɪn'djʊə	B	aushalten, ertragen
endurance	ɪn'djʊərəns	B	Ausdauer
enemy	'enəmɪ	B	Feind
energy	'enədʒɪ	B	Energie
energetic	enə'dʒetɪk	B	energisch
enforce	ɪn'fɔːs	C	erzwingen
engage	ɪn'geɪdʒ	B	an-, einstellen
engaged	ɪn'geɪdʒd	A	besetzt; verlobt B
engaged in		C	beschäftigt mit
engagement	ɪn'geɪdʒmənt	B	Verabredung; Verlobung
engine	'endʒɪn	A	(Verbrennungs-)Motor
engine driver		C	Lokomotivführer
engineer	endʒɪ'nɪə	A	Ingenieur
engineering	endʒɪ'nɪərɪŋ	C	Technik
England	'ɪŋglənd	A	England
English	'ɪŋglɪʃ	A	englisch
Englishman	'ɪŋglɪʃmən	A	Engländer
Englishwoman		A	Engländerin
he/she is English		A	er/sie ist Engländer(in)
enjoy	ɪn'dʒɔɪ	A	genießen, gern tun
enjoy o.s.		A	s. amüsieren
enjoyable	ɪn'dʒɔɪəbl	A	unterhaltsam, schön
enlarge	ɪn'lɑːdʒ	B	vergrößern
enormous	ɪ'nɔːməs	B	gewaltig, riesig
enough	ɪ'nʌf	A	genug
enquire(=i~)	ɪŋ'kwaɪə	B	s. erkundigen
enquiry(=i~)	ɪŋ'kwaɪərɪ	B	Anfrage; Telefonauskunft
enraged	ɪn'reɪdʒd	C	wütend
enrich	ɪn'rɪtʃ	C	bereichern

enrich

ensure	ɪnˈʃʊə C	gewährleisten	
enter	ˈentə A	be-, eintreten	
entrance	ˈentrəns A	Eingang; Eintritt	
entry	ˈentrɪ C	Eintritt; Eintragung	
enterprise	ˈentəpraɪz C	Unternehmen, Unternehmungsgeist	
entertain	entəˈteɪn A	unterhalten	
entertainment	entəˈteɪnmənt C	Unterhaltung	
enthusiasm	ɪnˈθjuːzɪæzm C	Begeisterung	
enthusiast	ɪnˈθjuːzɪæst C	Anhänger	
enthusiastic	ɪnθjuːzɪˈæstɪk C	begeistert	
entire	ɪnˈtaɪə A	ganz, vollständig	
entrust (with)	ɪnˈtrʌst C	be-, anvertrauen	
entitled	ɪnˈtaɪtld C	betitelt	
be entitled to	C	berechtigt sein, dürfen	
envelope	ˈenvələʊp A	Briefumschlag	
envy	ˈenvɪ B	Neid; beneiden	
envious (of)	ˈenvɪəs C	neidisch (auf)	
environment	ɪnˈvaɪərənmənt B	Umwelt	
equal (to)	ˈiːkwəl A	gleich; gleichkommen C	
equality	ɪˈkwɒlətɪ C	Gleichheit	
equator	ɪˈkweɪtə C	Äquator	
equip	ɪˈkwɪp C	ausrüsten	
equipped (with)	C	ausgestattet (mit)	
equipment	ɪˈkwɪpmənt C	Ausrüstung, Geräte	
equivalent	ɪˈkwɪvələnt C	gleichwertig; Gegenwert	
erase	ɪˈreɪz B	ausradieren; löschen	
eraser	ɪˈreɪzə C	Radiergummi	
erect	ɪˈrekt C	errichten	
error	ˈerə C	Irrtum, Fehler	
escalator	ˈeskəleɪtə B	Rolltreppe	
escape	ɪˈskeɪp A	fliehen, entkommen; Flucht	
it has escaped me	C	es ist mir entgangen	

episode
Episode, Begebenheit

epoch
/ˈiːpɒk/
Epoche, Zeitalter

Eskimo,(e)s	ˈeskɪməʊ C	Eskimo	
especial(ly)	ɪˈspeʃl(ɪ) A	besonders, namentlich	
essay	ˈeseɪ B	Aufsatz	
essential	ɪˈsenʃl B	wesentlich, notwendig	
establish	ɪˈstæblɪʃ B	gründen; einrichten	
establishment	ɪˈstæblɪʃmənt B	Einrichtung, Gründung	
estate	ɪˈsteɪt C	Gut, Besitzung	
estate agent	..ˈeɪdʒənt C	Grundstücksmakler	
housing estate	C	Siedlung	
estimate	ˈestɪmeɪt B	(ab)schätzen	
estimate	ˈestɪmət C	Schätzung, Voranschlag	
estuary	ˈestjʊərɪ C	breite Mündung	
etc.	etˈsetrə B	usw.	
eternal	iːˈtɜːnəl C	ewig	
eternity	iːˈtɜːnətɪ C	Ewigkeit	
ethnic	ˈeθnɪk C	ethnisch, rassisch	
Europe	ˈjʊərəp C	Europa	
European	jʊərəˈpiːən A	europäisch	
even	ˈiːvn A	sogar; gerade	
not even	A	nicht einmal	
even so	ˈiːvn ˈsəʊ B	trotzdem	
even number	..ˈ.. B	gerade Zahl	
even though	..ˈ.. B	obgleich, wenn auch	
evening	ˈiːvnɪŋ A	Abend	
event	ɪˈvent B	Ereignis; Veranstaltung	
eventually	ɪˈventʃʊəlɪ C	schließlich	
ever	ˈevə A	jemals, je	
for ever (= forever)	B	für immer	
ever since	A	seit, seitdem	
every	ˈevrɪ A	jede(r,s)	
every other day	B	jeden zweiten Tag	
everybody	ˈevrɪbɒdɪ A	jedermann	
everyday	ˈevrɪdeɪ B	alltäglich	
everyone	ˈevrɪwʌn A	jede(r,s)	
every one of	..ˈ.. C	jede(r,s) von	
everything	ˈevrɪθɪŋ A	alles	
everywhere	ˈevrɪweə A	überall	
evident	ˈevɪdənt B	offenbar	
evidence	ˈevɪdəns B	Beweis(e)	
evil	ˈiːvl C	Übel; böse	
ex-(champion)	eks... B	ehemaliger (Meister, Sieger)	
ex (factory)	W	ab (Werk)	
exact	ɪɡˈzækt A	genau; richtig	
exaggerate	ɪɡˈzædʒəreɪt B	übertreiben	
exaggeration	ɪɡzædʒəˈreɪʃn C	Übertreibung	
exam(ination)	ɪɡˈzæm(-ɪˈneɪʃn) A	Prüfung	
examine	ɪɡˈzæmɪn A	prüfen, untersuchen	
example	ɪɡˈzɑːmpl A	Beispiel	
for example	A	zum Beispiel	

To escape

An exam

exceed	ɪkˈsiːd	C	übertreffen
exceedingly	ɪkˈsiːdɪŋlɪ	C	außerordentlich
excellent	ˈeksələnt	A	ausgezeichnet
except	ɪkˈsept	A	außer
exception	ɪkˈsepʃn	A	Ausnahme
exceptional	ɪkˈsepʃənəl	B	außergewöhnlich
exchange (for)	ɪksˈtʃeɪndʒ	B	(aus)tauschen (gegen); (Aus-)Tausch
excited (about)	ɪkˈsaɪtɪd	A	begeistert (von)
excitement	ɪkˈsaɪtmənt	B	Begeisterung
exciting	ɪkˈsaɪtɪŋ	A	spannend
exclaim	ɪksˈkleɪm	C	ausrufen
exclamation mark	eksklәˈmeɪʃnˌmaːk	C	Rufzeichen
exclude	ɪksˈkluːd	C	ausschließen
exclusive	ɪksˈkluːsɪv	B	ausschließlich; exklusiv
excursion	ɪksˈkɜːʃn	C	Ausflug
excuse	ɪksˈkjuːs	A	Entschuldigung, Ausrede
excuse	ɪksˈkjuːz	A	entschuldigen
excuse me		A	Entschuldigung!
execute	ˈeksɪkjuːt	B	ausführen; hinrichten
execution	eksɪˈkjuːʃn	C	Hinrichtung; Erledigung
executive	ɪgˈzekjʊtɪv	C	Exekutive; Führungskraft
exercise	ˈeksәsaɪz	A	Übung; (aus)üben C
exercise-book	...bʊk	A	Schulheft
exhaust	ɪgˈzɔːst	C	erschöpfen
exhaust pipe	...paɪp	C	Auspuffrohr
exhausted	ɪgˈzɔːstɪd	B	erschöpft
exhibit	ɪgˈzɪbɪt	C	ausstellen
exhibition	eksɪˈbɪʃn	A	Ausstellung
exist	ɪgˈzɪst	A	vorhanden sein, bestehen
existence	ɪgˈzɪstәns	B	Existenz, Dasein
exit	ˈeksɪt	B	Ausgang
exotic	ɪgˈzɒtɪk	C	exotisch

expand	ɪkˈspænd	C	(s.) ausdehnen, erweitern
expansion	ɪkˈspænʃn	C	Ausdehnung, Erweiterung
expect	ɪkˈspekt	A	erwarten (von)
expectation	ekspekˈteɪʃn	B	Erwartung
expedition	ekspɪˈdɪʃn	B	(Forschungs-)Reise
expel	ɪkˈspel	C	ausschließen
expense(s)	ɪkˈspens(ɪz)	B	Ausgabe(n); Kosten
at the expense of		C	auf Kosten (von)
expensive	ɪkˈspensɪv	A	teuer
experience	ɪkˈspɪәrɪәns	A	Erfahrung, Erlebnis
experienced	ɪkˈspɪәrɪәnst	B	erfahren
experiment	ɪkˈsperɪmәnt	B	Versuch
expert	ˈekspɜːt	A	Fachmann
explain (to)	ɪkˈspleɪn	A	erklären
explanation	eksplәˈneɪʃn	A	Erklärung

An explanation

explode	ɪkˈsplәʊd	B	explodieren
explosion	ɪkˈsplәʊʒn	C	Explosion
exploit	ɪkˈsplɔɪt	C	ausbeuten
explore	ɪkˈsplɔː	A	erforschen
explorer	ɪkˈsplɔːrә	B	Erforscher
exploration	eksplәˈreɪʃn	B	Erforschung
export	ɪkˈspɔːt	A	ausführen
export	ˈekspɔːt	A	Ausfuhr, Export
exporter	ekˈspɔːtә	W	Exporteur
express	ɪkˈspres	A	ausdrücken, äußern
express letter	...letә	A	Eilbrief
express train	...treɪn	A	D-Zug
expression	ɪkˈspreʃn	B	Ausdruck, Redensart
exquisite	ekˈskwɪzɪt	C	(aus)erlesen, vorzüglich
extend (to)	ɪkˈstend	C	(s.) ausdehnen; s. erstrecken

extend

expedient
/ɪkˈspiːdjәnt/
zweckmäßig

extension

extension	ɪkˈstenʃn	C	Verlängerung; Nebenanschluß
extensive	ɪkˈstensɪv	C	ausgedehnt, umfassend
extent	ɪkˈstent	C	Ausmaß
to a large extent			in hohem Maße
external	ɪkˈstɜːnəl	C	äußerlich, Außen-
extinguish	ɪkˈstɪŋgwɪʃ	C	(aus)löschen
extra	ˈekstrə	A	besondere(r,s); Extra-
extraordinary	ɪkˈstrɔːdənrɪ	B	außergewöhnlich
extreme(ly)	ɪkˈstriːm(lɪ)	A	äußerst, höchst
eye	aɪ	A	Auge
eyebrow	ˈaɪbraʊ	C	Augenbraue
eyelid	ˈaɪlɪd	C	Augenlid
eye-witness	ˈaɪˌwɪtnəs	C	Augenzeuge

F

f	ef	A	f
fable	feɪbl	B	Fabel
fabric	ˈfæbrɪk	C	Stoff, Muster
fabulous	ˈfæbjʊləs	C	fabelhaft
face	feɪs	A	Gesicht; Fassade C; gegenüberliegen C
face (the truth)		B	(die Wahrheit) zur Kenntnis nehmen
facecloth	ˈfeɪsklɒθ	C	Waschlappen
facilities	fəˈsɪlətɪz	C	Möglichkeiten
fact	fækt	A	Tatsache
in fact		A	in der Tat, an sich
as a matter of fact		A	nebenbei bemerkt
factory	ˈfæktərɪ	A	Fabrik
fade	feɪd	C	verblassen; verwelken
fail	feɪl	A	versagen, durchfallen
fail to		C	etwas nicht tun
failure	ˈfeɪljə	B	Mißerfolg; Versagen
faint	feɪnt	C	schwach; ohnmächtig werden
fair	feə	A	Jahrmarkt, Messe; fair; blond
fair play		B	ehrliches Spiel
fairly	ˈfeəlɪ		ziemlich
fairness	ˈfeənɪs	B	Ehrlichkeit, Fairneß
fairy	ˈfeərɪ	C	Fee
fairy-tale	ˈfeərɪteɪl	C	Märchen
faith (in)	feɪθ	C	Glaube; Vertrauen
faithful	ˈfeɪθfʊl	B	treu; gewissenhaft
Yours faithfully		C	Hochachtungsvoll
fall	fɔːl	A	fallen; Fall;
fell	fel		(US) Herbst C
fallen	ˈfɔːlən		
fall asleep	ˌəˈsliːp	B	einschlafen
fall in love	ˌɪnˈlʌv	B	s. verlieben

To fall in love

fall ill	ˌɪl	B	krank werden
false	fɔːls	A	falsch; unaufrichtig
fame	feɪm	B	Ruhm, Ruf
famous (for)	ˈfeɪməs	A	berühmt
familiar (with)	fəˈmɪljə	B	vertraut (mit); bekannt
family	ˈfæm(ə)lɪ	A	Familie; Verwandte
fan	fæn	B	Fächer, Ventilator; Fan
fanatic	fəˈnætɪk	C	fanatisch, Fanatiker
fancy	ˈfænsɪ	B	s. vorstellen; mögen
fancy-dress	ˈfænsɪˈdres		Maskenkostüm
fancy goods		C	Geschenkartikel
fantastic	fænˈtæstɪk	A	phantastisch, toll
far	fɑː	A	weit, fern
far away (= off)		A	weit weg
as far as	əzˈfɑːrˌəz	A	bis zu; so weit wie
by far	baɪˌfɑː	B	bei weitem
so far	səʊˌfɑː	A	so weit; bis jetzt
fare	feə	A	Fahrpreis
farewell	feəˈwel	C	Lebewohl
farm	fɑːm	A	Bauernhof, Hof
farmer	ˈfɑːmə	A	Bauer, Landwirt
farming	ˈfɑːmɪŋ	B	Landwirtschaft
fascinating	ˈfæsɪneɪtɪŋ	B	faszinierend
fashion	fæʃn	A	Mode; Art und Weise
fashionable	ˈfæʃnəbl	B	modisch
fast	fɑːst	A	schnell; fest
fast asleep	ˌəˈsliːp	B	tief schlafend

fasten	fɑ:sn B	befestigen	
fat	fæt A	fett, dick; Fett C	
fate	feɪt C	Schicksal, Geschick	
fatal	feɪtl C	fatal, tödlich	
father	'fɑ:ðə A	Vater	
father-in-law	B	Schwiegervater	
fault	fɔ:lt A	Fehler, Schuld	
faulty	'fɔ:ltɪ C	fehler-, mangelhaft	
favour	'feɪvə C	Gunst, Gefallen; begünstigen C	
in favour of	C	zu Gunsten von	
favourable	'feɪvərəbl B	günstig	
favourite	'feɪvərɪt A	Lieblings-	
fear	fɪə B	Furcht; fürchten	
for fear of	fə'fɪər‿əv C	aus Angst vor	
feast	fi:st B	Fest	
feather	'feðə B	(Vogel-)Feder	
feature	'fi:tʃə B	(Charakter-)Zug; Merkmal; Hörbild C	
February	'februərɪ A	Februar	
federal	'fedrəl C	Bundes-	
Federal Republic	B	Bundesrepublik	
fee	fi: B	Gebühr, Honorar	
feeble	'fi:bl C	schwach	
feed	fi:d B	füttern; s. ernähren	
fed	fed		
fed			
be fed up with	B	etw. satt haben	
feel	fi:l A	fühlen; glauben	
felt	felt		
felt			
fell	fel C	fällen	
feel like	C	Lust haben zu	
feeling	'fi:lɪŋ A	Gefühl; Eindruck	
fellow	'feləʊ B	Kerl; Gefährte	
fellow passenger	C	Mitreisende(r)	
	'..‿pæsɪndʒə		
female	'fi:meɪl B	weiblich	
fence	fens A	Zaun	
ferry	'ferɪ A	Fähre	
car-ferry	'..‿.. A	Autofähre	
fertile	'fɜ:taɪl C	fruchtbar *fertility*	
festival	'festɪvəl C	Festival, Festspiele	
fetch	fetʃ A	holen, abholen	
few	fju: A	wenige	
a few	A	ein paar, einige	
fiancé, ée	fɪ'ɑ:nseɪ B	Verlobter, -e	
fibre	'faɪbə C	Faser	
fiction	fɪkʃn B	Romanliteratur	
science fiction	B	Science-fiction, Zukunftsroman(e)	
	'saɪəns‿fɪkʃn		
field	fi:ld A	Feld; Gebiet	
fierce	fɪəs C	wild; heftig	
fig	fɪg C	Feige	
five	faɪv A	fünf	
fifteen	fɪf'ti:n A	fünfzehn	
fifty	'fɪftɪ A	fünfzig	
fight	faɪt A	kämpfen; Kampf	
fought	fɔ:t		
fought			
figure	'fɪgə B	Gestalt, Figur; Zahl	
figure out	C	ausrechnen	
file	faɪl C	Feile; Ordner	
fill	fɪl A	(s.) füllen	
fill in	B	ausfüllen	
fill out	B	(US) ausfüllen	
fill up	B	ein-, auffüllen	
fillet	'fɪlɪt C	Filet	
filling	'fɪlɪŋ C	Füllung	
filling station	'..‿.. A	Tankstelle	
film	fɪlm A	Film, filmen	
film star	B	Filmstar	
filthy	'fɪlθɪ B	schmutzig, scheußlich	
final	'faɪnəl B	letzte(r, s), endgültig	
finally	'faɪnəlɪ A	schließlich, zuletzt	
finance	faɪ'næns C	finanzieren	
financial	faɪ'nænʃl B	finanziell	
find	faɪnd A	finden, suchen	
found	faʊnd		
found			
find out	B	ausfindig machen, entdecken	
fine	faɪn A	schön, fein; Bußgeld C	
be fined	C	Strafe zahlen (müssen)	
fine arts	.'ɑ:ts C	Schöne Künste	
finger	'fɪŋgə A	Finger	
fingerprint	'fɪŋgəprɪnt C	Fingerabdruck	
finish	'fɪnɪʃ A	(be)enden; Finish, Ziel	
finish off (= up)	C	beenden	
Finland	'fɪnlənd C	Finnland	
Finnish	'fɪnɪʃ C	finnisch	
fir(-tree)	fɜ: C	Tanne, Fichte	
fire	'faɪə A	Feuer; hinauswerfen C	
be on fire	B	brennen	
set on fire	C	in Brand setzen	

A family firm

set on fire

35

fire brigade (= fire service)	brɪˈgeɪd	C	Feuerwehr
fireman	ˈfaɪəmən	C	Feuerwehrmann
fireplace	ˈfaɪəpleɪs	B	offener Kamin
fireworks	ˈfaɪəwɜːks	C	Feuerwerk
firm	fɜːm	A	fest, standhaft; Firma
first	fɜːst	A	erste(r,s); zuerst
first of all	ˌ.əvˌɔːl	A	vor allem, zunächst
at first	ətˌ.	A	zuerst
at first sight	ətˌˌˈsaɪt	C	auf den ersten Blick
in the first place ɪnˌðəˌˈpleɪs		C	überhaupt
first-class	ˌ.ˈ..	B	erstklassig
first name	ˌ.ˈ.	A	Vorname
firstly	ˈfɜːstlɪ	B	erstens
fish	fɪʃ	A	Fisch(e); fischen B

To fish

fisherman	ˈfɪʃəmən	C	Fischer
fishmonger	ˈfɪʃmʌŋə	C	Fischhändler
fission	fɪʃn	C	Spaltung
fist	fɪst	B	Faust
fit	fɪt	A	passend; in Form; passen
fit in		C	einplanen
have a fit		C	einen Anfall haben
fitting	ˈfɪtɪŋ	C	Anprobe; Fassung
fix	fɪks	B	befestigen; festlegen; reparieren
flag	flæg	B	Fahne, Flagge
flame	fleɪm	C	Flamme
flash	flæʃ	B	blitzen, aufleuchten; Aufflammen, Blitz
flash(light)	ˈflæʃlaɪt	B	Blitzlicht
flat	flæt	A	flach; Wohnung
flatter	ˈflætə	B	schmeicheln
flavour	ˈfleɪvə	C	Geschmack, Aroma
flea	fliː	C	Floh
flee	fliː	B	fliehen
fled	fled		
fled			
fleet	fliːt	B	Flotte
flesh	fleʃ	C	(lebendes) Fleisch
flex	fleks	C	Kabel(schnur)
flexible	ˈfleksəbl	C	biegsam, flexibel
flight	flaɪt	A	Flug; Flucht C
flight attendant		B	Flugbegleiter(in)
fling	flɪŋ	C	schleudern
flung	flʌŋ		
flung			
flirt	flɜːt	C	flirten
float	fləʊt	B	treiben, schwimmen
flock	flɒk	C	Herde, Schar
flood	flʌd	C	Flut, Überschwemmung; überschwemmen
floodlight	ˈflʌdlaɪt	C	Flutlicht
floor	flɔː	A	(Fuß-)Boden; Stockwerk
flop	flɒp	C	Fehlschlag, Reinfall
florist	ˈflɒrɪst	C	Blumenhändler
flour	ˈflaʊə	A	Mehl
flourish	ˈflʌrɪʃ	B	blühen, gedeihen
flow	fləʊ	A	fließen, strömen
flow chart	ˈfləʊ tʃɑːt	C	Flußdiagramm
flower	ˈflaʊə	A	Blume, Blüte
flu	fluː	A	Grippe
fluency	ˈfluːənsɪ	C	fließende Beherrschung
fluent	ˈfluːənt	A	fließend
flute	fluːt	C	(Quer-)Flöte
fly	flaɪ	A	fliegen; (Fahne) wehen; Fliege
flew	fluː		
flown	fləʊn		
foam	fəʊm	C	Schaum
fog	fɒg	A	Nebel
foggy	ˈfɒgɪ	A	neblig
fold	fəʊld	B	falten; Falte
twofold	ˈtuːfəʊld	C	zweifach
folder	ˈfəʊldə	C	Aktendeckel; Prospekt W
folk	fəʊk	B	Leute, Volk(s-)
folk music		B	Volksmusik
follow	ˈfɒləʊ	A	folgen
follow up		C	nachfassen
following...		B	im Anschluß an...
the following		B	folgende(r,s)
as follows	əzˌˈfɒləʊz	C	wie folgt
follower	ˈfɒləʊə	B	Anhänger(in)
fond	fɒnd	A	lieb, zärtlich
be fond of		A	mögen, gern haben
food	fuːd	A	Nahrung, Lebensmittel
food mixer	ˈfuːdmɪksə	C	Küchenmaschine
fool	fuːl	B	Dummkopf, Narr; zum Narren halten
foolish	ˈfuːlɪʃ	C	töricht
foot, feet	fʊt, fiːt	A	Fuß

on foot	ɒnˌ. B	zu Fuß	
football	ˈfʊtbɔːl A	Fußball	
football ground	A	Fußballplatz	
football pools	B	Fußballtoto	
footballer	ˈfʊtbɔːlə B	Fußballer	
footbrake	ˈfʊtbreɪk C	Fußbremse	
footpath	ˈfʊtpɑːθ C	Fußweg	
footstep	ˈfʊtstep C	Schritt	
for	fɔː A	für; denn; seit	
as for	æzˌfə C	was... betrifft	
for good	fəˌgʊd C	für immer	
forbid	fəˈbɪd A	verbieten	
forbade	fəˈbæd		
forbidden	fəˈbɪdn		
force	fɔːs A	Kraft, Gewalt; zwingen	
be forced to	A	müssen	
forecast	ˈfɔːkɑːst B	vorhersagen; (Wetter-) Vorhersage	
forecast			
forecast			
forefathers	ˈfɔːfɑːðəz C	Vorfahren	
foreground	ˈfɔːgraʊnd C	Vordergrund	
forehead	ˈfɒrɪd C	Stirn	
foreign	ˈfɒrɪn A	fremd, ausländisch	
foreigner	ˈfɒrɪnə A	Ausländer(in)	
foreman	ˈfɔːmən C	Meister	
forest	ˈfɒrɪst A	Wald, Forst	
forever	fəˈrevə B	für immer	
foreword	ˈfɔːwɜːd B	Vorwort	
forget	fəˈget A	vergessen	
forgot	fəˈgɒt		
forgotten	fəˈgɒtn		
forgetful	fəˈgetfʊl B	vergeßlich	
forgive	fəˈgɪv A	vergeben, verzeihen	
forgave	fəˈgeɪv		
forgiven	fəˈgɪvn		
fork	fɔːk A	Gabel	
form	fɔːm A	Form(ular); Schulklasse; bilden	
formal	ˈfɔːməl C	förmlich, formell	
formality	fəˈmælətɪ C	Formalität	
former	ˈfɔːmə B	früher, ehemalig	
the former	B	erstere(r,s)	
forth	fɔːθ B	hervor, heraus	
and so forth	əndˌsəʊˌ. B	und so fort	
forthcoming	ˈfɔːθkʌmɪŋ C	bevorstehend	
fortnight	ˈfɔːtnaɪt B	vierzehn Tage	
fortress	ˈfɔːtrəs B	Festung	
fortunate	ˈfɔːtʃənət B	glücklich (dran)	
fortunately	ˈfɔːtʃnətlɪ A	glücklicherweise, zum Glück	
fortune	ˈfɔːtʃuːn B	Glück; Vermögen	
forward	ˈfɔːwəd B	vorwärts, voran; schicken W	
look forward to	A	s. freuen auf	
foul	faʊl B	Foul, Regelverstoß	
found	faʊnd B	gründen	
foundation	faʊnˈdeɪʃn C	Gründung; Stiftung	
founder	ˈfaʊndə C	Gründer	
four	fɔː A	vier	
fourteen	fɔːˈtiːn A	vierzehn	
forty	ˈfɔːtɪ A	vierzig	
fox	fɒks B	Fuchs	

Foxes

fraction	ˈfrækʃn C	Bruch(teil)	
fragment	ˈfrægmənt C	Bruchstück, Fragment	
frame	freɪm B	Rahmen; einrahmen	
frame of mind	C	Haltung, Einstellung	
France	frɑːns A	Frankreich	
frank	fræŋk B	offen, freimütig	
free	friː A	frei; befreien B	
freedom	ˈfriːdəm A	Freiheit	
freeze	friːz B	(ge)frieren	
froze	frəʊz		
frozen	frəʊzn		
freight(er)	ˈfreɪt(ə) C	Fracht(er)	
French	frentʃ A	französisch	
Frenchman	ˈfrentʃmən A	Franzose	
frequency	ˈfriːkwənsɪ C	Frequenz, Häufigkeit	
frequent	ˈfriːkwənt B	häufig	
fresh	freʃ A	frisch	
freshman (US)	ˈfreʃmən C	Schüler(in) oder Student(in) im 1. Studienjahr	
Friday	ˈfraɪdɪ,eɪ A	Freitag	
fridge	frɪdʒ A	Kühlschrank	
friend	frend A	Freund(in)	
make friends (with)	B	s. anfreunden (mit)	
friendly	ˈfrendlɪ A	freundlich	
friendliness	ˈfrendlɪnəs B	Freundlichkeit	
friendship	ˈfrendʃɪp A	Freundschaft	
fright	fraɪt C	Schrecken	
frighten	fraɪtn B	erschrecken	
frightful	ˈfraɪtfʊl B	schrecklich	
frog	frɒg B	Frosch	
from	frɒm, frəm A	von; aus; vor	

from now on

from now on		B	von nun an
front	frʌnt	A	Vorderseite
in front (of)		A	vorn; vor
frontier	ˈfrʌntɪə	A	Grenze
frost	frɒst	B	Frost; Reif
frown	fraʊn	C	die Stirne runzeln
frown on sth		C	etw. mißbilligen
fruit	fruːt	A	Frucht; Obst
fruit juice	ˈfruːt dʒuːs	A	Fruchtsaft
fruit-tree		B	Obstbaum
frustrating	frʌˈstreɪtɪŋ	C	frustrierend, entmutigend
fry	fraɪ	A	braten
fried eggs		B	Spiegeleier
frying-pan	ˈfraɪɪŋ pæn	B	Bratpfanne
fuel	ˈfjuːəl	B	Brenn-, Kraftstoff
fulfil	fʊlˈfɪl	B	erfüllen
full	fʊl	A	voll, vollständig
full stop	fʊlˈstɒp	B	Punkt
full time	ˈfʊltaɪm	B	ganztägig
full up		B	(voll)besetzt
fun	fʌn	A	Spaß, Scherz
it's fun		A	es macht Spaß
funny	ˈfʌnɪ	A	komisch
function	ˈfʌŋkʃn	B	funktionieren; Funktion
fundamental	ˌfʌndəˈmentl	B	grundlegend
funeral	ˈfjuːnərəl	C	Begräbnis
funds	fʌndz	C	Geldmittel
raise funds		C	Geld aufbringen
fur	fɜː	B	Pelz
furious	ˈfjʊərɪəs	C	wütend
furnish	ˈfɜːnɪʃ	B	ausstatten; liefern; möblieren
furniture	ˈfɜːnɪtʃə	A	Möbel
further	ˈfɜːðə	A	ferner, weiter
further on		B	weiter vorne
furthermore	fɜːðəˈmɔː	B	außerdem
fury	ˈfjʊərɪ	C	Wut
fuse	fjuːz	C	Sicherung
fusion	ˈfjuːʒn	C	Verschmelzung, Fusion
fuss	fʌs	B	Aufhebens; ein Getue machen
fussy	ˈfʌsɪ	C	übertrieben geschäftig; umständlich
future	ˈfjuːtʃə	A	Zukunft; zukünftig
in future		A	in Zukunft

College of Further Education
Fortbildungszentrum

Gaelic
/ˈɡælɪk, ˈɡeɪlɪk/
keltische Sprache
(Schottland, Irland)

gateau
/ˈɡætəʊ/
Torte

G

g	dʒiː	A	g
gadget	ˈɡædʒɪt	C	modernes Gerät
gain	ɡeɪn	A	gewinnen, erlangen; Gewinn
gale	ɡeɪl	B	Sturm
gallery	ˈɡælərɪ	A	Galerie
gallon	ˈɡælən	C	Gallone (=4,55 l; US: 3,78 l)
gamble	ɡæmbl	C	spielen (um Geld)
gambler	ˈɡæmblə	C	Spieler
game	ɡeɪm	A	Spiel; Wild C
gang	ɡæŋ	B	Gruppe, Bande
gangster	ˈɡæŋstə	C	Gangster
gangway	ˈɡæŋweɪ	B	Landebrücke, Durchgang
gaol (= jail)	dʒeɪl	C	Gefängnis; ins Gefängnis sperren
gap	ɡæp	B	Lücke, Spalte
garage	ˈɡærɑː(d)ʒ	A	Garage
garden	ˈɡɑːdn	A	Garten
gardener	ˈɡɑːdnə	B	Gärtner
gardening	ˈɡɑːdnɪŋ	B	Gartenarbeit
garment	ˈɡɑːmənt	C	Kleidungsstück
garter	ˈɡɑːtə	C	Strumpfband
Order of the Garter		C	Hosenbandorden
gas	ɡæs	A	Gas; (US) Benzin
gas station (US)		C	Tankstelle
gasoline (US)	ˈɡæsəliːn	C	Benzin
gasp	ɡɑːsp	C	keuchen
gate	ɡeɪt	A	Tor; Flugsteig C
gateway	ˈɡeɪtweɪ	C	Tor, Einfahrt
gather	ˈɡæðə	B	(s. ver)sammeln; pflücken

To gather

gay	ɡeɪ	B	heiter, lustig; homosexuell C
gaiety	ˈɡeɪətɪ	C	Fröhlichkeit
gaze (at)	ɡeɪz	C	starren (auf)
gear	ɡɪə	B	Zahnrad; Gang
change gear		B	schalten (Gang)
gearbox	ˈɡɪəbɒks	C	Getriebe

gear lever	ˈgɪəˌliːvə C	Schalthebel	
general	ˈdʒenərəl A	allgemein; General	
in general	B	im allgemeinen	
generally	B	in der Regel	
generation	dʒenəˈreɪʃn B	Generation	
generosity	dʒenəˈrɒsəti B	Großzügigkeit	
generous	ˈdʒenərəs B	großzügig	
genitive	ˈdʒenɪtɪv C	Genitiv, Besitzfall	
genius	ˈdʒiːnɪəs B	Genie; Genialität	
gentle	dʒentl B	sanft; freundlich	
gentleness	ˈdʒentlnəs C	Sanftheit; Freundlichkeit	
gentleman	ˈdʒentlmən A	Gentleman; Herr	
genuine	ˈdʒenjʊɪn C	echt	

Genuine

geography	dʒ(ɪ)ˈɒgrəfi A	Erdkunde	
geometry	dʒɪˈɒmətri C	Geometrie	
German	ˈdʒɜːmən A	deutsch	
Germany	ˈdʒɜːməni A	Deutschland	
Germanic	dʒəˈmænɪk C	germanisch	
gerund	ˈdʒerənd C	Gerund,-ing Form	
gesture	ˈdʒestʃə B	Geste, Gebärde	
get	get A	bekommen; holen; gelangen, veranlassen; werden	
got	gɒt		
got			
get along with	B	s. vertragen mit	
get away with	C	mit etw. davonkommen	
get (here, there)	A	(her-, hin-)kommen	
get in/out	A	ein-/aussteigen	
get on/off	A	ein-/aussteigen; vorwärts-/davonkommen	
get ready	B	s. fertigmachen	
get rid of	C	loswerden	
get together	B	s. treffen	
get up	A	aufstehen	
get to know	B	kennenlernen	
ghost	gəʊst B	Geist	
giant	ˈdʒaɪənt C	Riese; riesig	
gift	gɪft B	Geschenk, Gabe	
gifted	ˈgɪftɪd B	begabt	
gigantic	dʒaɪˈgæntɪk B	riesenhaft	

giggle	gɪgl C	kichern	
gin	dʒɪn C	Gin, Wacholderschnaps	
ginger	ˈdʒɪndʒə C	Ingwer	
ginger ale	eɪl C	Ingwergetränk	
gingerbread	ˈdʒɪndʒəbred C	Lebkuchen	
giraffe	dʒɪˈrɑːf C	Giraffe	
girl	gɜːl A	Mädchen	
girlfriend	A	feste Freundin	
Girl Guide	gɜːlˈgaɪd C	Pfadfinderin	
give	gɪv A	geben, schenken	
gave	geɪv		
given	gɪvn		
give away	B	weg-, preisgeben	
give in/way	B	nachgeben	
give up	A	aufgeben	
glad	glæd A	froh	
be glad	A	s. freuen	
gladly	ˈglædli B	gern	
glance (at)	glɑːns B	blicken (auf); flüchtiger Blick	
glass	glɑːs A	Glas	
(a pair of) glasses	A	Brille	
glide	glaɪd C	gleiten	
glider	ˈglaɪdə C	Segelflugzeug	
glimpse	glɪmps B	flüchtiger Blick	
glitter	ˈglɪtə C	glitzern	
globe	gləʊb B	Kugel; Globus	
global	ˈgləʊbl C	global, weltweit	
gloomy	ˈgluːmi C	düster	
glorious	ˈglɔːrɪəs C	prächtig; glorreich	
glory	ˈglɔːri B	Pracht; Ruhm	
glove	glʌv A	Handschuh	
glow	gləʊ C	glühen; Glut	
glue	gluː B	Klebstoff; kleben	
go	gəʊ A	gehen; fahren; werden	
went	went		
gone	gɒn		
go ahead	A	anfangen; weitermachen	
go away	A	weggehen, verreisen	
go in for	C	betreiben, gern tun	
go into	C	s. befassen mit, untersuchen	
go off	C	explodieren; vonstatten gehen	
go on	A	fortsetzen, weiterhin tun; geschehen	
go out	A	ausgehen	
go up	C	steigen (Preise)	
be going to	A	wollen, werden	
be gone	C	weg sein	
have a go (at)	C	angehen, beginnen	
go-ahead	ˈgəʊəhed C	fortschrittlich	
goal	gəʊl A	Ziel; Tor (Sport)	
goalkeeper	ˈgəʊlkiːpə A	Torwart	
goat	gəʊt B	Ziege	

God	gɒd A	Gott
godchild	ˈgɒdtʃaɪld C	Patenkind
godfather,	ˈgɒdfɑːðə C	Pate
godmother	ˈgɒdmʌðə C	Patin
gold	gəʊld A	Gold; golden
golden	ˈgəʊldən C	goldfarben
goldfish	ˈgəʊldfɪʃ C	Goldfisch
golf	gɒlf A	Golf
golfer	ˈgɒlfə C	Golfspieler
good	gʊd A	gut, brav
better	ˈbetə	
best	best	
good at	B	gut in
goods	gʊdz B	Güter, Waren
goodbye	gʊdˌbaɪ A	auf Wiedersehen
say goodbye	A	s. verabschieden
good-humoured	C	gutgelaunt
	.ˈhjuːməd	
good-looking	B	gutaussehend
goodness	ˈgʊdnəs C	Güte
goodwill	gʊdˈwɪl C	Sympathiebeweis
goose, geese	guːs, giːs B	Gans
gooseberry	ˈgʊzbərɪ B	Stachelbeere
gorgeous	ˈgɔːdʒəs B	herrlich, toll
gosh!	gɒʃ C	ach!
gospel	gɒspl B	Evangelium
gossip	ˈgɒsɪp C	Klatsch; ratschen

To gossip

Gothic	ˈgɒθɪk C	gotisch
govern	ˈgʌvən A	regieren
government	ˈgʌvnmənt A	Regierung
gown	gaʊn B	langes Gewand, Talar
dressing-gown	C	Morgenrock
evening gown	C	Abendkleid
grab	græb B	packen, schnappen
grace	greɪs C	Gunst; Anmut; Tischgebet
graceful	ˈgreɪsfʊl C	anmutig
gracious	ˈgreɪʃəs C	gnädig
good gracious!	C	mein Gott!
grade	greɪd B	Note; (US) Klasse
grade school	B	(US) Volksschule

governor
Gouverneur

gradual	ˈgrædʒʊəl B	allmählich
graduate	ˈgrædʒʊət C	Absolvent
	ˈgrædʒʊeɪt C	abschließen
grain	greɪn B	Korn; Getreide
grammar	ˈgræmə A	Grammatik
grammar school	A	Gymnasium
grammatical	B	grammatisch
	grəˈmætɪkəl	
gramophone	C	Plattenspieler
	ˈgræməfəʊn	
grand	grænd B	großartig
grandchild	ˈgræntʃaɪld A	Enkelkind
grandfather	A	Großvater
	ˈgræn(d)fɑːðə	
grandmother	A	Großmutter
	ˈgræn(d)mʌðə	
grandparents	A	Großeltern
	ˈgræn(d)peərənts	
granite	ˈgrænɪt C	Granit
grant	grɑːnt B	bewilligen; Stipendium
take for granted	C	als selbstverständlich ansehen
grapefruit	ˈgreɪpfruːt A	Grapefruit
grapes	greɪps A	Weintrauben
grasp	grɑːsp B	(be)greifen; packen
grass	grɑːs A	Gras
grateful	ˈgreɪtfʊl A	dankbar
gratitude	ˈgrætɪtjuːd B	Dankbarkeit
grave	greɪv C	Grab; ernsthaft
gravity	ˈgrævɪtɪ C	Schwerkraft
gravy	ˈgreɪvɪ B	Bratensoße
graze	greɪz C	grasen, weiden
great	greɪt A	groß, großartig
greatly	ˈgreɪtlɪ A	sehr
Great Britain	A	Großbritannien
Greece	griːs B	Griechenland
Greek	griːk B	griechisch; Grieche
greedy	ˈgriːdɪ C	gierig
green	griːn A	grün
greengrocer	A	Obst- und
	ˈgriːngrəʊsə	Gemüsehändler

The greenhouse

greenhouse	'gri:nhaʊs	C	Glas-, Gewächshaus
Greenland	'gri:nlənd	C	Grönland
greet	gri:t	A	(be)grüßen
greetings	'gri:tɪŋz	B	Grüße
grey, gray	greɪ	A	grau
greyhound	'greɪhaʊnd	C	Windhund
Greyhound bus		C	(US) Überlandbus
grief	gri:f	C	Kummer
grill	grɪl	C	Gitter; Grill; grillen
grim	grɪm	C	grimmig, finster
grin	grɪn	B	Grinsen; grinsen
grind	graɪnd	C	mahlen; schleifen
ground			
ground			
groan	grəʊn	C	stöhnen
grocer	'grəʊsə	A	Lebensmittelhändler
groceries	'grəʊsərɪz	C	Lebensmittel
gross weight	'grəʊs weɪt	W	Bruttogewicht
ground	graʊnd	A	(Erd-)Boden; Grund
ground floor	'graʊnd ˌflɔ:	A	Erdgeschoß
ground-plan		C	Grundriß
group	gru:p	A	Gruppe
grow	grəʊ	A	wachsen; züchten; werden
grew	gru:		
grown	grəʊn		
grow up		A	aufwachsen
grown-up	'grəʊnʌp	A	Erwachsene(r);
	'grəʊnˌʌp	A	erwachsen
growth	grəʊθ	B	Wachstum, Wuchs
growl	graʊl	B	knurren
grumble	grʌmbl	C	murren
guarantee	ˌgærən'ti:	B	Garantie; garantieren
guard	gɑ:d	B	bewachen; Wache; Zugschaffner
guard against		B	s. hüten vor
be on one's guard		C	auf der Hut sein
guardian	'gɑ:djən	B	Hüter; Vormund
guess	ges	A	(er)raten, vermuten; Vermutung
guest	gest	A	Gast
guesthouse	'gesthaʊs	A	Gästehaus
guidance	'gaɪdəns	C	Beratung, Hilfe
guide	gaɪd	A	führen, leiten; (Reise-, Fremden-)Führer
guided tour	'gaɪdɪdˌtʊə	C	Führung
guilt	gɪlt	B	Schuld (Verbrechen)
guilty	'gɪltɪ	A	schuldig
guitar	gɪ'tɑ:	A	Gitarre
Gulf Stream		B	Golfstrom
	'gʌlfˌstri:m		
gum	gʌm	C	(Kau-)Gummi
gun	gʌn	A	Schußwaffe, Geschütz
gunman	'gʌnmən	C	bewaffneter Bandit
Gunpowder Plot		C	Pulververschwörung
	ˌgʌnpaʊdəˌplɒt		
guy	gaɪ	B	(US) Kerl, junger Mann
gym(nastics)		B	Turnen
	dʒɪm('næstɪks)		
gymnasium	dʒɪm'neɪzɪəm	B	Turnhalle
gypsy (= gipsy)	'dʒɪpsɪ	C	Zigeuner(in)

H

h	eɪtʃ	A	h
habit	'hæbɪt	A	Gewohnheit
habitual	hə'bɪtjʊəl	C	gewohnt
haggis	'hægɪs	C	schott. Nationalgericht
hair	heə	A	Haar(e)
haircut	'heəkʌt	C	Haarschneiden, -schnitt
hairdo	'heədu:	C	Frisur
hairdresser	'heədresə	A	Friseur, Friseuse
hairdryer	'heədraɪə	C	Fön
half, ves	hɑ:f, vz	A	Hälfte; halb
halfway	'hɑ:fweɪ	A	halbwegs; auf halbem Wege
hall	hɔ:l	A	Halle; Hausflur
hallo, hello	hə'ləʊ	A	Hallo! Guten Tag!
halt	hɔ:lt	B	Halt; halten
halve	hɑ:v	C	halbieren
ham	hæm	A	Schinken
hamburger	'hæmbɜ:gə	B	»Hamburger«
hammer	'hæmə	C	Hammer; hämmern
hammock	'hæmək	C	Hängematte
hand	hænd	A	Hand; (Uhr)Zeiger; reichen
hand-made		C	handgefertigt
by hand		C	mit der Hand
give (= lend) a hand		B	behilflich sein
on the one hand		B	einerseits
on the other hand		B	andererseits
hand in		B	abgeben, -liefern
handbag	'hæn(d)bæg	A	Handtasche

group work
Gruppen-
arbeit

guitarist
/gɪ'tɑ:rɪst/
Gitarrist

handbag

a handful

a handful (of)		C	eine Handvoll
handicapped 'hændıkæpt		A	behindert
handkerchief,fs 'hæŋkətʃıf		B	Taschentuch
handle	hændl B		Griff, Henkel; behandeln
handlebars	'hændlbɑ:z C		Lenkstange
handout	'hændaʊt C		Begleitmaterial
handshake	'hændʃeık B		Händedruck
handsome	'hænsəm A		stattlich
(hand)writing 'hændraıtıŋ		C	Handschrift
handy	'hændı C		greifbar; praktisch
hang	hæŋ A		auf-, hinhängen
hung	hʌŋ		
hung			
hang (hanged)		C	hängen, hinrichten
hang about		C	s. herumtreiben
hang on		C	dableiben, warten
hang up		C	aufhängen, Hörer auflegen
hang-gliding 'hæŋglaıdıŋ		C	Drachenfliegen
hanger	'hæŋə C		(Kleider-)Bügel
hangover	'hæŋəʊvə C		Kater

A hangover

happen	hæpn A		s. ereignen, geschehen
happen to do		A	zufällig tun
happy	'hæpı A		glücklich
happily	'hæpılı B		glücklicherweise
happiness	'hæpınıs B		Glück
harbour	'hɑ:bə A		Hafen
hard	hɑ:d A		hart; schwer; heftig
work hard		A	hart arbeiten
hard of hearing		C	schwerhörig
hardly	'hɑ:dlı A		kaum
hardly any		B	fast kein(e)
hardly ever		B	fast nie

hardworking
fleißig

hardship	'hɑ:dʃıp B		Mühsal
hardware	'hɑ:dweə C		Eisenwaren; Hardware (=Geräte)
hare	heə B		Hase
harm	hɑ:m B		Schaden; schaden
harmful	'hɑ:mfʊl C		schädlich
harmless	'hɑ:mlıs B		unschädlich
harmony	'hɑ:mənı B		Harmonie, Einklang
harp	hɑ:p C		Harfe
harsh	hɑ:ʃ C		rauh, barsch
harvest	'hɑ:vıst B		Ernte; ernten
harvester	'hɑ:vıstə C		Erntemaschine
haste	heıst C		Eile, Hast
make haste		C	schnell machen
hasten	heısn C		s. beeilen
hat	hæt A		Hut
hat trick	'hæt‿trık C		3 aufeinanderfolgende Treffer
hatch	hætʃ C		ausbrüten
hatchet	'hætʃıt C		Beil
hate	heıt A		hassen; Haß C
hatred	'heıtrıd C		Haß
have	hæv, həv A		haben, besitzen
had	hæd, həd, (ə)d		
had			
have got	həv'gɒt A		haben, besitzen
had better		A	sollte lieber
have (got) to		A	müssen
have (=get) sth done		A	etw. machen lassen
have a look at		A	anschauen, betrachten
have a look round		A	sich umsehen
hay	heı B		Heu
make hay		C	heuen
hazard	'hæzəd C		Gefahr, Risiko
hazelnut	'heızlnʌt C		Haselnuß
he	hi:, hı A		er
head	hed A		Kopf; Haupt
head (for)		C	s. zubewegen (auf)
headache	'hedeık A		Kopfschmerzen
heading	'hedıŋ B		Überschrift
headlights	'hedlaıts C		Scheinwerfer (Auto)
headline	'hedlaın C		Schlagzeile
headmaster	hed'mɑ:stə A		Schulleiter
headmistress hed'mıstrıs		A	Schulleiterin
head office		W	Hauptbüro, Zentrale
headphones	'hedfəʊnz C		Kopfhörer
headquarters 'hedkwɔ:təz		B	Hauptquartier, Zentrale
headteacher	hed'ti:tʃə C		Schulleiter(in)
headscarf	'hedskɑ:f C		Kopftuch
heal	hi:l C		heilen
health	helθ A		Gesundheit
healthy	'helθı A		gesund

hear	hɪə A	hören; erfahren	
heard	hɜ:d		
heard			
hearing aid	'hɪərɪŋeɪd C	Hörapparat	
heart	hɑ:t A	Herz	
by heart	A	auswendig	
heart attack	ə'tæk C	Herzanfall	
hearty	'hɑ:tɪ A	herzlich, herzhaft	
heat	hi:t A	Hitze	
heating	'hi:tɪŋ A	Heizung	
heaven	hevn B	Himmel	
for heaven's sake!	C	um Himmels willen!	
good heavens!	C	du lieber Himmel!	
heavenly	'hevnlɪ C	himmlisch	
heavy	'hevɪ A	schwer, heftig	
hectic	'hektɪk C	hektisch	
hedge	hedʒ B	Hecke	
hedgehog	'hedʒhɒg C	Igel	
heel	hi:l B	Ferse; Absatz	
height	haɪt A	Höhe, Höhepunkt	
heir	eə B	Erbe	
helicopter	'helɪkɒptə B	Hubschrauber	
hell	hel C	Hölle	
hello	hə'ləʊ A	Hallo! Grüß Gott!	
helmet	'helmɪt C	Helm	
help	help A	Hilfe; helfen	
can't help...	B	nicht umhin können	
I can't help it	B	ich kann nichts dafür	
it can't be helped	B	es läßt s. nicht ändern	
help yourself (to)	C	bedienen Sie sich (mit)	

To help oneself

helping	'helpɪŋ C	Portion (Essen)	
helpful	'helpfʊl B	hilfreich	
helpless	'helpləs C	hilflos	
hen	hen B	Henne	
her	hɜ:, ɜ:, ə A	ihr, sie (Fürw.)	
herb	hɜ:b B	Heil-, Küchenkraut	
herd	hɜ:d B	Herde	
here	hɪə A	hier(her), da	
here you are	B	da; hier bitte!	
here's to you!	C	Prost!	
herewith	'hɪəwɪð C	hiermit	
heritage	'herɪtɪdʒ C	Erbe, Tadition	
hero, es	'hɪərəʊ B	Held	
heroic	hɪə'rəʊɪk C	heldenhaft	
hesitate	'hezɪteɪt A	zögern	
hesitation	hezɪ'teɪʃn C	Zögern, Bedenken	
hi	haɪ A	Grüß dich! Servus!	
hide	haɪd A	(s.) verstecken	
hid	hɪd		
hidden	hɪdn		
hi-fi	'haɪ ˌfaɪ C	Hochklang, Hifi	
high	haɪ A	hoch; Hoch	
highly	'haɪlɪ B	höchst, sehr	
Highland(s)	'haɪlənd(z) B	Hochland	
Highlander	C	Hochlandschotte	
highlight	'haɪlaɪt C	Höhepunkt	
hijack	'haɪdʒæk B	entführen, kapern	
hijacker	'haɪdʒækə B	Entführer	
highway	'haɪweɪ B	Landstraße	
hike	haɪk C	wandern	
hill	hɪl A	Hügel, Berg	
downhill	'daʊnhɪl C	bergab	
uphill	'ʌphɪl C	bergauf	
hillside	'hɪlsaɪd C	Abhang	
hill-walking	C	Bergwandern	
hilly	'hɪlɪ A	hügelig	
him	hɪm, ɪm A	ihn, ihm	
hind legs	'haɪndlegz C	Hinterbeine	
hint	hɪnt B	Wink, Andeutung	
hip	hɪp C	Hüfte	
hippopotamus	hɪpə'pɒtəməs	C	Nilpferd	
hire	haɪə A	mieten, anheuern	
hire-purchase	W	Ratenkauf	
	'haɪə 'pɜ:tʃɪs		
his	hɪz, ɪz A	sein (Fürwort)	
historic	hɪ'stɒrɪk B	historisch (berühmt)	
historical	hɪ'stɒrɪkl B	geschichtlich	
history	'hɪstərɪ A	Geschichte	
hit	hɪt A	schlagen, treffen;	
hit		Schlag(er), Treffer	
hit			
hitch-hike	'hɪtʃ ˌhaɪk A	per Anhalter reisen	
hoarse	hɔ:s C	heiser	
hobby	'hɒbɪ A	Steckenpferd	
hockey	'hɒkɪ B	Hockey	
hold	həʊld A	halten; Griff C	
held	held		
held			
hold on!	B	bleiben Sie am Apparat!	
hold up	B	aufhalten; überfallen	
hold-up	'həʊldʌp C	Überfall	

hectare /'hektɑ:/ Hektar

heliport Hubschrauberplatz

English	IPA	Level	German
catch/get hold of		C	ergreifen; erwischen
hole	həʊl	B	Loch, Höhle
holiday	ˈhɒlədɪ,eɪ	A	Feiertag; Urlaub
go on holiday		B	in Urlaub fahren
holidays	ˈhɒlədɪz,eɪz	A	Ferien
holiday-maker	ˈhɒlədɪˌmeɪkə	C	Urlauber
Holland	ˈhɒlənd	B	Holland
hollow	ˈhɒləʊ	C	hohl
holly	ˈhɒlɪ	C	Stechpalme

Holly

English	IPA	Level	German
holy	ˈhəʊlɪ	B	heilig
Holy Spirit (= Ghost)		C	Heiliger Geist
Holy Trinity	ˈ.. ˈtrɪnɪtɪ	C	Hl. Dreifaltigkeit
home	həʊm	A	Heim(at); nach Hause
at home		A	zu Hause
home appliance	əˈplaɪəns	C	Haushaltsgerät
home country		B	Heimat(land)
home-made		C	hausgemacht
Home Secretary		C	(GB)Innenminister
homesick	ˈhəʊmsɪk	C	heimwehkrank
homework	ˈhəʊmwɜːk	A	Hausaufgabe
homing pigeon	ˈpɪdʒən	C	Brieftaube
honest	ˈɒnɪst	B	ehrlich, aufrichtig
honestly	ˈɒnɪstlɪ	A	ehrlich (gesagt)
honesty	ˈɒnəstɪ	A	Aufrichtigkeit
honey	ˈhʌnɪ	A	Honig
honeymoon	ˈhʌnɪmuːn	C	Flitterwochen
honour	ˈɒnə	B	Ehre; ehren
honourable	ˈɒnərəbl	C	ehrenhaft, -wert
hood	hʊd	C	Kapuze; (US) Motorhaube
hoof, fs(ves)	huːf, vz	C	Huf
hook	hʊk	C	Haken; festhaken
hooligan	ˈhuːlɪɡən	C	Rowdy
hop	hɒp	C	hüpfen
hope	həʊp	A	hoffen; Hoffnung
hopeful	ˈhəʊpfʊl	B	hoffnungsvoll
hopefully	ˈhəʊpfʊlɪ	B	hoffentlich, wie zu hoffen ist
hopeless	ˈhəʊplɪs	B	hoffnungslos
hops	hɒps	C	Hopfen
hop-picking		C	Hopfenpflücken
horizon	həˈraɪzn	B	Horizont
horizontal	ˌhɒrɪˈzɒntl	B	horizontal; waagrecht
horn	hɔːn	C	Horn; Hupe
horoscope	ˈhɒrəskəʊp	C	Horoskop
horrible	ˈhɒrəbl	B	schrecklich
horrid	ˈhɒrɪd	C	abscheulich
horror	ˈhɒrə	C	Entsetzen, Abscheu
horse	hɔːs	A	Pferd
on horseback		B	zu Pferde
horsepower	ˈhɔːspaʊə	C	Pferdestärke
horseshoe	ˈhɔːʃʃuː	C	Hufeisen
hose	həʊz	C	Schlauch
hospitable	hɒˈspɪtəbl	B	gastfreundlich
hospitality	ˌhɒspɪˈtælətɪ	B	Gastfreundschaft
hospital	ˈhɒspɪtl	A	Krankenhaus
host, hostess	həʊst,ɪs	A	Gastgeber,-in
host family		A	Gastfamilie
hostage	ˈhɒstɪdʒ	C	Geisel
hostel	ˈhɒstl	A	Herberge, Heim
hostile	ˈhɒstaɪl	C	feindlich
hot	hɒt	A	heiß, warm; scharf
hot dog	ˈhɒtdɒɡ	B	Hotdog
hotel	həʊˈtel	A	Hotel, Gasthof

A hotel   *A hostel*

English	IPA	Level	German
hour	ˈaʊə	A	Stunde
hourly	ˈaʊəlɪ	B	stündlich
house	haʊs	A	Haus
House of Commons		A	Unterhaus
House of Lords	lɔːdz	A	Oberhaus
House of Representatives		B	(US) Repräsentantenhaus
household	ˈhaʊshəʊld	B	Haushalt
housewife	ˈhaʊswaɪf	B	Hausfrau
housework	ˈhaʊswɜːk	B	Hausarbeit
hovercraft	ˈhɒvəkrɑːft	C	Luftkissenfahrzeug
how	haʊ	A	wie
how are you?		A	wie geht es Ihnen?

how do you do		A	Guten Tag (bei der Vorstellung)
how do you know?		A	woher wissen Sie das?
however	haʊˈevə	A	jedoch; wie auch immer
howl	haʊl	C	heulen; Geheul
huge	hjuːdʒ	B	riesig
human	ˈhjuːmən	B	menschlich
humanity	hjuːˈmænəti	B	Menschheit
humble	hʌmbl	C	bescheiden, demütig
humour	ˈhjuːmə	A	Humor; Laune
humorous	ˈhjuːmərəs	B	humorvoll
hundred	ˈhʌndrəd	A	hundert
Hungary	ˈhʌŋgəri	C	Ungarn
Hungarian	hʌŋˈgeəriən	C	ungarisch
hunger	ˈhʌŋgə	B	Hunger
hungry	ˈhʌŋgri	A	hungrig
be hungry		A	Hunger haben
hunt	hʌnt	B	jagen; Jagd
hunter	ˈhʌntə	B	Jäger
hurricane	ˈhʌrikən	B	Orkan
hurry	ˈhʌri	A	Eile, Hast
hurry (up)		A	sich beeilen
be in a hurry		A	in Eile sein
hurried	ˈhʌrid	B	hastig, übereilt
hurt	hɜːt	A	verletzen, weh tun
hurt			
hurt			
hurt sb's feelings		C	jdn. kränken
husband	ˈhʌzbənd	A	(Ehe-)Mann
hush	hʌʃ	C	pst!
hut	hʌt	B	Hütte
hydrogen	ˈhaidrədʒən	C	Wasserstoff
hyphen	haifn	B	Bindestrich

I

i	ai	A	i
I	ai	A	ich
ice	ais	A	Eis
iceberg	ˈaisbɜːg	C	Eisberg
ice cream	aisˈkriːm	A	Speiseeis
ice-hockey	ˈaishɒki	B	Eishockey
Iceland	ˈaislənd	C	Island
ice skating	ˈais skeitiŋ	A	Eislaufen
icy	ˈaisi	A	eisig
ice-rink	ˈais ˌriŋk	C	Eisstadion,-bahn
idea	aiˈdiə	A	Gedanke, Idee
the idea is...	ðiˌaiˈdiə(r)ˌiz	C	es geht darum, daß...
ideal	aiˈdiəl	A	vorbildlich; Ideal
idealist	aiˈdiəlist	C	Idealist
identical	aiˈdentikl	C	identisch
identify	aiˈdentifai	C	identifizieren
identity	aiˈdentiti	C	Identität
identity card		C	Personalausweis
idiom	ˈidiəm	C	Idiom, sprachtypischer Ausdruck
idiomatic	idiəˈmætik	C	idiomatisch
idiot	ˈidiət	C	Idiot
idiotic	idiˈɒtik	C	idiotisch
idle	aidl	C	müßig, untätig
idleness	ˈaidlnəs	C	Müßiggang
idol	aidl	C	Idol
i.e. (= that is)		C	d. h. (das heißt)
if	if	A	wenn, falls; ob
if only		B	wenn (doch) nur
if so		C	wenn ja
ignite	igˈnait	C	(ent)zünden
ignition	igˈniʃn	C	Zündung
ignorant	ˈignərənt	C	unwissend
ignore	igˈnɔː	B	nicht beachten
ignorance	ˈignərəns	B	Unwissenheit
ill	il	A	krank
fall ill		B	krank werden
be taken ill		B	erkranken
illness	ˈilnis	B	Krankheit
illegal	iˈliːgəl	C	ungesetzlich
illegible	iˈledʒibl	C	unleserlich
illuminate	iˈluːmineit	B	beleuchten
illumination	iluːmiˈneiʃn	C	Beleuchtung
illustrate	ˈiləstreit	B	illustrieren
illustration	iləˈstreiʃn	C	Abbildung
illustrious	iˈlʌstriəs	C	hochangesehen
image	ˈimidʒ	C	Bild, Abbild
imagine	iˈmædʒin	A	s. vorstellen; s. einbilden
imagination	imædʒiˈneiʃn	B	Einbildungskraft, Phantasie
imitate	ˈimiteit	B	nachmachen
imitation	imiˈteiʃn	C	Imitation

To imitate

immediate(ly)

immediate(ly)	ɪˈmiːdɪət(lɪ)	A	unmittelbar, sofort
immense	ɪˈmens	B	unermeßlich
immigrant	ˈɪmɪgrənt	B	Einwanderer
immigrate	ˈɪmɪgreɪt	B	einwandern
immigration	ɪmɪˈgreɪʃn	B	Einwanderung
immoral	ɪˈmɒrəl	C	unmoralisch
impact	ˈɪmpækt	C	Aufprall; Einfluß
impatience	ɪmˈpeɪʃns	B	Ungeduld
impatient	ɪmˈpeɪʃnt	B	ungeduldig
impeccable	ɪmˈpekəbl	C	tadellos
imperative	ɪmˈperətɪv	B	Imperativ, Befehlsform
imperial	ɪmˈpɪərɪəl	C	Reichs-; kaiserlich
imperialism	ɪmˈpɪərɪəlɪzm	C	Imperialismus
impolite	ɪmpəˈlaɪt	B	unhöflich
import	ˈɪmpɔːt	A	Einfuhr
import	ɪmˈpɔːt	A	einführen, importieren
importer	ɪmˈpɔːtə	W	Importeur
imports	ˈɪmpɔːts	C	Importgüter
important	ɪmˈpɔːtənt	A	wichtig
importance	ɪmˈpɔːtəns	B	Wichtigkeit, Bedeutung
imposing	ɪmˈpəʊzɪŋ	C	eindrucksvoll
impossible	ɪmˈpɒsəbl	A	unmöglich
impress	ɪmˈpres	B	beeindrucken
impression	ɪmˈpreʃn	B	Eindruck
impressive	ɪmˈpresɪv	C	eindrucksvoll
imprison	ɪmˈprɪzn	C	inhaftieren
imprisonment	ɪmˈprɪznmənt	C	Inhaftierung, Haft
improbable	ɪmˈprɒbəbl	C	unwahrscheinlich
improve	ɪmˈpruːv	A	verbessern; s. bessern
improvement	ɪmˈpruːvmənt	B	(Ver-)Besserung
in	ɪn	A	in, an, auf; hinein
be in		B	da sein; modern sein
inauguration	ɪnɔːgjʊˈreɪʃn	C	Amtseinführung
Inaugural Address	ɪnˈɔːgjʊrəl	C	(US) Antrittsrede
incapable	ɪnˈkeɪpəbl	B	unfähig
inch	ɪntʃ	B	Zoll (2,54 cm)
incident	ˈɪnsɪdənt	C	Vorfall
incidentally	ɪnsɪˈdentlɪ	B	übrigens
inclined	ɪnˈklaɪnd	C	geneigt
be inclined to		C	geneigt sein
include	ɪnˈkluːd	B	einschließen, enthalten
including	ɪnˈkluːdɪŋ	B	einschließlich
income	ˈɪnkʌm	A	Einkommen
income tax	ˈɪnkʌm ˌtæks	C	Einkommensteuer
incomplete	ɪnkəmˈpliːt	B	unvollständig
incomprehensible	ɪnkɒmprɪˈhensəbl	C	unverständlich
inconvenient	ɪnkənˈviːnɪənt	B	ungelegen
inconvenience	ɪnkənˈviːnɪəns	B	Unannehmlichkeit
incorporate	ɪnˈkɔːpəreɪt	C	umfassen
incorrect	ɪnkəˈrekt	A	unrichtig
increase	ɪnˈkriːs	B	zunehmen; vergrößern
	ˈɪŋkriːs	B	Zunahme; Vergrößerung
incredible	ɪnˈkredəbl	B	unglaublich
indeed	ɪnˈdiːd	A	in der Tat, wirklich
indefinite	ɪnˈdefɪnɪt	B	unbestimmt
indefinite article		B	unbestimmter Artikel
independence	ɪndɪˈpendəns	A	Unabhängigkeit
independent	ɪndɪˈpendənt	A	unabhängig; selbständig
index	ˈɪndeks	C	Index; Register
index finger		C	Zeigefinger
India	ˈɪndjə	B	Indien
(india) rubber	ˈrʌbə	C	Radiergummi
Indian	ˈɪndjən	B	indisch; indianisch; Inder; Indianer
indicate	ˈɪndɪkeɪt	B	(an)zeigen, angeben

To indicate

indicator	ˈɪndɪkeɪtə	C	Blinker (Auto)
indifferent	ɪnˈdɪfərənt	B	gleichgültig
indignant	ɪnˈdɪgnənt	C	entrüstet, empört
indirect	ɪndɪˈrekt	B	indirekt, mittelbar
indirect speech	ˌ...ˈspiːtʃ	B	indirekte Rede
indispensable	ɪndɪˈspensəbl	C	unerläßlich
individual	ɪndɪˈvɪdjʊəl	B	Individuum; einzeln
indoor	ˈɪndɔː	B	Innen-, im Hause befindlich
indoors	ɪnˈdɔːz	B	im Hause, zu Hause
induce	ɪnˈdjuːs	C	bewegen, veranlassen

industry	ˈɪndəstrɪ A	Industrie	
industrial	ɪnˈdʌstrɪəl A	industriell	
industrial action	ækʃn C	gewerkschaftliche Maßnahmen	
industrialise(-ize)	ɪnˈdʌstrɪəlaɪz C	industrialisieren	
industrialisation	ɪndʌstrɪəlaɪˈzeɪʃn C	Industrialisierung	
industrialist	ɪnˈdʌstrɪəlɪst C	Industrieller	
industrious	ɪnˈdʌstrɪəs B	fleißig, arbeitsam	
inefficient	ɪnɪˈfɪʃnt B	untüchtig, unrationell	
inevitable	ɪnˈevɪtəbl B	unvermeidlich	
inexpensive	ɪnɪkˈspensɪv C	billig	
infant	ˈɪnfənt B	Kleinkind	
infant school		B	Grundschule
infectious	ɪnˈfekʃəs C	ansteckend	
inferior (to)	ɪnˈfɪərɪə B	minderwertig(er)	
infinite	ˈɪnfɪnɪt C	unendlich, unbegrenzt	
infinitive	ɪnˈfɪnɪtɪv B	Infinitiv	
inflation	ɪnˈfleɪʃn C	Inflation	
influence (on)	ˈɪnfluəns B	Einfluß (auf); beeinflussen	
influential	ɪnfluˈenʃl C	einflußreich	
inform (of/about)	ɪnˈfɔ:m A	benachrichtigen; unterrichten (von/über)	
information	ɪnfəˈmeɪʃn A	Auskunft, Information(en)	

Information

information office		A	Informationsbüro
informal	ɪnˈfɔ:məl C	form-, zwanglos	
ingenious	ɪnˈdʒi:nɪəs C	genial	
ingredient	ɪnˈgri:dɪənt C	Bestandteil, Zutat	
inhabit	ɪnˈhæbɪt C	(be)wohnen	
inhabitant	ɪnˈhæbɪtənt B	Einwohner(in), Bewohner(in)	
inherit	ɪnˈherɪt C	erben	
initial	ɪˈnɪʃl C	Anfangs-, anfänglich	
initials	ɪˈnɪʃlz C	Initialen, Anfangsbuchstaben	
initiative	ɪˈnɪʃɪətɪv C	Initiative	
inject	ɪnˈdʒekt C	einspritzen	
injection	ɪnˈdʒekʃn C	Injektion, Einspritz-	
injure	ˈɪndʒə A	verletzen	
injury	ˈɪndʒərɪ B	Verletzung	
injustice	ɪnˈdʒʌstɪs B	Ungerechtigkeit	
ink	ɪŋk A	Tinte; Druckerschwärze	
inland	ˈɪnlənd C	landeinwärts; Inland	
inn	ɪn C	Gasthof, Wirtshaus	
innkeeper	ˈɪnki:pə C	Gastwirt	
inner	ˈɪnə A	inner, inwendig	
innocence	ˈɪnəsəns C	Unschuld	
innocent	ˈɪnəsənt C	unschuldig	
innumerable	ɪˈnju:mərəbl B	unzählig, zahllos	
input	ˈɪnpʊt C	Eingabe	
inquire (about)	ɪŋˈkwaɪə B	s. erkundigen (über)	
inquiry	ɪŋˈkwaɪərɪ B	Anfrage, Erkundigung	
inquisitive	ɪnˈkwɪzɪtɪv C	neugierig	
insane	ɪnˈseɪn C	verrückt	
inscription	ɪnˈskrɪpʃn C	Inschrift	
insect	ˈɪnsekt A	Insekt	
inseparable	ɪnˈsepərəbl C	unzertrennlich	
insert	ɪnˈsɜ:t B	einfügen, einwerfen	
inside	ɪnˈsaɪd A	inner, innerhalb	
insist (on)	ɪnˈsɪst A	bestehen (auf)	
insolent	ˈɪnsələnt C	unverschämt, frech	
inspect	ɪnˈspekt C	be(auf)sichtigen	
inspector	ɪnˈspektə C	Aufseher, Inspektor	
install	ɪnˈstɔ:l C	einbauen, installieren	
instalment	ɪnˈstɔ:lmənt W	(Abzahlungs-)Rate	
instance	ˈɪnstəns B	Beispiel, Einzelfall	
for instance		A	zum Beispiel
instant	ˈɪnstənt C	Augenblick; sofortig	
instant coffee		C	Nescafé, Pulverkaffee
instantly	ˈɪnstəntlɪ B	sofort	
instead	ɪnˈsted B	dafür, statt dessen	
instead of		A	(an)statt
instinct	ˈɪnstɪŋkt C	Instinkt	
instinctive	ɪnˈstɪŋktɪv C	unwillkürlich, instinktiv	
institution	ɪnstɪˈtju:ʃn B	Einrichtung	
instruct	ɪnˈstrʌkt B	unterrichten, -weisen	
instruction	ɪnˈstrʌkʃn B	Unterweisung; Anweisung	
instructor	ɪnˈstrʌktə C	Ausbilder	
instrument	ˈɪnstrəmənt B	Instrument, Werkzeug	

instrument

insufficient	ɪnsəˈfɪʃnt	B	ungenügend, unzureichend	interrupt	ɪntəˈrʌpt	A	unterbrechen, stören
insult	ˈɪnsʌlt	C	Beleidigung	interruption	ɪntəˈrʌpʃn	B	Unterbrechung
	ɪnˈsʌlt	C	beleidigen	interval	ˈɪntəvəl	B	Zwischenraum; Pause
insure	ɪnˈʃʊə	B	versichern	interview	ˈɪntəvjuː	A	Interview; interviewen
insurance	ɪnˈʃʊərəns	B	Versicherung				
insurance company		W	Versicherungsgesellschaft	interviewer	ˈɪntəvjuːə	B	Interviewer
				intimate	ˈɪntɪmət	C	eng, vertraut
integrate	ˈɪntɪgreɪt	C	integrieren, eingliedern	into	ˈɪntʊ, ˈɪntə	A	in; in... hinein
				be into sth		C	von etwas begeistert sein
integration	ɪntɪˈgreɪʃn	C	Eingliederung				
intelligence	ɪnˈtelɪdʒəns	A	Intelligenz	introduce	ɪntrəˈdjuːs	A	einführen; vorstellen
intelligent	ɪnˈtelɪdʒənt	A	intelligent, gescheit				
intend	ɪnˈtend	A	beabsichtigen	introduction	ɪntrəˈdʌkʃn	A	Einführung, Einleitung; Vorstellung
intention	ɪnˈtenʃn	B	Absicht, Zweck				
intentional	ɪnˈtenʃnəl	C	absichtlich	invade	ɪnˈveɪd	B	einfallen
intent (on)	ɪnˈtent	C	gespannt, versessen (auf)	invader	ɪnˈveɪdə	C	Eindringling
				invalid	ɪnˈvælɪd	C	ungültig
intensive	ɪnˈtensɪv	C	intensiv, gründlich		ˈɪnvəlɪd	C	Versehrter
interchange	ˈɪntətʃeɪndʒ	C	(gegenseitiger) Austausch	invaluable	ɪnˈvæljuəbl	B	sehr wertvoll
				invariably	ɪnˈveərɪəblɪ	B	immer, ständig
intercontinental	ɪntəkɒntɪˈnentl	C	interkontinental	invasion	ɪnˈveɪʒn	B	Invasion
				invent	ɪnˈvent	A	erfinden
interest	ˈɪntrɪst	A	Interesse; Zins(en); interessieren	invention	ɪnˈvenʃn	B	Erfindung
				inventor	ɪnˈventə	B	Erfinder
take (=have) an interest (in)		B	s. interessieren (für)	inverted commas	ɪnˈvɜːtɪd	B	Anführungsstriche
interested	ˈɪntrɪstɪd	A	interessiert	invest		W	investieren
be interested (in)		A	s. interessieren (für)	investment	ɪnˈvestmənt	W	Investition
interesting	ˈɪntrɪstɪŋ	A	interessant	investigate	ɪnˈvestɪgeɪt	C	erforschen, untersuchen
interfere	ɪntəˈfɪə	B	s. einmischen				
interior	ɪnˈtɪərɪə	C	Innere(s); Innen-	investigation	ɪnvestɪˈgeɪʃn	C	Untersuchung
intermediate	ɪntəˈmiːdɪət	C	Mittel-, Zwischen-				
				invisible	ɪnˈvɪzəbl	C	unsichtbar
internal	ɪnˈtɜːnl	C	inner(lich)	invite	ɪnˈvaɪt	A	einladen
international	ɪntəˈnæʃnəl	A	international	invitation	ɪnvɪˈteɪʃn	A	Einladung
				invoice	ˈɪnvɔɪs	W	(Waren-)Rechnung
interpret	ɪnˈtɜːprɪt	B	auslegen; dolmetschen	involve	ɪnˈvɒlv	B	verwickeln
				be involved	ɪnˈvɒlvd	B	verwickelt sein, damit zu tun haben
interpreter	ɪnˈtɜːprɪtə	B	Dolmetscher(in)				
interpretation	ɪntɜːprɪˈteɪʃn	C	Interpretation, Auslegung	inward	ˈɪnwəd	C	inner(lich)
				Ireland	ˈaɪələnd	A	(Republik) Irland
interrogative pronoun	ɪntəˈrɒgətɪv	B	Fragepronomen	Northern Ireland		A	Nordirland
				Irish	ˈaɪərɪʃ	A	irisch
				Irishman	ˈaɪərɪʃmən	A	Ire
				iron	ˈaɪən	A	Eisen, eisern; Bügeleisen, bügeln
				irregular	ɪˈregjʊlə	B	unregelmäßig
				irrevocable	ɪˈrevəkəbl	C	unwiderruflich
				irritable	ˈɪrɪtəbl	C	gereizt
				irritate	ˈɪrɪteɪt	C	reizen, ärgern
				island	ˈaɪlənd	A	Insel
				isle	aɪl	B	Insel (in Namen)
				isolate	ˈaɪsəleɪt	C	isolieren, absondern
				Israel	ˈɪzreɪl	B	Israel
				Israeli	ɪzˈreɪlɪ	B	israelisch; Israeli

To interrupt

issue	ˈɪsjuː, ˈɪʃuː	B	Streitfrage; Problem; Ausgabe; (her)ausgeben
it/itself	ɪt, ɪtˈself	A	es (er, sie)/sich
its	ɪts	A	sein, ihr
Italy	ˈɪtəlɪ	A	Italien
Italian	ɪˈtæljən	A	italienisch; Italiener,-in
italics	ɪˈtælɪks	C	Schrägdruck
italicise (= ize)	ɪˈtælɪsaɪz	C	kursiv drucken
item	ˈaɪtəm	B	Posten, Punkt
ivy	ˈaɪvɪ	C	Efeu

J

j	dʒeɪ	A	j
jack	dʒæk	C	Wagenheber
jacket	ˈdʒækɪt	A	Jacke, Jackett
jackpot	ˈdʒækpɒt	C	Haupttreffer
jaguar	ˈdʒægjʊə	C	Jaguar
jail (= gaol)	dʒeɪl	B	Gefängnis
jam	dʒæm	A	Marmelade
traffic jam		B	Verkehrsstau
January	ˈdʒænjʊərɪ	A	Januar
Japan	dʒəˈpæn	B	Japan
Japanese	dʒæpəˈniːz	C	japanisch; Japaner,-in
jar	dʒɑː	C	Krug, Glas
jaw	dʒɔː	B	Kiefer, Kinnbacken
jazz	dʒæz	B	Jazz
jealous	ˈdʒeləs	B	eifersüchtig
jealousy	ˈdʒeləsɪ	B	Eifersucht
jeans	dʒiːnz	A	Jeans(hosen)
jelly	ˈdʒelɪ	B	Gelee
jersey	ˈdʒɜːzɪ	B	Jersey(stoff), Pullover
jet	dʒet	B	Düse, Strahl
jet engine		B	Düsenmotor
jet (plane)		B	Düsenflugzeug
Jew	dʒuː	B	Jude, Jüdin
Jewish	ˈdʒuːɪʃ	B	jüdisch
jewel	ˈdʒuːəl	B	Juwel, Edelstein
Crown Jewels		B	Kronjuwelen
jewellery, jewelry	ˈdʒuːəlrɪ	B	Juwelen, Schmuck
jigsaw (puzzle)	ˈdʒɪgsɔː	C	Zusammensetzspiel
job	dʒɒb	A	Arbeit, Stellung; Arbeitsplatz
jobcentre	ˈdʒɒbsentə	C	(GB) Arbeitsvermittlung
jockey	ˈdʒɒkɪ	B	Jockey, Rennreiter

Quite a job

join	dʒɔɪn	A	s. anschließen; verbinden
join in		B	dazukommen, mitmachen
joint	dʒɔɪnt	C	gemeinsam, verbunden; Gelenk; Bratenstück
joint-stock company		W	Aktiengesellschaft
joke	dʒəʊk	A	Scherz, Witz; scherzen
jolly	ˈdʒɒlɪ	C	lustig; sehr
joule	dʒuːl		Joule
journalist	ˈdʒɜːnəlɪst	B	Journalist(in)
journey	ˈdʒɜːnɪ	A	Reise, Fahrt
joy	dʒɔɪ	C	Freude
joyful	ˈdʒɔɪfʊl	C	freudig, froh
jubilee	ˈdʒuːbɪliː	C	Jubiläum
judge	dʒʌdʒ	B	Richter; beurteilen
judg(e)ment	ˈdʒʌdʒmənt	B	Urteil(sspruch)
jug	dʒʌg	C	Krug, Kännchen
juice	dʒuːs	A	Saft
fruit juice		A	Obstsaft
juicy	ˈdʒuːsɪ	C	saftig
July	dʒʊˈlaɪ	A	Juli
jumbo (jet)	ˈdʒʌmbəʊ	C	Jumbo-Jet
jump	dʒʌmp	A	springen; Sprung
jumper	ˈdʒʌmpə	B	Pulli
junction	ˈdʒʌŋkʃn	C	Kreuzung
June	dʒuːn	A	Juni
jungle	ˈdʒʌŋgl	C	Urwald, Dschungel
junior	ˈdʒuːnɪə	B	jünger; Unter-
junior high school		C	(US)Mittelschule
jury	ˈdʒʊərɪ	B	Jury; die Geschworenen
just	dʒʌst, dʒəst	A	gerade, nur
just	dʒʌst	B	gerecht
just as		B	ebenso
just now		B	eben jetzt, soeben
justice	ˈdʒʌstɪs	B	Gerechtigkeit
justify	ˈdʒʌstɪfaɪ	B	rechtfertigen
justly	ˈdʒʌstlɪ	C	mit Recht

K

k	keɪ	A	k
kangaroo	kæŋgər'u:	C	Känguruh
keen	ki:n	A	eifrig
be keen (on/to)		A	sehr interessiert sein (an)
keenness	'ki:nnəs	C	Eifer
keep kept kept	ki:p kept	A	(be)halten; aufbewahren
keep (on) doing		B	weiterhin, fortwährend tun
keep up (with)		C	beibehalten; Schritt halten mit
keeper	'ki:pə	B	Verwalter, Wärter; (Tor)Hüter

The keeper

ketchup	'ketʃʌp	C	Ketchup, Tomatensoße
kettle	ketl	B	Kessel
key	ki:	A	Schlüssel; Taste C
keyhole	'ki:həʊl	B	Schlüsselloch
kick	kɪk	B	mit dem Fuß stoßen; ausschlagen
(just) for kicks	kɪks	C	(nur) zum Spaß
kid	kɪd	B	Zicklein; Kind
kidnap	'kɪdnæp	B	entführen
kidnapper	'kɪdnæpə	B	Entführer
kidney	'kɪdnɪ	C	Niere
kill	kɪl	A	töten
killer	'kɪlə	C	Mörder
kilo	'ki:ləʊ	A	Kilo
kilogram	'kɪləgræm	B	Kilogramm
kilometre	'kɪləmi:tə	B	Kilometer
kilt	kɪlt	B	Kilt (Schottenrock)
kind	kaɪnd	A	Art, Sorte; freundlich
kindness	'kaɪndnəs	B	Freundlichkeit
kindergarten	'kɪndəga:tn	B	Kindergarten
king	kɪŋ	A	König
kingdom	'kɪŋdəm	B	Königreich
kiosk	'ki:ɒsk	C	Kiosk
kiss	kɪs	A	Kuß; (s.) küssen
kit	kɪt	C	Ausrüstung
kite	kaɪt	C	Drachen
kitchen	'kɪtʃɪn	A	Küche
knee	ni:	A	Knie
kneel knelt knelt	ni:l nelt	B	knien
knife, ves	naɪf, vz	A	Messer
knight	naɪt	B	Ritter
knit	nɪt	B	stricken
knob	nɒb	C	(Dreh-)Knopf
knock	nɒk	A	klopfen, stoßen; Klopfen, Schlag
knock down		B	niederschlagen
knock over		B	umstoßen, umwerfen
knock out		B	k.o. schlagen
knot	nɒt	B	Knoten; einen Knoten machen
know knew known	nəʊ nju: nəʊn	A	wissen; kennen; können
know-how	'nəʊˌhaʊ	B	technisches Können
known for		B	bekannt für
knowledge	'nɒlɪdʒ	A	Kenntnisse, Wissen
kohlrabi	kəʊl'ra:bɪ	C	Kohlrabi

L

l	el	A	l
label	leɪbl	B	Etikett
laboratory (lab)	lə'bɒrətrɪ læb	A	Labor
labour	'leɪbə	C	Arbeit, Mühe; Arbeitskräfte
Labour Party		A	brit. Arbeiterpartei
labourer	'leɪbərə	B	Hilfsarbeiter
lace	leɪs	C	Spitze(n)
shoe laces	'ʃu:ˌleɪsɪz	C	Schuhbänder
lack	læk	B	Mangel; ermangeln
for lack of		C	mangels
lad	læd	C	Bursche
ladder	'lædə	B	Leiter; Laufmasche C
lady	'leɪdɪ	A	Dame

Lack of cooperation

lager	'lɑ:gə	C	(GB) helles Bier
lake	leɪk	A	See
lamb	læm	A	Lamm, Lammfleisch
lame	leɪm	C	lahm
lamp	læmp	A	Lampe
lampshade	'læmpʃeɪd	C	Lampenschirm
land	lænd	A	Land, Boden; landen
landing	'lændɪŋ	B	oberer Gang
landing-card		B	Landekarte
landlady	'lændleɪdɪ	A	Zimmerwirtin
landlord	'lændlɔ:d	A	Hauswirt
landmark	'lændmɑ:k	C	Markstein, Landmarke
landscape	'lændskeɪp	B	Landschaft
landslide	'lændslaɪd	C	Erdrutsch
lane	leɪn	B	Gasse, Fahrspur
language	'læŋgwɪdʒ	A	Sprache
lantern	'læntən	C	Laterne
lap	læp	C	Schoß
larder	'lɑ:də	C	Speis(ekammer)
large	lɑ:dʒ	A	groß, weit
largely	'lɑ:dʒlɪ	A	weitgehend
last	lɑ:st	A	letzte(r,s); vorig; zuletzt; dauern
last but not least		B	nicht zuletzt
last but one	ˌ...ˌ 'li:st	C	vorletzte(r,s)
at last	ət ˈlɑ:st	A	endlich, zuletzt
last name		A	Zu-, Familienname
last night		A	gestern abend
lasting	'lɑ:stɪŋ	B	bleibend, dauerhaft
lastly	'lɑ:stlɪ	C	zuletzt, schließlich
late	leɪt	A	spät, verspätet
be late		A	zu spät kommen
lately	'leɪtlɪ	A	unlängst, kürzlich
later on	leɪtəˈr ɒn	A	später, nachher
latest	'leɪtəst	A	späte(r,s); neueste(r,s)
at the latest		C	spätestens
lathe	leɪð	C	Drehbank, -maschine
Latin	'lætɪn	B	Latein; lateinisch
the latter	'lætə	B	letztere(r)
laugh (at, about)	lɑ:f	A	lachen (über); Lachen
laughter	'lɑ:ftə	C	Gelächter, Lachen
launch	lɔ:ntʃ	B	vom Stapel lassen, starten
launderette	lɔ:nˈdret	C	Waschsalon
laundry	'lɔ:ndrɪ	B	Wäsche(rei)
lavatory	'lævətrɪ	A	Toilette, W.C.
law	lɔ:	A	Gesetz, Recht
lawful	'lɔ:fəl	C	rechtmäßig
father-in-law		B	Schwiegervater
lawn	lɔ:n	A	Rasen
lawn-mower	'lɔ:nməʊə	B	Rasenmäher
lawyer	'lɔ:jə	B	Jurist, Anwalt
lay	leɪ	A	legen, stellen, setzen
laid	leɪd		
laid			
lay the table		B	den Tisch decken
layer	'leɪə	C	Lage, Schicht
laziness	'leɪzɪnəs	B	Faulheit
lazy	'leɪzɪ	A	faul, träge
lb. (pound)	paʊnd	B	Pfund (454g)
lead	led	C	Blei
lead	li:d	C	Leine; Kabel
lead	li:d	A	führen, leiten
led	led		
led			
lead the way		B	vorausgehen
leader	'li:də	B	Führer, Leiter
leadership	'li:dəʃɪp	C	Leitung, Führung
leading	'li:dɪŋ	B	führend, Haupt-
leaf, ves	li:f, vz	A	Blatt
leaflet	'li:flət	C	Broschüre, Prospekt
league	li:g	C	Liga, Bund
lean (against)	li:n	B	(s.) (an)lehnen (an)
leant(-ed)	lent, li:nd		
leant(-ed)			
leap	li:p	B	springen, hüpfen; Sprung
leapt(-ed)	lept, li:pt		
leapt(-ed)			
leap year	'li:p jɪə	C	Schaltjahr
learn	lɜ:n	A	lernen; erfahren
learnt(-ed)			
learnt(-ed)	lɜ:nt, lɜ:nd		
learned	'lɜ:nɪd	C	gelehrt
learner	'lɜ:nə	B	Anfänger, Lernender
least	li:st	A	kleinste(r,s); am wenigsten
at least		A	mindestens, wenigstens
not in the least		B	nicht im geringsten

not in the least

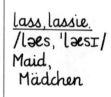

lass, lassie.
/læs, 'læsɪ/
Maid,
Mädchen

leather

leather	'leðə	A	Leder
leave	li:v	A	verlassen, überlassen; Urlaub
left	left		
left			
leave alone		B	in Ruhe lassen
leave behind		B	zurücklassen; verlieren
leave for		B	abfahren nach
leave off		C	aufhören (mit)
leave out		B	auslassen
lecture	'lektʃə	B	Vorlesung
lecturer	'lektʃərə	B	Dozent
left	left	A	linke(r,s); übrig
on the left		A	links
left-handed		C	linkshändig
there's not much left		B	es ist nicht viel übrig
left luggage	'lʌgɪdʒ	C	Gepäckaufgabe
leg	leg	A	Bein
pull sb's leg		C	jd. auf den Arm nehmen
legal	'li:gəl	B	legal, rechtlich
legend	'ledʒənd	B	Legende
legislation	ledʒɪs'leɪʃn	C	Gesetzgebung
legislative	'ledʒɪslətɪv	C	legislativ, gesetzgebend
legislature	'ledʒɪslətʃə	B	Legislatur, Gesetzgebung
leisure	'leʒə	B	Muße
lemon	'lemən	A	Zitrone
lemonade	lemə'neɪd	B	Limonade
lend	lend	A	(ver)leihen
lent	lent		
lent			
length	leŋθ	B	Länge
lengthen	'leŋθən	C	verlängern
leopard	'lepəd	C	Leopard
less	les	A	kleiner, geringer, weniger
less and less		A	immer weniger
lessen	lesn	C	verringern
lesson	lesn	A	Lektion; Unterrichtsstunde
lessons	lesnz	A	Unterricht
let	let	A	lassen, zulassen; vermieten B
let			
let			
let alone		B	in Ruhe lassen; geschweige denn...
let down		C	versetzen, enttäuschen
let go		C	loslassen
let know		B	Bescheid geben
letter	'letə	A	Brief; Buchstabe
letter-box		A	Briefkasten
lettuce	'letɪs	B	Kopfsalat
level	levl	B	Niveau, Höhe
lever	'li:və	C	Hebel

to liberate befreien

Let

liar	'laɪə	C	Lügner(in)
liberal	'lɪbərəl	C	liberal; freigebig
Liberal Party		B	Liberale Partei (GB)
liberty	'lɪbətɪ	B	Freiheit
library	'laɪbrərɪ	A	Bücherei, Bibliothek
librarian	laɪ'breərɪən	B	Bibliothekar(in)
licence (US) license	'laɪsəns	A	Lizenz, Genehmigung
lick	lɪk	C	lecken
lid	lɪd	C	Deckel
lie	laɪ	A	liegen
lay	leɪ		
lain	leɪn		
lie down		A	s. hinlegen
lie	laɪ	A	Lüge; lügen
life, ves	laɪf, vz	A	Leben
lifebelt	'laɪfbelt	C	Rettungsgürtel
lifeboat	'laɪfbəʊt	C	Rettungsboot
lifetime	'laɪftaɪm	C	Lebenszeit
lift	lɪft	A	(auf)heben; Lift
give a lift		A	(im Auto) mitnehmen

Can you give me a lift?

light	laɪt	A	anzünden; Licht;
lit(-ed)	lɪt, 'laɪtɪd		Feuer; hell; leicht
lit(-ed)			
light-hearted		C	sorglos
lightbulb	'bʌlb	C	Glühbirne
lighter	'laɪtə	C	Feuerzeug

lighthouse	'laɪthaʊs	C	Leuchtturm
lightning	'laɪtnɪŋ	A	Blitz
lightning conductor	kən'dʌktə	C	Blitzableiter
lightweight	'laɪtweɪt	B	aus leichtem Material
like	laɪk	A	gernhaben, mögen; wie
I like it		A	es gefällt mir
what is it like?		A	wie sieht es aus?
and the like		B	und dergleichen
likely	'laɪklɪ	B	wahrscheinlich
be likely to		B	wird wahrscheinlich
likewise	'laɪkwaɪz	B	gleichfalls, ebenso
limb	lɪm	B	(Körper-)Glied
lime	laɪm	C	Limone
lime juice		C	Limonensaft
lime-tree		C	Linde(nbaum)
limelight	'laɪmlaɪt	C	Rampenlicht
limerick	'lɪmərɪk	C	Limerick (Scherzgedicht)
limit	'lɪmɪt	B	Grenze, Begrenzung; begrenzen, beschränken
limited	'lɪmɪtɪd	C	beschränkt, begrenzt
limited company (Ltd)		W	AG, GmbH
line	laɪn	A	Linie, Zeile; Strecke; Branche W
line up		C	s. aufstellen, antreten
in line with		C	in Übereinstimmung mit
linen	'lɪnɪn	B	Leinen
linesman	'laɪnzmən	C	Linienrichter
link	lɪŋk	B	(Binde-)Glied; verbinden
lion	'laɪən	B	Löwe
lioness	'laɪənes	C	Löwin
lip	lɪp	A	Lippe
lipstick	'lɪpstɪk	C	Lippenstift
liquid	'lɪkwɪd	B	flüssig; Flüssigkeit
list	lɪst	A	Liste, Verzeichnis; verzeichnen B
listen (to)	lɪsn	A	zuhören
listener	'lɪsnə	B	Zuhörer
literal(ly)	'lɪtrəl(ɪ)	C	wörtlich
literary	'lɪtrərɪ	C	literarisch
literature	'lɪtrətʃə	B	Literatur
litre	'li:tə	B	Liter
litter	'lɪtə	B	Abfall
litter-bin	'..bɪn	C	Abfallkorb
little	lɪtl	A	klein; wenig
a little		A	ein wenig, ein bißchen
little by little		C	nach und nach
live	lɪv	A	leben; wohnen
live	laɪv	A	lebend, direkt
lively	'laɪvlɪ	B	lebhaft, temperamentvoll
livelihood	'laɪvlɪhʊd	C	Lebensunterhalt
liver	'lɪvə	B	Leber
living	'lɪvɪŋ	A	lebendig; Lebensunterhalt
living-room	'..rʊm	A	Wohnzimmer
living standard	'..stændəd	C	Lebensstandard
load	ləʊd	B	Last, Ladung; beladen
a load of		C	eine Menge von
loaf, ves	ləʊf	B	(Brot-)Laib
loan	ləʊn	C	Anleihe; Darlehen
lobster	'lɒbstə	B	Hummer
local	ləʊkl	B	örtlich
located	ləʊ'keɪtɪd	B	gelegen
be located		B	liegen, s. befinden
loch	lɒx	B	See (Schottland)
lock	lɒk	A	(Tür-)Schloß; Schleuse C; verschließen, absperren
lock out		C	aussperren
lockout	'lɒkaʊt	C	Aussperrung
lock up		B	ein-, zusperren
locker	'lɒkə	C	Schließfach
locomotive	ləʊkə'məʊtɪv	B	Lokomotive
lodge	lɒdʒ	B	(in Miete) wohnen
lodger	'lɒdʒə	C	(Unter-)Mieter
lodging	'lɒdʒɪŋ	B	Unterkunft
loft	lɒft	C	Speicher
log cabin	lɒg ˌkæbɪn	B	Blockhaus
logic	'lɒdʒɪk	C	Logik
logical	'lɒdʒɪkl	C	logisch
lollipop	'lɒlɪpɒp	C	Lutscher
lonely	'ləʊnlɪ	B	einsam
loneliness	'ləʊnlɪnəs	B	Einsamkeit
long	lɒŋ	A	lang(e), weit; s. sehnen C
before long		B	bald
so long!		A	auf Wiedersehen!
as (=so) long as		B	solange; falls
look	lʊk	A	Blick; sehen, blicken
look after		A	aufpassen, sorgen für
look at, have a look at		A	ansehen
look for		A	suchen
look forward to		A	s. freuen auf
look like		A	aussehen wie
look up		A	aufschauen; nachsehen
loose	lu:s	A	lose, locker
loosen	lu:sn	C	lösen, lockern

not long ago — unlängst

53

lord			
lord	lɔ:d	B	Herr, Lord
Lord		B	Gott der Herr
good Lord!		C	(ach du) großer Gott!
Lord Mayor	ˌmeə	C	Oberbürgermeister
lorry	ˈlɒrɪ	A	Lastwagen, Lkw
lose	lu:z	A	verlieren
lost	lɒst		
lost			
be (get) lost		A	verlorengehen; s. verirren
lose one's way		A	s. verirren
loser	ˈlu:zə	B	Verlierer
loss	lɒs	B	Verlust
be at a loss (to)		B	in Verlegenheit sein
lost property (office)	ˈlɒst ˈprɒpətɪ	A	Fundbüro

(at) Lord's (Londoner Kricket-stadion)

Lost property

lot	lɒt	B	Los; Anteil
a lot of		A	eine Menge, sehr viel(e)
lots of		B	sehr viel(e)
the lot		C	alle(s) (zusammen)
loud	laʊd	A	laut; grell
(loud)speaker	ˈspi:kə	B	Lautsprecher
lounge	laʊndʒ	A	Salon, Wohnzimmer
lousy	ˈlaʊzɪ	C	gemein, schäbig

magistrate Magistrats-richter (1. Instanz)

Magna Carta engl. Frei-heitsakte (1215)

Love of animals

love	lʌv	A	Liebe; lieben
be in love (with)		A	verliebt sein (in)
fall in love (with)		A	s. verlieben (in)
lover	ˈlʌvə	C	Liebende(r); Liebhaber
lovely	ˈlʌvlɪ	A	reizend, sehr nett
low	ləʊ	A	niedrig, tief; leise
lower	ˈləʊə	C	herunterlassen, senken
Lowlands	ˈləʊləndz	C	(schott.) Tiefland
loyal	ˈlɔɪəl	B	treu
loyalty	ˈlɔɪəltɪ	B	Treue
L-plate	ˈel pleɪt	C	„Anfänger"-Schild
luck	lʌk	A	Glück(sfall)
good luck/bad luck		A	Glück; Pech
lucky	ˈlʌkɪ	A	vom Glück begünstigt
be lucky		A	Glück haben
luckily	ˈlʌkɪlɪ	B	zum Glück
luggage	ˈlʌgɪdʒ	A	Gepäck
lump	lʌmp	C	Klumpen, Stück
lunar	ˈlu:nə	C	Mond-
lunch	lʌntʃ	A	Mittagessen
have lunch		A	zu Mittag essen
lung	lʌŋ	C	Lunge
luxurious	lʌgˈzjʊərɪəs	B	üppig, luxuriös
luxury	ˈlʌkʃərɪ	B	Luxus, Pracht
lyrics	ˈlɪrɪks	C	Liedtext

M

m	em	A	m
machine	məˈʃi:n	A	Maschine
machinery	məˈʃi:nərɪ	B	Maschinen
mad	mæd	A	wahnsinnig, verrückt
be mad about		B	wahnsinnig gern mögen (tun)
madam	ˈmædəm	A	gnädige Frau, gnädiges Fräulein
madness	ˈmædnəs	C	Wahnsinn, Verrücktheit
magazine	mægəˈzi:n	A	Zeitschrift; Magazin
magic	ˈmædʒɪk	B	Zauberei; Zauber-
magician	məˈdʒɪʃn	C	Zauberer
magnificent	məgˈnɪfɪsənt	B	großartig, prächtig
magnify	ˈmægnɪfaɪ	C	vergrößern
maid	meɪd	B	Dienstmädchen
maiden name	ˈmeɪdn ˌneɪm	C	Mädchenname

mail	meɪl	A	Post(sendung);(US) Post aufgeben
mail-order firm		C	Versandhaus
main	meɪn	A	Haupt-
mainly	'meɪnlɪ	A	hauptsächlich
mainland	'meɪnlənd	C	Festland
main clause	ˌ'klɔːz	C	Hauptsatz
mains	meɪnz	C	(Strom-)Netz
maintain	meɪn'teɪn	B	aufrechterhalten; behaupten
majesty	'mædʒəstɪ	B	Majestät; Erhabenheit
majestic	mə'dʒestɪk	C	majestätisch, erhaben
major	'meɪdʒə	B	größer; Major C; Dur C
majority	mə'dʒɒrətɪ	B	Mehrheit
make made made	meɪk meɪd	A	machen, veranlassen; Fabrikat C
make for		C	zugehen auf
make it		B	es schaffen
make out		B	erkennen, entziffern
make up		B	herrichten; s. versöhnen C
make up for		C	wettmachen
make sure		A	s. versichern; aufpassen
maker	'meɪkə	C	Hersteller
make-up	'meɪk ʌp	A	Schminke, Make-up
male	meɪl	B	männlich
man (men)	mæn (men)	A	Mann, Mensch
manage (to)	'mænɪdʒ	A	es schaffen, gelingen
management	'mænɪdʒmənt	B	(Geschäfts-)Leitung
manager	'mænɪdʒə	A	Leiter, Manager
managing director	...dɪ'rektə	W	Geschäftsleiter
mankind	'mæn'kaɪnd	B	Menschheit
manner	'mænə	B	Art, Weise
manners	'mænəz	B	Benehmen, Manieren
manpower	'mænpaʊə	C	Arbeitskräfte
mansion	'mænʃn	C	Herrschaftssitz
mantelpiece	'mæntlpiːs	C	Kaminsims
manual	'mænjʊəl	C	manuell; Handbuch
manufacture	ˌmænjʊ'fæktʃə	B	herstellen
manufacturer	ˌmænjʊ'fæktʃərə	B	Hersteller
manuscript	'mænjʊskrɪpt	C	Manuskript
many	'menɪ	A	viele
many a		A	manche(r,s)
a good many		B	ziemlich viele
a great many		B	sehr viele

The mantelpiece

map	mæp	A	Landkarte, Stadtplan
marble	mɑːbl	C	Marmor
March	mɑːtʃ	A	März
march	mɑːtʃ	B	Marsch; marschieren
margarine	ˌmɑːdʒə'riːn	B	Margarine
margin	'mɑːdʒɪn	C	Rand
mark	mɑːk	B	Zeichen, Merkmal; (Schul-)Note; kennzeichnen; benoten
market	'mɑːkɪt	A	Markt(platz)
Common Market		B	Gemeinsamer Markt
marketing	'mɑːkɪtɪŋ	W	Absatzpolitik, Marketing
marmalade	'mɑːməleɪd	A	Zitrusmarmelade
marriage	'mærɪdʒ	A	Heirat, Ehe
marry	'mærɪ	A	(ver)heiraten
get married		A	(s. ver-)heiraten
martial law	ˌmɑːʃl 'lɔː	C	Kriegsrecht
marvellous	'mɑːvələs	A	wunderbar
masculine	'mæskjʊlɪn	C	männlich
mash(ed) potatoes	mæʃ(t)	C	Kartoffelpüree
mask	mɑːsk	B	Maske; maskieren
mason	meɪsn	C	Maurer, Steinmetz
mass	mæs	B	Masse, Menge; Messe
mass production	ˌprə'dʌkʃn	B	Massenfertigung
mass media	ˌ'miːdɪə	B	Massenmedien
master	'mɑːstə	A	Meister, Herr; bewältigen, meistern
masterpiece	'mɑːstəpiːs	B	Meisterstück
mat	mæt	B	Matte
match	mætʃ	A	Wettspiel; Streichholz; zusammenpassen C
matchbox	'mætʃbɒks	B	Streichholzschachtel

marathon
/'mærəθn/
Marathon-
lauf

mate

media
/ˈmiːdɪə/
Medien

English	Pronunciation	Level	German
mate	meɪt	C	Gefährte, Kamerad
material	məˈtɪərɪəl	A	Stoff; Material
raw material		B	Rohstoff
mathematical		C	mathematisch
	ˌmæθɪˈmætɪkl		
math(ematic)s		A	Mathematik
	mæθs, ˌmæθɪˈmætɪks		
matter	ˈmætə	A	Sache, Angelegenheit; Materie C; von Bedeutung sein
as a matter of fact		B	nebenbei bemerkt
for that matter		C	was das betrifft
no matter what		A	ganz gleich was
that doesn't matter		A	das macht nichts
what's the matter?		A	was ist los?
mattress	ˈmætrəs	B	Matratze
mature	məˈtjʊə	B	reif
maximum	ˈmæksɪməm	B	Maximum, Maximal-
May	meɪ	A	Mai
may	meɪ	A	kann, darf; wird vielleicht
maybe	ˈmeɪˈbiː	A	vielleicht
mayor	meə	B	Bürgermeister
me	miː, mɪ	A	mich, mir
meadow	ˈmedəʊ	B	Wiese
meal	miːl	A	Mahl(zeit), Essen
mean, meant, meant	miːn, ment	A	meinen; bedeuten; beabsichtigen B
meaning	ˈmiːnɪŋ	A	Bedeutung; Absicht
mean	miːn	B	geizig; gemein
meanness	ˈmiːnnəs	C	Geiz
(a) means (of)	miːnz	A	Mittel
by means of	baɪ ... əv	A	mittels
by all means	baɪ ... ɔːl	B	auf alle Fälle
by no means	baɪ ... nəʊ	B	keinesfalls
(in the) meantime		A	inzwischen
meanwhile	ˈmiːnwaɪl	A	inzwischen
measles	ˈmiːzlz	C	Masern
measure	ˈmeʒə	B	Maß(nahme); messen
measurements	ˈmeʒəmənts	C	Maße, Abmessungen
meat	miːt	A	Fleisch
mechanic	mɪˈkænɪk	B	Mechaniker
mechanical	mɪˈkænɪkl	C	mechanisch
mechanical engineering	... ˌendʒɪˈnɪərɪŋ	C	Maschinenbau
medal	medl	B	Medaille
medieval	ˌmedɪˈiːvl	C	mittelalterlich
medical	ˈmedɪkl	C	ärztlich, medizinisch
medicine	ˈmedsn, ˈmedɪsn	C	Medizin
Mediterranean	ˌmedɪtəˈreɪnɪən	C	Mittelmeer
medium	ˈmiːdɪəm	C	Mittel
medium wave	... weɪv	C	Mittelwelle
meet, met, met	miːt, met	A	(s.) treffen, s. versammeln; begegnen, kennenlernen
meeting	ˈmiːtɪŋ	A	Versammlung; Begegnung
melody	ˈmelədɪ	B	Melodie
melt	melt	B	schmelzen
melting-pot	ˈmeltɪŋ pɒt	C	Schmelztiegel
member	ˈmembə	A	Mitglied
membership		B	Mitgliedschaft
membership card	... kɑːd	C	Mitgliedsausweis
memorable	ˈmemərəbl	C	denkwürdig
memorial	məˈmɔːrɪəl	C	Denkmal
memorise(-ize)	ˈmeməraɪz	C	s. merken, lernen
memory	ˈmemərɪ	B	Gedächtnis, Erinnerung
in memory of		C	zur Erinnerung an
mend	mend	B	ausbessern, reparieren
mental	mentl	B	geistig
mentally handicapped	... ˈhændɪkæpt	B	geistig behindert
mention	ˈmenʃn	A	erwähnen
don't mention it		A	keine Ursache, bitte
menu	ˈmenjuː	A	Speisekarte
merchant	ˈmɜːtʃənt	C	Kaufmann
mercy	ˈmɜːsɪ	B	Gnade, Mitleid
mere(ly)	ˈmɪə(lɪ)	B	bloß, lediglich
merge	mɜːdʒ	C	s. zusammenschließen, fusionieren
merit	ˈmerɪt	C	Wert, Verdienst
Merry (= Happy) Christmas	ˈmerɪ	B	Frohe Weihnachten!
mess	mes	B	Durcheinander, Schlamassel
mess up		C	durcheinanderbringen, verpfuschen

To measure

56

message	'mesɪdʒ A	Botschaft, Mitteilung
messenger	'mesɪndʒə B	Bote
metal	metl A	Metall
metallic	mə'tælɪk C	metallisch; Metall-
meter	'mi:tə C	Meßgerät, Zähler, (US) Meter
method	'meθəd B	Methode
metre	'mi:tə A	Meter
metric system	'metrɪk C	metrisches System
Mexico	'meksɪkəʊ C	Mexiko
Mexican	'meksɪkən C	mexikanisch
microprocessor	'maɪkrəʊprəʊsesə C	Mikroprozessor
microphone	'maɪkrəfəʊn B	Mikrofon
microscope	'maɪkrəskəʊp C	Mikroskop
mid-(August)	mɪd A	Mitte (August)
midday	'mɪdeɪ B	Mittag
middle	mɪdl A	Mitte
in the middle (of)	A	mitten in (unter)
middle-aged	C	mittleren Alters
the Middle Ages	C	Mittelalter
middle-class	C	Mittelstand, mittelständisch
the Midlands	'mɪdləndz C	Mittelengland
midnight	'mɪdnaɪt B	Mitternacht
the Midwest (= Middle West)	C	(US) der Mittelwesten
midwife	'mɪdwaɪf C	Hebamme
might	maɪt A	könnte (vielleicht), dürfte; Macht C
mighty	'maɪtɪ C	mächtig, gewaltig
mike	maɪk C	Mikro(fon)
mild	maɪld A	mild, sanft
mile	maɪl A	Meile
military	'mɪlɪtərɪ C	militärisch, Militär-
milk	mɪlk A	Milch; melken C
milkman	'mɪlkmən B	Milchmann
Milky Way	'mɪlkɪ weɪ C	Milchstraße
mill	mɪl B	Mühle; Fabrik
million	'mɪljən A	Million
millionaire	mɪljə'neə C	Millionär
mince	mɪns B	zerkleinern, zerhacken
minced meat	mɪnst C	Hackfleisch
mincemeat	'mɪnsmi:t C	Pastetenfüllung
mind	maɪnd A	Verstand, Geist; etw. ausmachen, betreuen
bear (= keep) in mind	A	s. merken; bedenken
change one's mind	A	es s. anders überlegen
have in mind	B	im Sinn haben
make up one's mind	A	s. entschließen
never mind!	A	macht nichts!
to my mind	tə'maɪ C	meiner Meinung nach
would you mind...?	A	würden Sie bitte...?
I don't mind	A	meinetwegen
mind you!	ju: C	wohlgemerkt!
mine	maɪn C	Bergwerk; Mine; mein(er,-e,es)

They're mine

miner	'maɪnə C	Bergmann
mineral	'mɪnərəl C	Mineral; mineralisch
mineral water	B	Mineralwasser
miniature	'mɪnɪtʃə C	Kleinst-
minibus	'mɪnɪbʌs C	Kleinbus
minimum	'mɪnɪməm B	Minimum; Mindest-
minister	'mɪnɪstə B	Minister; ev. Pfarrer C
Prime Minister	B	Premierminister
ministry	'mɪnɪstrɪ C	Ministerium
mink	mɪŋk C	Nerz
minor	'maɪnə B	kleiner, geringer; Minderjährige(r); Moll
minority	maɪ'nɒrətɪ B	Minderheit
mint	mɪnt B	Minze
mint sauce	sɔ:s C	Minzsoße
minus	'maɪnəs A	minus
minute	'mɪnɪt B	Minute
	maɪ'nju:t C	winzig, genau
(the) minutes	'mɪnɪts W	Protokoll
miracle	'mɪrəkl B	Wunder
mirror	'mɪrə A	Spiegel
mischief	'mɪstʃɪf C	Unfug
miserable	'mɪzərəbl B	elend, kläglich
misery	'mɪzərɪ B	Elend, Not
misfortune	mɪs'fɔ:tʃn C	Unglück(sfall), Mißgeschick
misleading	mɪs'li:dɪŋ B	irreführend
misprint	'mɪsprɪnt C	Druckfehler
miss, Miss	mɪs A	Fräulein
miss	mɪs A	vermissen; versäumen
be missing	A	fehlen

missile	ˈmɪsaɪl C	Rakete(nwaffe)
mission	ˈmɪʃn C	Mission, Auftrag
missionary	ˈmɪʃnrɪ C	Missionar
mist	mɪst B	Nebel
misty	ˈmɪstɪ B	neblig
mistake	mɪsˈteɪk A	Fehler; Irrtum
by mistake		B	aus Versehen
be mistaken		C	s. irren
mistletoe	ˈmɪsltəʊ C	Mistel(zweig)
mistress	ˈmɪstrɪs B	Herrin; Lehrerin
misunderstand mɪsʌndəˈstænd		B	mißverstehen
misunderstanding mɪsʌndəˈstændɪŋ		B	Mißverständnis
mix	mɪks A	(s.) (ver)mischen
mix up	.ˈ. A	verwechseln
mix-up	ˈ.. B	Verwechslung
mixture	ˈmɪkstʃə B	Mischung
mob	mɒb C	Pöbel
mobile	ˈməʊbaɪl C	beweglich
mock	mɒk C	(ver)spotten
mockery	ˈmɒkərɪ C	Spott
model	mɒdl A	Modell; vorbildlich
moderate	ˈmɒd(ə)rət B	mäßig, gemäßigt
modern	ˈmɒd(ə)n A	modern, zeitgemäß, neuzeitlich
modernise(-ize) ˈmɒdənaɪz		C	modernisieren
modest	ˈmɒdɪst B	bescheiden; gering
modesty	ˈmɒdəstɪ C	Bescheidenheit
modify	ˈmɒdɪfaɪ C	(ab)ändern
modification mɒdɪfɪˈkeɪʃn		C	(Ab-)Änderung
moist	mɔɪst C	feucht, naß
moisture	ˈmɔɪstʃə C	Feuchtigkeit, Nässe
mole	məʊl C	Maulwurf
moment	ˈməʊmənt A	Augenblick
at the moment	ətˈðəˈ.. A	im Augenblick, z.Zt.
monarch	ˈmɒnək B	Monarch
monarchy	ˈmɒnəkɪ B	Monarchie
monastery	ˈmɒnəstrɪ B	Kloster
Monday	ˈmʌndɪ,eɪ A	Montag
money	ˈmʌnɪ A	Geld

Monday morning

make (= earn) money		A	Geld verdienen
monk	mʌŋk B	Mönch
monkey	ˈmʌŋkɪ B	Affe
monopoly	məˈnɒpəlɪ C	Monopol
monster	ˈmɒnstə B	Ungeheuer
monstrous	ˈmɒnstrəs C	ungeheuer(lich)
month,s	mʌnθ,θs A	Monat
monthly	ˈmʌnθlɪ A	monatlich; Monatszeitschrift
monument	ˈmɒnjʊmənt B	Denkmal, Monument
mood	muːd B	Stimmung, Laune
moon	muːn A	Mond
full moon		C	Vollmond
new moon		C	Neumond
moonlight	ˈmuːnlaɪt C	Mondschein
moor	mʊə C	Hochmoor, Heideland
moped	ˈməʊped B	Moped
moral	ˈmɒrəl C	moralisch; Moral
more	mɔː A	mehr
more and more mɔːrˌəndˈmɔː		A	immermehr
more or less mɔːrˌəˈles		A	mehr oder weniger
no more; not any more		A	nicht mehr
once more	wʌnsˈmɔː A	noch einmal
moreover	mɔːˈrəʊvə B	außerdem, ferner
morning	ˈmɔːnɪŋ A	Morgen; Vormittag
morning paper ..ˈpeɪpə		B	Tages-, Morgenzeitung
mortal	ˈmɔːtl C	sterblich
mosque	mɒsk C	Moschee
most	məʊst A	meist(e); äußerst
most of all		A	vor allem, am meisten
at (the) most	ətˈðəˈ. C	höchstens
for the most part		B	größtenteils
make the most of		C	das Beste machen aus
mostly	ˈməʊstlɪ B	meist(ens)
motel	məʊˈtel C	Motel
mother	ˈmʌðə A	Mutter
mother-in-law		B	Schwiegermutter
mother tongue ˈ..tʌŋ		A	Muttersprache
motion	ˈməʊʃn B	Bewegung; Antrag C
in slow motion	.ˈ.ˈ.. C	in Zeitlupe
motionless	ˈməʊʃnləs B	bewegungslos
motive	ˈməʊtɪv B	Beweggrund, Motiv
motor	ˈməʊtə A	Motor, Elektromotor
motorbike	ˈməʊtəbaɪk A	Motorrad
motorcar	ˈməʊtəkɑː A	Auto
motorcycle	ˈməʊtəsaɪkl A	Motorrad
motorist	ˈməʊtərɪst B	Kraftfahrer
motorway	ˈməʊtəweɪ A	Autobahn
motto	ˈmɒtəʊ C	Motto, Wahlspruch

To mount

mount	maʊnt	C	Berg (in Namen); besteigen; montieren C
mountain	ˈmaʊntən	A	Berg
mountainous	ˈmaʊntənəs	B	gebirgig
mountaineer	ˌmaʊntəˈnɪə	C	Bergsteiger
mourn	mɔːn	C	(be)trauern
mourning	ˈmɔːnɪŋ	C	Trauer
mouse, mice	maʊs, maɪs	A	Maus
moustache	məˈstɑːʃ	C	Schnurrbart
mouth,s	maʊθ, ðz	A	Mund; Mündung C
by word of mouth		B	mündlich
move	muːv	A	(s.) bewegen; umziehen B; Maßnahme C
move in/out		B	ein-, ausziehen
movement	ˈmuːvmənt	B	Bewegung
movie	ˈmuːvɪ	A	(US) Film
movie theater		C	(US) Kino
mow	məʊ	C	mähen
mowed	məʊd		
mown, mowed	məʊn		
Mr(.)	ˈmɪstə	A	Herr (+ Name)
Mrs(.)	ˈmɪsɪz	A	Frau (+ Name)
Ms(.)	mɪz, məz	A	Frau (+ Name)
much	mʌtʃ	A	viel; sehr
(as) much as...	(..)ˈ..əz	A	so sehr (auch)...
how much is it?		A	wieviel kostet es?
mud	mʌd	B	Schlamm, Schmutz
muddle	ˈmʌdl	C	Verwirrung
mudguard	ˈmʌdgɑːd	C	Schutzblech
muddy	ˈmʌdɪ	B	schlammig, schmutzig
multiply	ˈmʌltɪplaɪ	B	multiplizieren; (s.) vermehren
multi-purpose	ˌmʌltɪˈpɜːpəs	C	Mehrzweck-
multiple choice test	ˈmʌltɪplˌtʃɔɪs	C	Auswahltest
2 multiplied by 3		B	2 mal 3
mum(my)	ˈmʌm(ɪ)	A	Mutti, Mami
murder	ˈmɜːdə	B	Mord; ermorden
murderer	ˈmɜːdərə	B	Mörder
murmur	ˈmɜːmə	B	murmeln; Gemurmel
muscle	ˈmʌsl	B	Muskel
museum	mjuːˈzɪəm	A	Museum
mushroom	ˈmʌʃrʊm	B	Pilz, Schwammerl
music	ˈmjuːzɪk	A	Musik; Noten
musical	ˈmjuːzɪkl	A	musikalisch; Musical
musician	mjuːˈzɪʃn	B	Musiker(in)
must	mʌst	A	muß
must not		A	darf nicht
a must	əˈ..	C	Muß, Notwendigkeit
mustard	ˈmʌstəd	B	Senf
mutter	ˈmʌtə	C	murmeln, murren
mutton	mʌtn	A	Hammelfleisch
mutual	ˈmjuːtʃʊəl	B	gegenseitig, gemeinsam
my/mine	maɪ, maɪn	A	mein(e)
myself	maɪˈself	A	ich (selbst); mich
by myself		A	(ich) allein
all by myself		A	(ich) ganz allein
mysterious	mɪˈstɪərɪəs	C	geheimnisvoll, rätselhaft
mystery	ˈmɪstərɪ	C	Geheimnis, Rätsel

N

n	en	A	n
nail	neɪl	A	Nagel
naive	naɪˈiːv	C	naiv, einfältig
naked	ˈneɪkɪd	C	nackt
name	neɪm	A	Name; (be)nennen
named ...	neɪmd	A	genannt ...
namely	ˈneɪmlɪ	A	nämlich
nap	næp	B	Schläfchen, Nickerchen
napkin	ˈnæpkɪn	B	Serviette
narrow	ˈnærəʊ	A	eng, schmal
have a narrow escape (= to escape narrowly)		B	knapp entgehen
nasty	ˈnɑːstɪ	B	boshaft, schlimm
nation	neɪʃn	A	Volk, Nation
nation-wide	ˈneɪʃnˌwaɪd	C	landesweit, überregional
national	ˈnæʃnəl	A	national; Volks-, Staats-
nationality	næʃəˈnælətɪ	A	Staatsangehörigkeit

nationalise

A narrow escape

nationalise(-ize)	ˈnæʃnəlaɪz	C	verstaatlichen
native	ˈneɪtɪv	A	einheimisch, gebürtig; Eingeborener
native language	..ˈ..	A	Muttersprache
native speaker	..ˈ..	A	Muttersprachler
nature	ˈneɪtʃə	B	Natur; Beschaffenheit
by nature		C	von Natur aus
natural	ˈnætʃərəl	B	natürlich
natural gas	...ˈgæs	C	Erdgas
naturally	ˈnætʃərəlɪ	B	naturgemäß
naughty	ˈnɔːtɪ	B	ungezogen, böse
navy	ˈneɪvɪ	B	Marine
near	nɪə	A	nahe (bei)
nearby	nɪəˈbaɪ	B	in der Nähe
nearly	ˈnɪəlɪ	A	beinahe, fast
neat	niːt	B	sauber, ordentlich
necessary	ˈnesəsrɪ	A	notwendig, nötig
necessarily		A	notwendigerweise
ˈnesəsrəlɪ, nesəˈserəlɪ			
not necessarily		A	nicht unbedingt
necessity	nɪˈsesətɪ	B	Notwendigkeit; Bedürfnis
neck	nek	A	Hals
necklace	ˈnekləs	B	Halskette
need	niːd	A	brauchen; Bedarf B
need not		A	muß nicht
needle	ˈniːdl	B	Nadel
needlework	ˈniːdlwɜːk	B	Handarbeit
negative	ˈnegətɪv	A	negativ; Negativ
neglect	nɪˈglekt	C	vernachlässigen
negligent	ˈneglɪdʒənt	C	unachtsam, leichtsinnig
negotiate	nɪˈgəʊʃɪeɪt	B	verhandeln
negotiation		B	Verhandlung
nɪgəʊʃɪˈeɪʃn			
negro,es	ˈniːgrəʊ,z	A	Neger
neighbour	ˈneɪbə	A	Nachbar(in)
neighbourhood		A	Nachbarschaft
neighbouring	ˈneɪbərɪŋ	B	benachbart
neither	ˈnaɪðə, (US) ˈniːðə	A	keine(r,s) (von beiden); auch nicht
neither... nor		A	weder... noch
nephew	ˈnevjuː,-f-	A	Neffe
nerve	nɜːv	B	Nerv
nervous	ˈnɜːvəs	A	nervös, reizbar
nest	nest	B	Nest
net	net	B	Netz; netto
netball	ˈnetbɔːl	C	Netzball
network	ˈnetwɜːk	B	Netz, System
Netherlands	ˈneðələndz	B	Niederlande
neutral	ˈnjuːtrəl	C	neutral
never	ˈnevə	A	nie(mals); noch nie
never mind	..ˈmaɪnd	A	macht nichts!
nevertheless	nevəðəˈles	A	dennoch
new	njuː	A	neu
newly	ˈnjuːlɪ	B	neu, frisch
news (sg.)	njuːz	A	Nachrichten
newsagent	ˈnjuːzeɪdʒənt	A	Zeitungshändler
newspaper	ˈnjuːspeɪpə	A	Zeitung
newsvendor	ˈnjuːzvendə	C	Zeitungsverkäufer
New Zealand	njuːˈziːlənd	B	Neuseeland
next	nekst	A	nächste(r,s); zunächst
next but one		C	übernächste(r,s)
next door		A	nebenan
next to		A	neben, bei
nib	nɪb	C	Schreibfeder
nice	naɪs	A	hübsch, nett, fein
nickel	ˈnɪkl	C	Nickel, (US) 5 Cent
nickname	ˈnɪkneɪm	B	Spitzname
niece	niːs	A	Nichte
Nigeria	naɪˈdʒɪərɪə	C	Nigeria
night	naɪt	A	Nacht; Abend
all night		A	die ganze Nacht
at/by night		B	abends; nachts
last night		A	gestern abend
goodnight		A	Gute Nacht!
nightcap	ˈnaɪtkæp	C	Gutenacht-Drink
nightmare	ˈnaɪtmeə	B	Alptraum
nil	nɪl	C	Null (Torergebnis)
nine	naɪn	A	neun
nineteen	naɪnˈtiːn	A	neunzehn
ninety	ˈnaɪntɪ	A	neunzig
ninth	naɪnθ	A	neunte(r,s)
no	nəʊ	A	nein; kein(e,-er,-es)
no less		A	nicht weniger
no more (=longer)		A	nicht mehr
no one (=no-one)		A	niemand
no smoking		B	Rauchen verboten
be no good		B	(zu) nichts taugen
it's no good (saying it)		B	es ist sinnlos (das zu sagen)
nobility	nəʊˈbɪlətɪ	C	Adel

noble	nəʊbl	B	adlig; großzügig, edel
nobleman	ˈnəʊblmən	B	Adliger
nobody	ˈnəʊbədɪ	A	niemand
nod	nɒd	C	nicken
noise	nɔɪz	A	Geräusch, Lärm
noisy	ˈnɔɪzɪ	A	laut, lärmend

Noisy

noiseless	ˈnɔɪzləs	B	geräuschlos
nominate	ˈnɒmɪneɪt	B	nominieren, aufstellen
nomination	nɒmɪˈneɪʃn	B	Ernennung
none	nʌn	A	keine(r,s)
nonetheless	nʌnðəˈles	B	nichtsdestoweniger
nonsense	ˈnɒnsəns	A	Unsinn
non-smoker	nɒnˈsməʊkə	C	Nichtraucher
non-stop	ˈnɒnˌstɒp	B	Nonstop-
noon	nuːn	B	Mittag
nor	nɔː	A	auch nicht
normal	ˈnɔːml	A	normal
normally		A	normalerweise
Norman	ˈnɔːmən	C	normannisch
north	nɔːθ	A	Nord(en); nördlich
northern	ˈnɔːðən	A	nördlich
northward(s)	ˈnɔːθwəd(z)	C	Richtung Norden
Norway	ˈnɔːweɪ	C	Norwegen
Norwegian	nɔːˈwiːdʒən	C	norwegisch; Norweger(in)
nose	nəʊz	A	Nase
not	nɒt	A	nicht
not at all	nɒt ət ˈɔːl	B	überhaupt nicht
not... either	ˈaɪðə	A	auch nicht
not in the least		A	nicht im geringsten
not only... but also		A	nicht nur... sondern auch
not until		A	nicht vor, erst wenn
not yet		A	noch nicht
notably	ˈnəʊtəblɪ	C	insbesondere
note	nəʊt	B	Notiz; (Musik)Note; beachten
notebook	ˈnəʊtbʊk	B	Notizheft

nothing	ˈnʌθɪŋ	A	nichts
nothing but		B	nichts als, nur
for nothing		B	umsonst
nothing doing		C	nichts zu machen
notice	ˈnəʊtɪs	A	Notiz; Hinweis(-schild); bemerken
at short notice		C	kurzfristig
until further notice		C	bis auf weiteres
without notice		C	fristlos
give notice		C	kündigen
take notice		C	etw. beachten
noticeable	ˈnəʊtɪsəbl	C	bemerkenswert, beachtlich
notion	ˈnəʊʃn	C	Begriff, Vorstellung
nought	nɔːt	C	Null
noun	naʊn	B	Hauptwort, Substantiv
nourish	ˈnʌrɪʃ	B	(er)nähren
novel	ˈnɒvl	A	Roman
novelist	ˈnɒvəlɪst	C	Romanschriftsteller
novelty	ˈnɒvəltɪ	C	Neuheit
November	nəʊˈvembə	A	November
now	naʊ	A	jetzt, nun, eben
by now		B	jetzt (schon)
from now on		A	von jetzt an
just now		A	soeben, gerade
up to now		B	bis jetzt
now and then		B	hin und wieder
now that	naʊ ðət	B	jetzt, wo; da (nun)
nowadays	ˈnaʊədeɪz	A	heutzutage
nowhere	ˈnəʊweə	A	nirgends
nuclear	ˈnjuːklɪə	C	nuklear; Kern-
nuclear power	ˌ..ˈpaʊə	B	Kernkraft
nucleus	ˈnjuːklɪəs	C	(Atom-)Kern
nuisance	ˈnjuːsəns	B	Ärgernis; Unfug
number	ˈnʌmbə	A	Nummer, Zahl; numerieren B
a number of		A	einige, etliche
numerous	ˈnjuːmərəs	B	zahlreich(e)
nun	nʌn	B	Nonne
nurse	nɜːs	A	Krankenpfleger(in); Kinderschwester; pflegen C

A nursery rhyme

nursery	nursery	ˈnɜːsərɪ C	Kinderzimmer, Krippe
	nursery rhyme	ˈ...ˌraɪm C	Kinderlied,-vers
	nursery school	C	Vorschule
	nut	nʌt A	Nuß; Schraubenmutter C
	nutshell	ˈnʌtʃel C	Nußschale
	in a nutshell	C	kurz zusammengefaßt
	nylon	ˈnaɪlən C	Nylon

O

o	əʊ A	o
oh	əʊ B	oh; ach
oh dear!	əʊˌdɪə B	ach, du liebe Zeit!
oak (tree)	əʊk C	Eiche
oar	ɔː C	Ruder
oath,s	əʊθ,ðz C	Eid
oats	əʊts B	Hafer
oatmeal	ˈəʊtmiːl C	Hafermehl
obedient	əˈbiːdɪənt C	gehorsam
obedience	əˈbiːdɪəns C	Gehorsam
obey	əˈbeɪ B	gehorchen
object	ˈɒbdʒɪkt A	Objekt, Gegenstand
object (to)	əbˈdʒekt B	dagegen sein
objection	əbˈdʒekʃn B	Einwand
objective	əbˈdʒektɪv C	objektiv; Ziel
obligation	ɒblɪˈgeɪʃn C	Verpflichtung
obligatory	əˈblɪgətrɪ C	obligatorisch, Pflicht-
oblige	əˈblaɪdʒ C	einen Gefallen tun
obliged	əˈblaɪdʒd B	verbunden, dankbar
be obliged (to)	A	müssen
observe	əbˈzɜːv B	beobachten; beachten
observation	ɒbzəˈveɪʃn C	Beobachtung; Bemerkung
observer	əbˈzɜːvə C	Beobachter
obstacle	ˈɒbstəkl B	Hindernis
obtain	əbˈteɪn B	erlangen, erhalten
obvious	ˈɒbvɪəs A	offensichtlich, einleuchtend
occasion	əˈkeɪʒn B	Gelegenheit; Anlaß
occasional(ly)	əˈkeɪʒnəl(ɪ) B	gelegentlich
occupy	ˈɒkjʊpaɪ B	beschäftigen; besetzen

occupation	ɒkjʊˈpeɪʃn B	Beruf, Beschäftigung; Besetzung C
occur	əˈkɜː B	s. ereignen, vorkommen
it occurs to me	C	es fällt mir ein
occurrence	əˈkʌrəns C	Vorkommen, Vorfall
ocean	ˈəʊʃn A	Ozean, Meer
o' clock	əˈklɒk A	... Uhr
October	ɒkˈtəʊbə A	Oktober
odd	ɒd B	seltsam, sonderbar
odd number	C	ungerade Zahl
oddly enough	C	eigenartigerweise
of	ɒv,əv A	von, über
of course	əvˈkɔːs A	natürlich, selbstverständlich
off	ɒf A	fort; unweit
a day off	B	ein freier Tag
I'm off	B	ich gehe jetzt
well-off	welˌɒf C	wohlhabend
offence	əˈfens C	Beleidigung; Vergehen
take offence	C	Anstoß nehmen
offend	əˈfend A	beleidigen
offensive	əˈfensɪv C	beleidigend; anstößig
offer	ˈɒfə A	Angebot; anbieten

To offer

office	ˈɒfɪs A	Amt; Dienst; Büro
officer	ˈɒfɪsə A	Beamte(r); Offizier
official	əˈfɪʃl B	Beamte(r); Funktionär; offiziell
offshore	ɒfˈʃɔː C	vor der Küste (liegend)
often	ɒfn,ˈɒftən A	oft
more often than not	C	in aller Regel
oil	ɔɪl A	Öl; ölen
oil refinery	ˈ...rɪfaɪnərɪ C	Ölraffinerie
oil rig	ˈ...rɪg C	Bohrturm
crude oil	kruːd C	Rohöl
OK, okay	əʊˈkeɪ A	in Ordnung! einverstanden; gutheißen C

old	əʊld	A	alt
old age		B	hohes Alter
old-fashioned	ˌəʊldˈfæʃnd	A	altmodisch
O-levels		C	mittlerer Schulabschluß
Olympic Games	əˈlɪmpɪk	C	Olympiade
omelet(te)	ˈɒmlət	A	Omelette
omission	əʊˈmɪʃn	C	Aus-, Unterlassung
omit	əʊˈmɪt	B	aus-, unterlassen
on	ɒn	A	auf; an
it's on		B	es findet statt; es ist in Betrieb
on + ing form		B	(gleich) nachdem...
onto (= on to)	ˈɒntʊ, ˈɒntə	A	auf... hinauf
once	wʌns	A	einmal; einst; sobald
once again		A	nochmal, erneut
once more		A	noch einmal
once and for all		C	ein für allemal
once in a while		B	hin und wieder
once upon a time...		C	es war einmal...
at once		A	sofort; gleichzeitig
one	wʌn	A	eins; ein(e,er); man
one another		A	einander, sich
one day		A	eines Tages
one-man...	ˈwʌnmæn	B	Einmann-
one-time		C	einst(ig), ehemalig
one-way street		B	Einbahnstraße
oneself	wʌnˈself	A	sich
(all) by oneself		A	(ganz) allein
onion	ˈʌnjən	B	Zwiebel
onlooker	ˈɒnlʊkə	C	Zuschauer
only	ˈəʊnli	A	nur, erst; einzig B
onward(s)	ˈɒnwəd(z)	C	vorwärts, weiter
open	ˈəʊpən	A	offen, öffnen
in the open (air)		A	im Freien
open-air	..ˈeə	A	Freiluft-
opener	ˈəʊpənə	C	Öffner
opening	ˈəʊpənɪŋ	B	Öffnung; Eröffnung
opera	ˈɒpərə	A	Oper
opera house		A	Oper(nhaus)
operate	ˈɒpəreɪt	B	bedienen, handhaben
operate on sb		C	jd. operieren
operation	ˌɒpəˈreɪʃn	B	Bedienung, Handhabung; Operation
operator	ˈɒpəreɪtə	B	Bedienungsmann; Vermittlung
operating instructions		C	Bedienungsanleitung
opinion	əˈpɪnjən	A	Meinung
in my opinion		A	meiner Meinung nach
opinion poll	..ˌpəʊl	C	Meinungsumfrage
opponent	əˈpəʊnənt	B	Gegner, Widersacher
opportunity	ˌɒpəˈtjuːnəti	B	(günstige) Gelegenheit
oppose	əˈpəʊz	B	s. widersetzen
be opposed (to)	əˈpəʊzd	B	dagegen sein
opposite	ˈɒpəzɪt	A	Gegenteil; gegenüber, entgegengesetzt
opposition	ˌɒpəˈzɪʃn	B	Opposition, Widerstand
optical	ˈɒptɪkl	C	optisch
optimist	ˈɒptɪmɪst	C	Optimist
optional	ˈɒpʃənəl	C	wahlweise, Wahl-
optional subject		C	Wahlfach
or	ɔː	A	oder; sonst
or else	ˈɔːrels	A	sonst, andernfalls
...or so	ɔːˈsəʊ	B	etwa, an die...
oral	ˈɔːrəl	B	mündlich
orange	ˈɒrɪndʒ	A	Orange; orange
orbit	ˈɔːbɪt	B	Umlaufbahn; umkreisen
orchard	ˈɔːtʃəd	C	Obstgarten
orchestra	ˈɔːkɪstrə	B	Orchester
order	ˈɔːdə	A	Ordnung; Befehl; Auftrag; Bestellung; befehlen, bestellen
in order that		B	damit
in order to		A	um... zu
out of order		A	außer Betrieb
orderly	ˈɔːdəli	C	ordentlich
ordinal number	ˈɔːdɪnəl	C	Ordnungszahl
ordinary	ˈɔːdnri	B	gewöhnlich
ordinarily	ˈɔːdnərɪli	B	gewöhnlich, in der Regel
ore	ɔː	C	Erz
organ	ˈɔːgən	C	Organ; Orgel
organic	ɔːˈgænɪk	C	organisch
organise(-ize)	ˈɔːgənaɪz	A	organisieren
organisation(-z)	ˌɔːgənaɪˈzeɪʃn	A	Organisation

organisation

Old Bailey (zentraler Gerichtshof in London)

to opt (for) sich entscheiden für

to opt out "aussteigen", "ausflippen"

oriental

oriental	ɔːrɪˈentl	B	orientalisch
origin	ˈbrɪdʒɪn	B	Ursprung
original	əˈrɪdʒɪnəl	B	ursprünglich; Original; originell
originally		B	am Anfang
originate	əˈrɪdʒɪneɪt	C	herstammen, entstehen
ornament	ˈɔːnəmənt	C	Ornament, Verzierung
orphan	ˈɔːfən	C	Waise
osprey	ˈɒspreɪ	C	Fischadler
other	ˈʌðə	A	andere(r,s), weitere
each other		A	einander
every other		B	jeder zweite
somehow or other		B	irgendwie
the other day		A	neulich
other than		C	außer
(the) others		A	(die) andere(n)
otherwise	ˈʌðəwaɪz	A	andernfalls, sonst
ouch	aʊtʃ	C	au!
ought to	ɔːt	A	sollte, müßte
ought to (have done)		A	hätte (tun) sollen
ounce (oz.)	aʊns	B	Unze (= 28,35 g)
our, ours	ˈaʊə, ˈaʊəz	A	unser(e)
ourselves	aʊəˈselvz	A	uns (selbst)
out	aʊt	A	aus; hinaus; heraus
outdated	aʊtˈdeɪtɪd	C	veraltet, überholt
out of doors; outdoors		B	im Freien

(at) the Oval (Londoner Kricket-platz)

Outdoor exercises

eat out		C	auswärts essen
outbreak	ˈaʊtbreɪk	C	Ausbruch
outcome	ˈaʊtkʌm	C	Folge, Ergebnis
outdo	aʊtˈduː	C	übertreffen
outdoor	ˈaʊtdɔː	B	Außen-
outer	ˈaʊtə	B	äußere(r,s)
outfit	ˈaʊtfɪt	B	Ausrüstung, Ausstattung
outing	ˈaʊtɪŋ	C	Ausflug
outlaw	ˈaʊtlɔː	C	Geächtete(r); ächten
outline	ˈaʊtlaɪn	B	Umriß, Skizze; umreißen
outlive	aʊtˈlɪv	C	überleben
outlook	ˈaʊtlʊk	C	Ausblick, Aussicht(en)
out-of-date	ˌaʊt əv ˈdeɪt	A	veraltet, altmodisch
outnumber	aʊtˈnʌmbə	C	zahlenmäßig übertreffen
outpatient	ˈaʊtpeɪʃnt	C	Ambulanter
output	ˈaʊtpʊt	C	Produktion; Ausgabe
outside	aʊtˈsaɪd ˈaʊtsaɪd	A	außerhalb; (nach) draußen; Äußere(s)
outskirts	ˈaʊtskɜːts	B	Außenbezirke, Vororte
outstanding	aʊtˈstændɪŋ	B	herausragend; geschuldet W
outward	ˈaʊtwəd	B	äußere(r,s)
outwards	ˈaʊtwədz	C	nach außen
oval	ˈəʊvl	B	oval
oven	ˈʌvn	B	Bratrohr, Backofen
over	ˈəʊvə	A	über, hinüber
over and over (again)		B	immer wieder
over here		A	hier (herüben)
over there		A	dort (drüben)
overall	ˈəʊvərɔːl	C	Gesamt; Arbeitsanzug
overboard	ˈəʊvəbɔːd	C	über Bord
overcast	ˈəʊvəkɑːst	C	bewölkt
overcoat	ˈəʊvəkəʊt	B	Mantel
overcome	əʊvəˈkʌm	C	überwinden, überwältigen
overcrowded	əʊvəˈkraʊdɪd	A	überfüllt
overdo	əʊvəˈduː	C	übertreiben
overdue	əʊvəˈdjuː	C	überfällig
overhead	əʊvəˈhed	C	(dr)oben; Ober-
overhead projector	prəˈdʒektə	C	Tageslichtprojektor
overhear	əʊvəˈhɪə	C	zufällig hören, belauschen
overlook	əʊvəˈlʊk	C	übersehen; Aussicht bieten auf
overnight	əʊvəˈnaɪt	C	über Nacht
overpower	əʊvəˈpaʊə	C	überwältigen
overseas	əʊvəˈsiːz	B	in (nach) Übersee; überseeisch, ausländisch
oversight	ˈəʊvəsaɪt	C	Versehen
oversleep	əʊvəˈsliːp	B	verschlafen
overtake	əʊvəˈteɪk	C	ein-, überholen
overtime	ˈəʊvətaɪm	A	Überstunden
overwhelm	əʊvəˈwelm	C	überwältigen
overwhelming	əʊvəˈwelmɪŋ	B	überwältigend
ow!	aʊ	C	au!

owe	əʊ A	schulden, verdanken
owing to	'əʊɪŋtə B	infolge, dank
owl	aʊl B	Eule
own	əʊn A	eigen; besitzen
my own bike		A	mein eigenes Rad
a bike of one's own		A	ein eigenes Rad
(all) on one's own		A	allein, ohne Hilfe
owner	'əʊnə A	Eigentümer(in); Inhaber(in)
ox, oxen	ɒks, ɒksn B	Ochse
oxygen	'ɒksɪdʒən B	Sauerstoff

P

p	piː A	p; Penny, Pence
pace	peɪs C	Schritt; Tempo
keep pace		C	Schritt halten
Pacific (Ocean)	pə'sɪfɪk	C	Stiller Ozean
pack	pæk A	(ein)packen; Pack(en); Rudel C
package	'pækɪdʒ B	Paket, Packung
package tour	'.. tʊə B	Pauschalreise
packet	'pækɪt A	Paket, Packung
pad	pæd C	Polster; Schreibblock; polstern
page	peɪdʒ A	Seite; Blatt
turn the page		B	umblättern
pail	peɪl C	Eimer
pain	peɪn A	Schmerz
take pains		C	s. Mühe geben
painful	'peɪnfəl C	schmerzhaft, schmerzlich
paint	peɪnt A	Farbe; (an)streichen; malen
wet paint	wet'peɪnt C	frisch gestrichen!
painter	'peɪntə A	Maler(in)
painting	'peɪntɪŋ A	Gemälde
pair	peə A	Paar
a pair of scissors	'sɪzəz A	eine Schere
a pair of trousers	'traʊzəz	A	eine Hose
in pairs		C	paarweise
palace	'pæləs B	Palast, Schloß
pale (with)	peɪl A	blaß, bleich (vor)
palm	pɑːm C	Palme; Handfläche
pan	pæn C	Pfanne
pancake	'pænkeɪk C	Pfannkuchen
panic	'pænɪk C	Panik; in Panik geraten
pants	pænts B	Unterhose; (US)Hose
paper	'peɪpə A	Papier; Zeitung; Schriftstück

Reading the papers

paperback	'peɪpəbæk B	Taschenbuch
parachute	'pærəʃuːt C	Fallschirm
parade	pə'reɪd C	Parade; paradieren
paradise	'pærədaɪs C	Paradies
paragraph	'pærəgrɑːf A	Absatz; Abschnitt
parallel	'pærəlel C	parallel
paraphrase	'pærəfreɪz C	Umschreibung; umschreiben
parcel	pɑːsl A	Paket
pardon	pɑːdn A	Verzeihung, Begnadigung; verzeihen, begnadigen
I (do) beg your pardon		A	Entschuldigung!
(I beg your) pardon?		A	wie bitte?
parents	'peərənts A	Eltern
parish	'pærɪʃ C	(Pfarr-)Gemeinde
park	pɑːk A	Park; parken
car park		B	Parkplatz
no parking	'pɑːkɪŋ A	Parken verboten!
parking lot		C	(US) Parkplatz
parking meter		C	Parkuhr
parking space		C	Parkplatz, -lücke
parliament	'pɑːləmənt A	Parlament
parrot	'pærət B	Papagei
parsley	'pɑːslɪ B	Petersilie
parsnips	'pɑːsnɪps C	Pastinaken
part	pɑːt A	Teil; Rolle
part-time		A	Teilzeit(-)
part (with)		B	s. trennen (von)
for the most part		B	meist, größtenteils
in part, partly		B	zum Teil, teilweise
take part in		A	teilnehmen an
take sb's part		C	jds. Partei ergreifen
spare parts	speə'pɑːts C	Ersatzteile
partial	pɑːʃl C	teilweise; parteiisch
participant	pɑːˈtɪsɪpənt C	Teilnehmer(in)

participant

pair work
Partnerarbeit

English	Pronunciation	Level	German
participation	pɑːtɪsɪˈpeɪʃn	C	Teilnahme
participate	pɑːˈtɪsɪpeɪt	C	teilnehmen; teilhaben
participle	ˈpɑːtɪsɪpl	B	Partizip
particle	ˈpɑːtɪkl	C	Teilchen
particular	pəˈtɪkjʊlə	B	besondere(r,s)
in particular		C	insbesondere
particularly	pəˈtɪkjʊləlɪ	A	besonders
parting	ˈpɑːtɪŋ	C	Trennung; Scheitel
partition	pɑːˈtɪʃn	C	Trennwand
partly	ˈpɑːtlɪ	B	zum Teil, teils
partner	ˈpɑːtnə	A	Teilhaber, Partner
partnership	ˈpɑːtnəʃɪp	C	Teilhaberschaft, Partnerschaft
partridge	ˈpɑːtrɪdʒ	C	Rebhuhn
party	ˈpɑːtɪ	A	Partei; Party, Feier; Gruppe
pass	pɑːs	A	Paß; Ausweis; vorübergehen; überreichen; bestehen
pass away		C	fortgehen; sterben
pass by		B	vorbeigehen
pass for		C	gelten als
pass on		B	weitersagen, -geben
passage	ˈpæsɪdʒ	B	Durchgang, Überfahrt; (Text-)Passage
passenger	ˈpæsɪndʒə	A	Passagier; Reisende(r)
passer-by	ˈpɑːsəbaɪ	C	Vorübergehende(r)
passion	ˈpæʃn	C	Leiden(schaft), Zorn
passion play		C	Passionsspiele
passionate	ˈpæʃənət	C	leidenschaftlich
passive	ˈpæsɪv	B	passiv; Passiv
passport	ˈpɑːspɔːt	A	(Reise-) Paß
past	pɑːst	A	vergangen; Vergangenheit; vorüber; nach
pastime	ˈpɑːstaɪm	B	Zeitvertreib
pastry	ˈpeɪstrɪ	B	Gebäck
pasture	ˈpɑːstʃə	C	Weide(land)
pat	pæt	B	tätscheln; Klaps
patch	pætʃ	C	Fleck
path,s	pɑːθ,ðz	A	Pfad, Weg
patience	ˈpeɪʃns	B	Geduld
patient	ˈpeɪʃnt	A	geduldig; Patient(in)
patriotic	pætrɪˈɒtɪk	C	patriotisch
patron saint	ˈpeɪtrənˌseɪnt	C	Schutzheiliger, -patron
pattern	ˈpætən	B	Muster
pause	pɔːz	B	Pause; zögern, verweilen
pave	peɪv	C	pflastern
pave the way		C	den Weg bereiten
pavement	ˈpeɪvmənt	A	Pflaster; Gehsteig
paw	pɔː	C	Pfote, Tatze
pay	peɪ	A	(be)zahlen;
paid	peɪd		s. lohnen C;
paid			Bezahlung, Lohn B
pay attention	əˈtenʃn	A	aufpassen
pay a visit	ˈvɪzɪt	B	einen Besuch machen

Paying a visit

English	Pronunciation	Level	German
pay back/off		B	zurück-/abzahlen
payable	ˈpeɪəbl	C	zahlbar, fällig
paying guest	ˈpeɪɪŋˌgest	C	zahlender Gast
payment	ˈpeɪmənt	A	Zahlung
pay rise	ˌraɪz	B	Lohnerhöhung
P.E. (= Physical Education)	piːˈiː	C	Schulsport, Gymnastik
pea	piː	B	Erbse
peace	piːs	A	Friede; Ruhe
peaceful	ˈpiːsfəl	B	friedlich
peach	piːtʃ	B	Pfirsich
peak	piːk	C	Gipfel, Spitze
peak hours		C	Spitzenzeiten
peanut	ˈpiːnʌt	C	Erdnuß
pear	peə	A	Birne
pearl	pɜːl	B	Perle
peasant	ˈpeznt	C	Bauer
pebble	ˈpebl	C	Kiesel
peculiar	pɪˈkjuːljə	C	eigentümlich; besonder(s)
pedal	ˈpedl	C	Pedal; treten
pedestrian	pɪˈdestrɪən	A	Fußgänger(in)
pedestrian zone		C	Fußgängerzone
peel	piːl	C	schälen; Schale
peer	pɪə	C	Adliger; Mitglied des Oberhauses
pen	pen	A	(Schreib-)Feder, Füller, Stift
pen pal	ˈpenpæl	B	(US)Brieffreund(in)
penfriend	ˈpenfrend	A	Brieffreund(in)
penalty	ˈpenəltɪ	C	Strafe, Strafstoß
pence (p)	pens, piː	A	Pence

To peel

pencil	pensl	A	Bleistift
pencil-case	'penslkeɪs	B	Federmäppchen
peg	peg	C	Haken
off the peg		C	von der Stange
penetrate	'penɪtreɪt	C	ein-, durchdringen
penguin	'peŋgwɪn	C	Pinguin
penicillin	penɪ'sɪlɪn	C	Penicillin
peninsula	pɪ'nɪnsjʊlə	C	Halbinsel
penniless	'penɪləs	C	mittellos
penny (p)	'penɪ, piː	A	Penny (0,01 Pfund)
pension	penʃn	B	Pension, Rente
people	piːpl	A	Leute; Volk
pepper	'pepə	A	Pfeffer
peppermint	'pepəmɪnt	C	Pfefferminze
per	pɜː,pə	B	per, pro, für
per cent	pə'sent	B	Prozent
percentage	pə'sentɪdʒ	W	Prozentsatz
percussion instrument	pə'kʌʃn...	C	Schlaginstrument
perfect	'pɜːfɪkt	A	vollkommen; perfekt
perfection	pə'fekʃn	C	Vollkommenheit
perform	pə'fɔːm	B	auf-, ausführen; leisten
performance	pə'fɔːməns	B	Auf-, Ausführung; Leistung
perfume	'pɜːfjuːm	B	Parfüm
perhaps	pə'hæps	A	vielleicht
period	'pɪərɪəd	A	Periode, Zeitraum
periodical	pɪərɪ'ɒdɪkl	B	Zeitschrift
perish	'perɪʃ	C	verderben
permanent	'pɜːmənənt	B	(an)dauernd, beständig
perm	pɜːm	C	Dauerwelle
permission	pə'mɪʃn	B	Erlaubnis, Genehmigung
permit	pə'mɪt	B	erlauben
be permitted to		B	dürfen
permit	'pɜːmɪt	C	(Erlaubnis-)Schein
persecute	'pɜːsɪkjuːt	C	verfolgen
persecution	pɜːsɪ'kjuːʃn	C	Verfolgung
person	pɜːsn	A	Person
in person		C	selber, persönlich
personal	'pɜːsnəl	A	persönlich, privat
personality	pɜːsə'nælətɪ	B	Persönlichkeit
personnel	pɜːsə'nel	C	Personal
personnel manager		W	Personalleiter
persuade	pə'sweɪd	A	überreden, überzeugen C
persuasion	pə'sweɪʒn	C	Überredung
pessimist	'pesɪmɪst	C	Pessimist
pessimistic	pesɪ'mɪstɪk	B	pessimistisch
pet	pet	A	Heimtier; Lieblings- C
petrol	'petrəl	A	Benzin
petrol station		A	Tankstelle
petroleum	pɪ'trəʊlɪəm	C	Erdöl
petticoat	'petɪkəʊt	C	Unterrock
pharmacy	'fɑːməsɪ	C	Apotheke
pharmacist	'fɑːməsɪst	C	Apotheker(in)
philosophy	fɪ'lɒsəfɪ	C	Philosophie
philosopher	fɪ'lɒsəfə	B	Philosoph
phone	fəʊn	A	Telefon; telefonieren
phone booth	...buːð	A	Telefonzelle
phone call	...kɔːl	A	Anruf
phonetic	fə'netɪk	C	phonetisch, lautlich
photocopy	'fəʊtəkɒpɪ	B	Fotokopie; fotokopieren
photo(graph)		A	Foto;
	'fəʊtəgrɑːf		fotografieren
take a photo		A	fotografieren
(=photos)			
photographer	fə'tɒgrəfə	C	Fotograf(in)
photography	fə'tɒgrəfɪ	C	Fotografie(ren)
phrase	freɪz	B	Ausdruck, Redensart
physical	'fɪzɪkl	B	körperlich; physikalisch
physician	fɪ'zɪʃn	B	Arzt, Ärztin
physicist	'fɪzɪsɪst	C	Physiker(in)
physics	'fɪzɪks	B	Physik
piano,s	pɪ'ænəʊ	A	Klavier
pianist	'pɪənɪst	B	Pianist(in)
pick	pɪk	B	pflücken; auswählen
pick out		C	heraussuchen
pick up		A	aufheben; abholen
picket	'pɪkɪt	C	Streikposten
pickpocket	'pɪkpɒkɪt	C	Taschendieb
picnic	'pɪknɪk	A	Picknick
picture	'pɪktʃə	A	Bild
take a picture		A	eine Aufnahme machen
go to the pictures		A	ins Kino gehen
picture postcard	...pəʊstkɑːd	B	Ansichtskarte
picturesque	pɪktʃə'resk	C	malerisch

picturesque

pie

The pickpocket

pie	paɪ	B	Pastete
piece	piːs	A	Stück
two-piece	ˈtuːˌpiːs	C	zweiteilig
take to pieces		C	auseinandernehmen, zerlegen
pierce	pɪəs	C	durchbohren, durchdringen
pig	pɪg	A	Schwein
pigsty	ˈpɪgstaɪ	C	Schweinestall
pigeon	ˈpɪdʒən	B	Taube
pigeonhole		C	Fach (für Briefe etc.)
pile	paɪl	B	Haufen, Stoß
pile up	paɪl ˌʌp	C	aufhäufen
pile-up	ˈpaɪl ˌʌp	C	Auffahrunfall
pilgrim	ˈpɪlgrɪm	B	Pilger, Wallfahrer
pill	pɪl	A	Pille
pillar	ˈpɪlə	C	Pfeiler, Säule
pillar-box		B	(öffentl.) Briefkasten
pillow	ˈpɪləʊ	B	Kissen
pillow-case	ˈpɪləʊkeɪs	C	Kissenbezug
pilot	ˈpaɪlət	A	Pilot; Lotse
pin	pɪn	B	(An-)Stecknadel; Reißzwecke; befestigen
pincers	ˈpɪnsəz	C	(Kneif-)Zange
pinch	pɪntʃ	C	Prise; klauen
pine(tree)	paɪn	C	Kiefer (Baum)
pineapple	ˈpaɪnæpl	B	Ananas
ping-pong	ˈpɪŋˈpɒŋ	C	Tischtennis
pink	pɪŋk	A	rosa
pint	paɪnt	A	Flüssigkeitsmaß (= 0,568 l)
pioneer	paɪəˈnɪə	B	Pionier
pipe	paɪp	A	Pfeife; Rohr
pipes	paɪps	C	Dudelsack
piper	ˈpaɪpə	C	Dudelsackpfeifer
pipeline	ˈpaɪplaɪn	C	Pipeline, Ölleitung
be in the pipeline		C	bevorstehen
pirate	ˈpaɪrət	C	Pirat
pistol	ˈpɪstl	B	Pistole
piston	ˈpɪstn	C	Kolben
pit	pɪt	C	Grube, Schacht
pitch (tent)	pɪtʃ	C	(Zelt) aufschlagen
pity	ˈpɪtɪ	A	Mitleid; bemitleiden
what a pity!		A	wie schade!
placard	ˈplækɑːd	C	Plakat
place	pleɪs	A	Platz, Ort; setzen, stellen, tun
in place of		B	an Stelle von
in the first place		B	erst, überhaupt
be out of place		C	unangebracht sein
take place		A	stattfinden
places of interest		B	Sehenswürdigkeiten
plain	pleɪn	B	flach; häßlich; Ebene
plan	plæn	A	Plan, Entwurf; planen
plane	pleɪn	A	Flugzeug
go by plane		A	fliegen
planet	ˈplænɪt	B	Planet
plant	plɑːnt	A	Pflanze; Fabrik C; pflanzen
plantation	plænˈteɪʃn	B	Pflanzung; Plantage
plaster	ˈplɑːstə	C	Putz, Gips
plastic	ˈplæstɪk	A	Plastik; plastisch
plate	pleɪt	A	Teller; Platte
chrome-plated	ˌkrəʊmˈpleɪtɪd	C	verchromt
platform	ˈplætfɔːm	A	Bahnsteig; Plattform
play	pleɪ	A	(Schau-)Spiel; spielen
play fair	ˌfeə	C	ehrlich sein
play truant	ˌtruːənt	C	Schule schwänzen

To play truant

player	ˈpleɪə	A	Spieler
playful	ˈpleɪfəl	C	verspielt
playground	ˈpleɪgraʊnd	A	Spielplatz
playing-field	ˈpleɪɪŋ fiːld	B	Spielfeld
playwright	ˈpleɪraɪt	C	Bühnenschriftsteller
plead	pliːd	C	plädieren; verteidigen

plead guilty	ˈgɪltɪ	C	s. schuldig erklären	polite	pəˈlaɪt	A	höflich
pleasant	pleznt	A	angenehm; freundlich	politeness	pəˈlaɪtnəs	B	Höflichkeit
				political	pəˈlɪtɪkl	A	politisch
please	pliːz	A	bitte; erfreuen C	politician	pɒlɪˈtɪʃn	C	Politiker(in)
be pleased with		A	s. freuen über	politics	ˈpɒlɪtɪks	A	Politik
pleasing	ˈpliːzɪŋ	B	ansprechend	poll	pəʊl	C	Wahl; Meinungsumfrage
pleasure	ˈpleʒə	A	Vergnügen, Freude				
take (have) pleasure in		C	Freude haben an	polling-day	ˈpəʊlɪŋˌdeɪ	C	Wahltag
plenty (of)	ˈplentɪ	A	viel(e), reichlich	pollute	pəˈluːt	B	verschmutzen
plentiful	ˈplentɪfəl	C	reichlich	pollution	pəˈluːʃn	A	(Umwelt-)Verschmutzung
pliers	ˈplaɪəz	C	Zange				
plot	plɒt	B	Komplott; Handlung	Polytechnic	pɒlɪˈteknɪk	C	Fachhochschule
				pompous	ˈpɒmpəs	C	pompös, aufgeblasen
plough	plaʊ	C	Pflug; pflügen				
pluck	plʌk	C	pflücken; rupfen	pond	pɒnd	C	Teich
pluck up courage		C	Mut fassen	pony	ˈpəʊnɪ	B	Pony
plug	plʌg	C	(Elektro-)Stecker	pool	puːl	B	(Schwimm-, Sammel-)Becken
plug in		C	einstecken				
plum	plʌm	A	Pflaume, Zwetschge	poor	pʊə	A	arm; dürftig
plum pudding		C	Plumpudding	poverty	ˈpɒvətɪ	B	Armut
plumber	ˈplʌmə	B	Spengler, Installateur	Pope	pəʊp	B	Papst
				pop in	pɒpˌ	C	vorbeischauen
plunge	plʌndʒ	C	(ein)tauchen; s. stürzen	pop (music)		A	Popmusik
					ˈpɒpˌmjuːzɪk		
plural	ˈplʊərəl	B	Plural	pop singer	ˈpɒpˌsɪŋə	A	Popsänger
plus	plʌs	B	plus	pop star	ˈpɒpˌstaː	A	Schlagerstar
p.m.	piːˈem	A	nachmittags	popular	ˈpɒpjʊlə	A	beliebt
poached egg	pəʊtʃt	C	pochiertes, verlorenes Ei	popularity	pɒpjʊˈlærətɪ	B	Beliebtheit
				population	pɒpjʊˈleɪʃn	A	Bevölkerung
pocket	ˈpɒkɪt	A	(Hosen-, Mantel- etc.) Tasche	porch	pɔːtʃ	C	Veranda
				pork	pɔːk	B	Schweinefleisch
pocket money		A	Taschengeld	porridge	ˈpɒrɪdʒ	A	Haferbrei
poem	ˈpəʊɪm	A	Gedicht	port	pɔːt	A	Hafen(stadt); Portwein C
poet	ˈpəʊɪt	A	Dichter				
poetry	ˈpəʊɪtrɪ	A	Dichtung	portable	ˈpɔːtəbl	B	tragbar
point	pɔɪnt	A	Punkt; Spitze	porter	ˈpɔːtə	A	Portier, Träger
point at (= to)		B	(hin-)zeigen (auf)	portion	ˈpɔːʃn	B	Teil, Anteil
point of view		B	Standpunkt, Gesichtspunkt	portrait	ˈpɔːtrɪt	B	Porträt
				Portugal	ˈpɔːtjʊgəl	B	Portugal
point out		C	klarmachen, aufzeigen	Portuguese	pɔːtjʊˈgiːz	B	portugiesisch
				position	pəˈzɪʃn	B	Lage; Stellung
be on the point of		C	im Begriff sein zu	be in a position to		C	in der Lage sein zu
there is no point (in)		B	es hat keinen Sinn	positive	ˈpɒzətɪv	B	positiv; sicher
to the point		C	treffend, präzis	possess	pəˈzes	B	besitzen
pointed	ˈpɔɪntɪd	C	spitz	possession	pəˈzeʃn	C	Besitz
poison	pɔɪzn	B	Gift; vergiften	possessive	pəˈzesɪv	C	besitzanzeigend
poisonous	ˈpɔɪzənəs	B	giftig	possibility	pɒsəˈbɪlətɪ	A	Möglichkeit
polar	ˈpəʊlə	B	polar	possible	ˈpɒsəbl	A	möglich
polar bear	ˌbeə	C	Eisbär	possibly	ˈpɒsəblɪ	B	möglicherweise, eventuell
pole	pəʊl	B	Pol; Stange				
Pole	pəʊl	B	Pole, Polin	post	pəʊst	A	Post; Posten; Pfosten; zur Post geben
Poland	ˈpəʊlənd	B	Polen				
Polish	ˈpəʊlɪʃ	B	polnisch				
police (pl.)	pəˈliːs	A	Polizei	post office	ˈpəʊstˌɒfɪs	A	Postamt
police station	ˌsteɪʃn	A	Polizeirevier	postage	ˈpəʊstɪdʒ	B	Porto
policeman; -woman		A	Polizist; -in	postcard	ˈpəʊs(t)kɑːd	A	Postkarte
policy	ˈpɒləsɪ	B	Politik; Police W	postcode	ˈpəʊs(t)kəʊd	B	Postleitzahl
polish	ˈpɒlɪʃ	B	glätten, polieren	(US) zip code	ˈzɪpˌkəʊd		

the point is... entscheidend ist, daß...

pointless sinnlos

poster	ˈpəʊstə	A	Plakat, Poster
postman	ˈpəʊstmən	A	Postbote
postpone	pəʊs(t)ˈpəʊn	A	ver-, aufschieben
postponement	pəʊs(t)ˈpəʊnmənt	C	Verschiebung
pot	pɒt	A	Topf, Kanne
pottery	ˈpɒtərɪ	C	Töpferwaren
potato, es	pəˈteɪtəʊ	A	Kartoffel
pound	paʊnd	A	Pfund
a pound note		A	eine Pfundnote
pour	pɔː	A	gießen, schütten
pour with rain		C	in Strömen regnen

It's pouring

poverty	ˈpɒvətɪ	B	Armut
powder	ˈpaʊdə	A	Staub, Pulver; Puder; pudern
power	ˈpaʊə	A	Macht; Kraft
power station	ˌ..ˌ..	B	Kraftwerk
powerful	ˈpaʊəfəl	B	mächtig; leistungsfähig
practical	ˈpræktɪkl	A	praktisch, brauchbar
practically	ˈpræktɪkəlɪ	B	praktisch, so gut wie
practice	ˈpræktɪs	A	Übung; Praxis
practise	ˈpræktɪs	A	üben; ausüben
prairie	ˈpreərɪ	B	Grasebene
praise	preɪz	B	loben; Lob
pram	præm	B	Kinderwagen
US: baby carriage			
prawn	prɔːn	C	Krabbe
pray	preɪ	B	beten
prayer	preə	B	Gebet
preach	priːtʃ	C	predigen
precede	prɪˈsiːd	C	voran-, vorausgehen
precious	ˈpreʃəs	B	kostbar, edel
precious stone	..ˌ.	B	Edelstein
precise	prɪˈsaɪs	B	genau, präzis
precision	prɪˈsɪʒn	C	Genauigkeit, Präzision
predecessor	ˈpriːdɪsesə	B	Vorgänger(in)
predict	prɪˈdɪkt	C	voraussagen
prediction	prɪˈdɪkʃn	C	Voraussage

prefect	ˈpriːfekt	C	Präfekt
prefer	prɪˈfɜː	A	vorziehen, lieber tun
preferable	ˈprefərəbl	B	vorzuziehen
preferably	ˈprefərəblɪ	B	am liebsten
preference	ˈprefərəns	C	Vorzug; Vorliebe
prefix	ˈpriːfɪks	C	Präfix, Vorsilbe
pregnant	ˈpregnənt	C	schwanger
prejudice	ˈpredʒədɪs	B	Vorurteil
prejudiced	ˈpredʒədɪst	C	voreingenommen
preparation	prepəˈreɪʃn	B	Vorbereitung
prepare	prɪˈpeə	A	vorbereiten
be prepared to		B	bereit sein zu
preposition	prepəˈzɪʃn	B	Präposition, Verhältniswort
prescription	prɪˈskrɪpʃn	B	Rezept; Verordnung
presence	prezns	B	Gegenwart; Anwesenheit
presence of mind		B	Geistesgegenwart
present	preznt	A	anwesend; gegenwärtig; Präsens B; Geschenk
at present	ətˈpreznt	B	im Augenblick
at the present time		B	gegenwärtig
for the present		C	vorläufig
presently	ˈprezntlɪ	C	sofort
present	prɪˈzent	B	vorstellen; schenken
preserve	prɪˈzɜːv	C	bewahren, erhalten
president	ˈprezɪdənt	A	Präsident, Vorsitzender
presidential	prezɪˈdenʃl	C	Präsidenten-
Presidency	ˈprezɪdənsɪ	C	Präsidentschaft
press	pres	A	Presse; drücken, drängen; bügeln C
press shop	ˈpresˌʃɒp	C	Stanzerei
pressure	ˈpreʃə	C	Druck
prestige	preˈstiːʒ	C	Prestige, Ansehen
presume	prɪˈzjuːm	C	vermuten
presumably	prɪˈzjuːməblɪ	C	vermutlich
pretend	prɪˈtend	C	vorgeben, so tun

To pretend

pretext	ˈpriːtekst	C	Vorwand
pretty	ˈprɪtɪ	A	hübsch; ziemlich
prevent (from)	prɪˈvent	B	abhalten (von), hindern (an)
prevention	prɪˈvenʃn	C	Verhütung
previous	ˈpriːvɪəs	B	vorhergehend
previously	ˈpriːvɪəslɪ	B	vorher
prey	preɪ	B	Beute, Raub
bird of prey		B	Raub-, Greifvogel
price	praɪs	A	Preis
price tag	ˈ.. tæg	B	Preisschild
pride	praɪd	B	Stolz
take pride in		C	stolz sein auf
priest	priːst	B	Priester
primary	ˈpraɪmərɪ	C	frühest, ursprünglich
primary school		A	Grundschule
primarily	ˈpraɪmərɪlɪ, praɪˈmerɪlɪ	C	in erster Linie
prime minister	praɪm ˈmɪnɪstə	B	Premier (minister,in)
prince	prɪns	B	Prinz
princess	prɪnˈses	B	Prinzessin
principal	ˈprɪnsɪpl	B	hauptsächlich, Haupt-; Direktor
principle	ˈprɪnsɪpl	B	Prinzip
print	prɪnt	A	Druck; Abzug (phot.); drucken
printed matter	ˈprɪntɪd ˈmætə	W	Drucksache
prior to	ˈpraɪə tə	C	vor, bevor
priority	praɪˈɒrɪtɪ	C	Vorrecht, Vorzug
prison	prɪzn	A	Gefängnis
prisoner	ˈprɪznə	A	Gefangene(r), Häftling
private	ˈpraɪvɪt	A	privat; persönlich
privacy	ˈprɪvəsɪ, ˈpraɪ-	C	Privatleben

Privacy

privilege	ˈprɪvɪlɪdʒ	B	Vorrecht, Privileg
prize	praɪz	A	Preis, Prämie
probable	ˈprɒbəbl	A	wahrscheinlich
probably	ˈprɒbəblɪ	A	wahrscheinlich (adv.)
probability	ˌprɒbəˈbɪlɪtɪ	C	Wahrscheinlichkeit
problem	ˈprɒbləm	A	Problem; Aufgabe
procedure	prəˈsiːdʒə	C	Vorgehen, Verfahren
proceed	prəˈsiːd	C	vorgehen; fortschreiten
process	ˈprəʊses	B	Verfahren; verarbeiten
procession	prəˈseʃn	C	Prozession, Umzug
produce	prəˈdjuːs	A	erzeugen, herstellen; vorzeigen C
	ˈprɒdjuːs		(Agrar-)Produkt(e)
producer	prəˈdjuːsə	C	Erzeuger, Hersteller
product	ˈprɒdʌkt	A	Produkt, Erzeugnis
production	prəˈdʌkʃn	A	Produktion
mass production	ˈmæs ...	B	Massenproduktion
production line	ˈ... laɪn	C	Fließband
profession	prəˈfeʃn	A	(bes. akad.) Beruf
professional	prəˈfeʃnəl	A	beruflich; »Profi«
professor	prəˈfesə	C	Professor
profit	ˈprɒfɪt	A	Gewinn, Nutzen; nützen; profitieren
profitable	ˈprɒfɪtəbl	C	nutzbringend, vorteilhaft
profound	prəˈfaʊnd	C	tief(gründig)
program(me)	ˈprəʊgræm	A	Programm; programmieren C
programmer	ˈprəʊgræmə	C	Programmierer
progress	ˈprəʊgres	B	Fortschritt(e)
progressive	prəˈgresɪv	B	progressiv, fortschreitend
progressive form	... ˈfɔːm	C	Verlaufsform
prohibit	prəˈhɪbɪt	C	verbieten, untersagen
prohibition	ˌprəʊɪˈbɪʃn	C	Verbot
project	ˈprɒdʒekt	B	Plan, Projekt
	prəˈdʒekt	B	projizieren
projector	prəˈdʒektə	B	Projektor
prolong	prəˈlɒŋ	C	verlängern
prominent	ˈprɒmɪnənt	B	prominent, hervorragend
promise	ˈprɒmɪs	A	versprechen; Versprechen
promising	ˈprɒmɪsɪŋ	C	vielversprechend
promote	prəˈməʊt	C	befördern, fördern
promotion	prəˈməʊʃn	C	Beförderung, Förderung
prompt	prɒm(p)t	C	schnell, unverzüglich
pronoun	ˈprəʊnaʊn	B	Pronomen
pronounce	prəˈnaʊns	A	aussprechen
pronunciation	prəˌnʌnsɪˈeɪʃn	A	Aussprache

pronunciation

proof	pru:f	B	Beweis; Probeabzug
waterproof 'wɔːtəˌpruːf		C	wasserabstoßend
prop word	'prɒpˌwɜːd		Stützwort
proper	'prɒpə	B	passend; richtig
property	'prɒpəti	B	Besitz; Eigenschaft
proportion	prə'pɔːʃn	C	Verhältnis; Anteil
out of proportion to		C	in keinem Verhältnis zu
proportional representation		C	Verhältniswahlrecht
propose	prə'pəʊz	B	vorschlagen; einen Heiratsantrag machen
proposal	prə'pəʊzl	C	Vorschlag
pros and cons 'prəʊzˌəndˌ'kɒnz		C	Für und Wider
prospect	'prɒspekt	C	Aussicht
prosper	'prɒspə	C	gedeihen, blühen
prosperity	prɒ'sperəti	C	Gedeihen; Wohlstand
prosperous	'prɒspərəs	C	wohlhabend; erfolgreich
protect (from)	prə'tekt	A	schützen (vor)
protection	prə'tekʃn	B	Schutz
protest	'prəʊtest	A	Protest, Einspruch;
	prə'test	A	protestieren
Protestant	'prɒtɪstənt	B	Protestant; protestantisch
proton	'prəʊtɒn	C	Proton
proud (of)	praʊd	A	stolz (auf)
prove	pruːv	A	beweisen; s. erweisen
proverb	'prɒvɜːb	B	Sprichwort
provide (with)	prə'vaɪd	B	beschaffen; versorgen (mit)
provided (that)		B	vorausgesetzt, daß
province	'prɒvɪns	B	Provinz
provincial	prə'vɪnʃl	C	provinziell
Prussian	prʌʃn	C	preußisch; Preuße
P.S. (=postscript) piːˌes		C	P.S.

psychology	saɪ'kɒlədʒɪ	C	Psychologie
psychological saɪkə'lɒdʒɪkl		C	psychologisch
psychologist saɪ'kɒlədʒɪst		C	Psychologe
pub	pʌb	A	Pub, Kneipe
public	'pʌblɪk	A	öffentlich
the public		A	die Öffentlichkeit
in public		A	in der Öffentlichkeit
public conveniences ..ˌkən'viːnɪənsɪz		C	öffentl. Toilette(n)
public opinion ..ˌə'pɪnɪən		A	öffentl. Meinung
public school '..ˌskuːl		B	(GB) priv. höhere Schule
	..ˌ'skuːl		(US) öffentliche Schule
publication	pʌblɪ'keɪʃn	A	Veröffentlichung, Schrift
publish	'pʌblɪʃ	A	veröffentlichen
publisher	'pʌblɪʃə	A	Verleger, Verlag
pudding	'pʊdɪŋ	A	Pudding, Süßspeise
puddle	'pʌdl	C	Pfütze, Lache
pull	pʊl	A	ziehen, reißen, zerren
pull o.s. together		A	s. zusammennehmen
pull sb's leg		C	jd. veräppeln
pull up		C	vor-, heranfahren
pullover	'pʊləʊvə	A	Pullover
pulse	pʌls	B	Puls
pump	pʌmp	C	Pumpe; pumpen
pun	pʌn	C	Wortspiel
punch	pʌntʃ	B	lochen; Locher
punch(ed) card '..ˌkɑːd		W	Lochkarte
punctual	'pʌŋktjʊəl	B	pünktlich
punctuality pʌŋktjʊ'æləti		C	Pünktlichkeit
punctuation pʌŋktjʊ'eɪʃn		C	Zeichensetzung
puncture	'pʌŋktʃə	A	(Reifen-)Panne
punish	'pʌnɪʃ	A	bestrafen
punishment 'pʌnɪʃmənt		B	Strafe
punk	pʌŋk	C	Punkanhänger
punk rock		C	Punk-Rock
pupil	'pjuːpl	A	Schüler(in)
puppet	'pʌpɪt	B	Marionette
puppy	'pʌpɪ	C	junger Hund
purchase	'pɜːtʃəs	B	Kauf; kaufen
pure	pjʊə	B	rein, echt
Puritan	'pjʊərɪtən	C	Puritaner
purple	pɜːpl	C	violett
purpose	'pɜːpəs	B	Zweck; Absicht
on purpose		B	absichtlich
purse	pɜːs	A	Geldbeutel, Börse
pursue	pə'sjuː	C	verfolgen; nachgehen (einer Tätigkeit)

pursuit (of)	pə'sju:t	C	Verfolgung; Streben (nach)
push	pʌʃ	A	stoßen; schieben; drängen
give a push		A	(Auto) anschieben
push-button	'puʃbʌtn	C	Druckknopf
pushcart	'puʃka:t	C	Einkaufswagen
pushing	'puʃɪŋ	C	energisch, strebsam
put	put	A	setzen, stellen, legen
put			
put			
put down		B	heruntertun; aufschreiben
put off		A	ver-, aufschieben
put on		A	einschalten, auflegen (Band, Platte); inszenieren (Stück) C
put on weight		C	zunehmen (Gewicht)
put out		A	auslöschen, -machen
put right		C	richtigstellen, berichtigen
put through		B	verbinden (Telefon)
put up		A	unterbringen
put up with		C	s. abfinden mit
puzzle	pʌzl	A	Rätsel
puzzling	'pʌzlɪŋ	C	rätselhaft, verwirrend
puzzled	pʌzld	C	verwirrt
pyjamas	pə'dʒa:məz	A	Schlafanzug
(US auch: pajamas)			

Quarrelsome

queer	kwɪə	C	sonderbar; homosexuell
question	'kwestʃn	A	Frage; befragen; in Frage stellen C
question mark	'kwestʃn‿ma:k	B	Fragezeichen
question tag	'kwestʃn‿tæg	B	Frageanhängsel
question word		B	Fragewort
questionnaire	kwestʃə'neə	C	Fragebogen
queue	kju:	A	Schlange; Schlange stehen
quick	kwɪk	A	schnell, rasch
quiet	'kwaɪət	A	ruhig, still; Ruhe
quit	kwɪt	B	verlassen; aufgeben
quit, quitted			
quit, quitted			
quite	kwaɪt	A	ganz; ziemlich
quiz	kwɪz	A	Fragespiel
quotation	kwəʊ'teɪʃn	B	Zitat
quotation marks		B	Anführungsstriche
quote	kwəʊt	B	zitieren; (Preis) angeben W

quilt /kwɪlt/ Steppdecke

Q

q	kju:	A	q
qualify	'kwɒlɪfaɪ	B	s. qualifizieren; näher bestimmen
qualification	kwɒlɪfɪ'keɪʃn	B	Qualifikation, Befähigung
quality	'kwɒlətɪ	A	Eigenschaft; Qualität
quantity	'kwɒntətɪ	A	Menge
quarrel	'kwɒrəl	A	streiten; Streit
quarrelsome	'kwɒrəlsəm	C	zänkisch
quarter	'kwɔ:tə	A	Viertel; (US) 25 Cent
quarterly	'kwɔ:təlɪ	C	vierteljährlich
quay	ki:	C	Kai, Uferstraße
queen	kwi:n	A	Königin

R

r	a:	A	r
rabbit	'ræbɪt	B	Kaninchen
rabies	'reɪbi:z	C	Tollwut
race	reɪs	A	(Wett-)Rennen; Rasse; um die Wette rennen
racing car	'reɪsɪŋka:	C	Rennwagen
racial	reɪʃl	C	Rassen-, rassisch

rack

rack	ræk	C	(Gepäck-)Ständer; Zahnstange
rack railway		C	Zahnradbahn
racism	'reɪsɪzm	C	Rassismus
racist	'reɪsɪst	C	Rassist, rassistisch
racket	'rækɪt	B	(Tennis-)Schläger
radar	'reɪdɑ:	C	Radar
radiator	'reɪdɪeɪtə	B	Heizkörper, Kühler
radical	'rædɪkl	C	radikal; Radikale(r)
radio	'reɪdɪəʊ	A	Radio; Rundfunk
radioactive	reɪdɪəʊ'æktɪv	C	radioaktiv
rag	ræg	C	Lumpen, Fetzen
ragged	'rægɪd	C	zerlumpt
ragtime	'rægtaɪm	C	Ragtime(-Jazz)
rage	reɪdʒ	B	Wut; wüten
raid	reɪd	C	Überfall

A raid

rail	reɪl	B	Schiene
by rail		W	mit der Bahn
railing	'reɪlɪŋ	C	Gitter; Geländer
railways; (US) railroad	'reɪlweɪz, 'reɪlrəʊd	A	Eisenbahn
railway station	'..⌣..	A	Bahnhof
rain	reɪn	A	Regen; regnen
rainy	'reɪnɪ	B	regnerisch
rainbow	'reɪnbəʊ	B	Regenbogen
raincoat	'reɪnkəʊt	A	Regenmantel
raise	reɪz	A	hochheben, erhöhen
raise a family		B	eine Familie ernähren
raise a question		B	eine Frage aufwerfen
raise one's voice		B	lauter reden
rally	'rælɪ	C	Kundgebung; Rallye
ranch	rɑːntʃ	B	(US) Rinderfarm
rancher	'rɑːntʃə	B	(US) Viehzüchter
at random	ət 'rændəm	C	willkürlich
range	reɪndʒ	B	Bereich; s. erstrecken
ranger	'reɪndʒə	C	(US) Förster, Waldheger
rank	ræŋk	C	Rang; rangieren

ransom	'rænsəm	C	Lösegeld
rape	reɪp	C	vergewaltigen; Vergewaltigung
rapid	'ræpɪd	B	schnell, rasch
rare	reə	A	selten; kostbar
rasher	'ræʃə	C	Speckscheibe, -schnitte
raspberry	'rɑːzbərɪ	C	Himbeere
rat	ræt	C	Ratte
rate	reɪt	C	Verhältnis; Tarif; Tempo
at any rate		B	auf jeden Fall
rate of exchange		C	Wechselkurs
rate of interest		W	Zinssatz
rather	'rɑːðə	A	eher, lieber; ziemlich
rather than		B	anstatt, statt
rather too...		B	(wohl) etwas zu...
or rather		B	oder vielmehr
I would rather		A	ich würde lieber
rational	'ræʃnəl	C	rational; vernünftig
rationalisation	ˌræʃnəlaɪ'zeɪʃn	C	Rationalisierung
raven	'reɪvn	C	Rabe
raw	rɔ:	B	roh; rauh
raw material		B	Rohstoff
ray	reɪ	C	Strahl
razor	'reɪzə	C	Rasierapparat
reach	riːtʃ	A	erreichen; s. erstrecken
out of (one's) reach		B	unerreichbar
within easy reach		B	leicht erreichbar
react (to)	rɪ'ækt	A	reagieren (auf)
reaction	rɪ'ækʃn	B	Reaktion
read	riːd	A	lesen
read	red		
read			
reader	'riːdə	B	Leser(in); Lesebuch
reading	'riːdɪŋ	B	Lesen; Lese-; Lektüre
reading-room	'..⌣.	B	Lesesaal, Lesezimmer
ready	'redɪ	A	fertig; bereit
get ready		A	(s.) fertigmachen
ready-made	ˌredɪ'meɪd	C	Fertig-
readily	'redɪlɪ	C	bereitwillig, gerne
readiness	'redɪnəs	C	Bereitschaft; Bereitwilligkeit
real	rɪəl	A	wirklich, tatsächlich; echt
really	'rɪəlɪ	A	wirklich, wahrhaftig
realism	'rɪəlɪzm	C	Realismus, Wirklichkeitssinn
realistic	rɪə'lɪstɪk	C	realistisch
reality	rɪ'ælətɪ	A	Wirklichkeit
realise(-ize)	'rɪəlaɪz	A	einsehen; merken
realisation (-iz-)		B	Einsicht, Erkennen
rear	rɪə	B	Rückseite, Rück-

rear lights	rɪəˌlaɪts B	Rücklicht(er)
rear wheel	rɪəˌwiːl B	Hinterrad
reason	riːzn A	Grund, Vernunft; gut zureden C
reasonable	ˈriːznəbl B	vernünftig; angemessen
rebel	rebl B	Rebell(in)
	rɪˈbel C	rebellieren, meutern
rebellion	rɪˈbeljən B	Rebellion
rebuild	riːˈbɪld C	wiederaufbauen
recall	rɪˈkɔːl B	s. erinnern an
receive	rɪˈsiːv A	empfangen, erhalten
receiver	rɪˈsiːvə B	Empfänger; Telefonhörer
receipt	rɪˈsiːt B	Empfang; Quittung
recent(ly)	ˈriːsnt(lɪ) A	kürzlich
reception	rɪˈsepʃn B	Aufnahme; Empfang
receptionist	rɪˈsepʃnɪst B	Empfangsdame
recession	rɪˈseʃn W	Rezession, Wirtschaftsflaute
recharge	riːˈtʃɑːdʒ C	(Batterie) aufladen
recipe	ˈresɪpɪ A	(Koch-)Rezept
recite	rɪˈsaɪt C	aufsagen, rezitieren
reckon	rekn C	rechnen; meinen
recognise(-ize)	ˈrekəgnaɪz A	(wieder)erkennen; anerkennen
recognition	rekəgˈnɪʃn B	Anerkennung
recommend	rekəˈmend A	empfehlen
recommendation	rekəmenˈdeɪʃn B	Empfehlung
reconcile	ˈrekənsaɪl C	s. versöhnen
reconciliation	rekənsɪlɪˈeɪʃn C	Versöhnung
record	ˈrekɔːd A	Rekord; Schallplatte
record player	A	Plattenspieler
record	rɪˈkɔːd A	aufzeichnen, -nehmen
recorder	rɪˈkɔːdə C	Blockflöte
tape recorder	A	Tonbandgerät
recording	rɪˈkɔːdɪŋ B	Aufnahme (Ton)
recover	rɪˈkʌvə B	wiedererlangen; s. erholen
recovery	rɪˈkʌvərɪ B	Genesung
recreation	rekrɪˈeɪʃn B	Erholung
rectangle	ˈrektæŋgl C	Rechteck
rectangular	rekˈtæŋgjʊlə C	rechteckig
red	red A	rot
Red Cross	redˌkrɒs C	Rotes Kreuz
redcurrants	redˈkʌrənts C	rote Johannisbeeren
red tape	redˌteɪp C	Papierkram
reduce	rɪˈdjuːs B	ermäßigen, senken
reduction	rɪˈdʌkʃn B	Ermäßigung
redundant	rɪˈdʌndənt C	überzählig
refer (to)	rɪˈfɜː B	s. beziehen (auf); verweisen (auf)
reference	ˈrefrəns B	Bezug; Referenz
with reference to	C	mit Bezug auf
reference book	B	Nachschlagewerk
referee	refəˈriː C	Schiedsrichter (Fußball)
refined	rɪˈfaɪnd C	verfeinert
refinery	rɪˈfaɪnərɪ C	Raffinerie
reflect	rɪˈflekt B	widerspiegeln; überlegen
reflection (reflexion)	rɪˈflekʃn C	Reflexion; Überlegung
reflector	rɪˈflektə C	Rückstrahler
reflexive pronoun	rɪˈfleksɪv C	Reflexivpronomen, rückbez. Fürwort
reform	rɪˈfɔːm C	Verbesserung, Reform; umgestalten
reformation	refəˈmeɪʃn C	Umgestaltung; Reformation
refrain from	rɪˈfreɪn C	s. enthalten
refresh	rɪˈfreʃ C	(s.) erfrischen
refreshments	B	Erfrischungen
refrigerator	rɪˈfrɪdʒəreɪtə A	Kühlschrank
refugee	refjuːˈdʒiː C	Flüchtling
refuse	rɪˈfjuːz A	s. weigern; ablehnen

Reference books

To refuse

refuse

refusal	rɪˈfjuːzl B	Weigerung; Ablehnung	
regain	rɪˈgeɪn C	wiedererlangen	
regard (as)	rɪˈgɑːd A	betrachten, ansehen (als)	
as regards; regarding	C	angesichts	
with regard to	C	bezüglich	
(kind) regards	B	(freundliche) Grüße	
regards to ...	A	(schönen) Gruß an ...	
regatta	rɪˈgætə C	Regatta	
region	ˈriːdʒn B	Gegend, Gebiet	
regional	ˈriːdʒnəl C	regional, örtlich	
register	ˈredʒɪstə B	Verzeichnis; registrieren	
cash register	ˌkæʃ ˈredʒɪstə C	Registrierkasse	
registered letter	ˈredʒɪstəd ... B	Einschreibebrief	
registration	redʒɪˈstreɪʃn C	Registrierung	
regret	rɪˈgret B	bedauern; Bedauern	
regrettable	rɪˈgretəbl C	bedauerlich	
regular	ˈregjʊlə A	regelmäßig; normal	
regulate	ˈregjʊleɪt B	regeln	
regulation	regjʊˈleɪʃn B	Vorschrift	
rehearse	rɪˈhɜːs C	proben, einstudieren	
rehearsal	rɪˈhɜːsl C	Probe	
dress rehearsal	C	Generalprobe	
reign	reɪn B	Regierungszeit; regieren	
reject	rɪˈdʒekt C	verwerfen; ablehnen	
related	rɪˈleɪtɪd B	verwandt; in Beziehung stehend	
relating to	rɪˈleɪtɪŋtə C	betreffend	
relation	rɪˈleɪʃn B	Verwandte(r); Beziehung	
relationship	rɪˈleɪʃnʃɪp B	Beziehung	
relative	ˈrelətɪv A	Verwandte(r); relativ	
relative pronoun	B	Relativpronomen; bezügliches Fürwort	
relatively	ˈrelətɪvlɪ B	verhältnismäßig	
relax	rɪˈlæks A	(s.) entspannen	
release	rɪˈliːs C	Freilassung; herausbringen, freilassen	
relevant	ˈrelɪvənt C	relevant, zutreffend	
reliable	rɪˈlaɪəbl B	zuverlässig	
relief	rɪˈliːf C	Erleichterung; Hilfe	
relieve	rɪˈliːv C	erleichtern; befreien	
be relieved	C	erleichtert sein	
religion	rɪˈlɪdʒn A	Religion	
religious	rɪˈlɪdʒəs A	religiös	
reluctance	rɪˈlʌktəns C	Widerstreben	
reluctant	rɪˈlʌktənt C	zögernd, widerwillig	
rely (on)	rɪˈlaɪ A	s. verlassen (auf)	
reliable	rɪˈlaɪəbl A	zuverlässig	
reliability	rɪlaɪəˈbɪlətɪ B	Zuverlässigkeit	
remain	rɪˈmeɪn A	bleiben; übrigbleiben	
remainder	rɪˈmeɪndə C	Rest	
remains	rɪˈmeɪnz C	Überreste	
remark	rɪˈmɑːk B	bemerken; Bemerkung	
remarkable	rɪˈmɑːkəbl B	bemerkenswert, beachtlich	
remedy	ˈremɪdɪ B	(Heil-)Mittel	
remember	rɪˈmembə A	s. erinnern an	
remembrance	rɪˈmembrəns C	Erinnerung; Gedächtnis	
remind (of)	rɪˈmaɪnd A	jd. erinnern (an)	
that reminds me	C	dabei fällt mir ein	
reminder	rɪˈmaɪndə C	Hinweis; Mahnung W	
remit	rɪˈmɪt W	überweisen	
remittance	rɪˈmɪtəns W	Überweisung	
remote	rɪˈməʊt B	fern, entfernt	
remote control	C	Fernsteuerung	
remove	rɪˈmuːv B	entfernen, beseitigen	
removal	rɪˈmuːv(ə)l C	Beseitigung; Umzug	
removal van	... væn C	Möbelwagen	
Renaissance	rɪˈneɪsəns C	Renaissance	
render	ˈrendə C	erweisen; machen zu	
render a service	ˈsɜːvɪs C	einen Dienst erweisen	
renew	rɪˈnjuː C	erneuern	
renewal	rɪˈnjuːəl C	Erneuerung; Verlängerung	
renounce	rɪˈnaʊns C	verzichten auf	
renovate	ˈrenəveɪt C	renovieren	
rent	rent A	Miete; mieten	
rent (to)	A	vermieten (an)	
repair	rɪˈpeə A	reparieren; Reparatur	
repay	rɪˈpeɪ C	zurückzahlen	
repeat	rɪˈpiːt A	wiederholen	
repeatedly	rɪˈpiːtɪdlɪ C	wiederholt, mehrmals	
repetition	repɪˈtɪʃn A	Wiederholung	
replace	rɪˈpleɪs B	ersetzen	
replacement	rɪˈpleɪsmənt C	Ersatz(-)	
reply (to)	rɪˈplaɪ A	erwidern; Antwort	
report	rɪˈpɔːt A	Bericht; berichten; s. melden	
reporter	rɪˈpɔːtə A	Reporter	

represent	rɪˈprɪzent	B	vertreten; darstellen
representative	reprɪˈzentətɪv	B	Vertreter
reproach	rɪˈprəʊtʃ	C	Vorwurf; vorwerfen
reproachful	rɪˈprəʊtʃfl	C	vorwurfsvoll
reproduce	riːprəˈdjuːs	C	wiedergeben
reproduction	riːprəˈdʌkʃn	C	Nachbildung; Nacherzählung
republic	rɪˈpʌblɪk	B	Republik
republican	rɪˈpʌblɪkən	B	republikanisch
reputation	repjuːˈteɪʃn	B	Ruf, Ansehen
request	rɪˈkwest	B	Bitte, Gesuch; ersuchen
request stop	..ˈstɒp	B	Bedarfshaltestelle
require	rɪˈkwaɪə	A	verlangen; benötigen
requirement	rɪˈkwaɪəmənt	B	Anforderung; Bedarf
rescue	ˈreskjuː	A	retten; Rettung
research	rɪˈsɜːtʃ	B	Forschung
resemble	rɪˈzembl	B	ähneln, gleichen
resemblance	rɪˈzembləns	C	Ähnlichkeit
resent	rɪˈzent	C	übelnehmen
reserve	rɪˈzɜːv	A	reservieren; Reserve
reserved	rɪˈzɜːvd	C	reserviert; kühl
reservation	rezəˈveɪʃn	B	Reservierung; Vorbehalt C
residence	ˈrezɪdəns	B	Wohnsitz; Aufenthalt
resident	ˈrezɪdənt	C	ortsansässig; Einwohner
resign	rɪˈzaɪn	C	zurücktreten
resignation	rezɪgˈneɪʃn	C	Resignation; Rücktritt
resist	rɪˈzɪst	B	widerstehen

To resist

resistance	rɪˈzɪstəns	B	Widerstand
resolution	rezəˈljuːʃn	C	Entschluß; Entschlossenheit
resolve	rɪˈzɒlv	C	beschließen
resort	rɪˈzɔːt	B	Zuflucht
seaside resort	ˈsiːsaɪd..	B	Seebad
resource	rɪˈzɔːs	B	Hilfsquelle, Hilfsmittel
mineral resources	ˈmɪnrəl rɪˈzɔːsɪz	B	Bodenschätze
respect	rɪˈspekt	B	Achtung; Hinsicht; achten
in every respect		C	in jeder Beziehung
respectable	rɪˈspektəbl	B	achtbar
respectful	rɪˈspektfl	C	ehrerbietig
respective	rɪˈspektɪv	C	entsprechend, jeweilig
respond (to)	rɪˈspɒnd	B	reagieren; antworten (auf)
response	rɪˈspɒns	B	Antwort; Reaktion
responsible	rɪˈspɒnsəbl	A	verantwortlich
responsibility	rɪspɒnsəˈbɪlətɪ	B	Verantwortung
rest	rest	A	Rest; Ruhe; Stütze C; (aus)ruhen
restaurant	ˈrestrɑːŋ	A	Restaurant, Gaststätte
restful	ˈrestfʊl	C	ruhig, friedlich
restless	ˈrestləs	C	ruhelos, rastlos
restore	rɪˈstɔː	C	wiederherstellen, sanieren
restrict	rɪˈstrɪkt	C	einschränken
restrictive	rɪˈstrɪktɪv	C	einschränkend
restriction	rɪˈstrɪkʃn	C	Einschränkung
result	rɪˈzʌlt	A	Ergebnis; Folge; resultieren C
as a result		A	als Folge, infolge
resume	rɪˈzjuːm	C	wiederaufnehmen
resumption	rɪˈzʌmpʃn	C	Wiederaufnahme
retailer	ˈriːteɪlə	W	Einzelhändler
retail trade	..ˈ..	W	Einzelhandel
retain	rɪˈteɪn	C	zurückhalten; behalten
retell	rɪˈtel	C	wieder erzählen, nacherzählen
retire	rɪˈtaɪə	B	s. zurückziehen, in Pension gehen
retirement	rɪˈtaɪəmənt	B	Pensionierung
retired	rɪˈtaɪəd	C	im Ruhestand
retreat	rɪˈtriːt	C	Rückzug; s. zurückziehen
return	rɪˈtɜːn	A	zurückkehren, -geben; Rückkehr
return ticket	..ˈtɪkɪt	A	Rückfahrkarte
in return		C	als Gegenleistung; dafür
reveal	rɪˈviːl	C	enthüllen; verraten
revenge	rɪˈvendʒ	C	Rache; rächen
reverse	rɪˈvɜːs	C	umgekehrt
reverse gear	..ˈgɪə	C	Rückwärtsgang
reverse side	..ˈsaɪd	C	Rückseite
reversed charge call		C	R-Gespräch

reversed charge call

review	rɪˈvju:	B	Kritik; besprechen
revision	rɪˈvɪʒn	C	Überprüfung, Wiederholung
revive	rɪˈvaɪv	C	wiederbeleben
revival	rɪˈvaɪv(ə)l	C	Wiederbelebung
revolt	rɪˈvəʊlt	C	Aufruhr; revoltieren
revolution	revəˈlu:ʃn	B	Revolution; Umsturz
revolutionary	revəˈlu:ʃnərɪ	C	revolutionär, Revolutions-
revolver	rɪˈvɒlvə	B	Revolver
reward	rɪˈwɔ:d	A	Belohnung; belohnen

ring (up)/give a ring		A	anrufen
ring back	ˌbæk	A	zurückrufen
rinse	rɪns	C	ausspülen
riot	ˈraɪət	C	Aufruhr; Ausschreitungen begehen
ripe	raɪp	B	reif
ripen	ˈraɪp(ə)n	C	reifen
rise	raɪz	A	s. erheben,
rose	rəʊz		steigen; Zunahme
risen	rɪzn		
risk	rɪsk	B	Wagnis; riskieren
run a risk		C	ein Risiko eingehen

A reward

To run no risk

rewarding	rɪˈwɔ:dɪŋ	A	lohnend
rewind	rɪˈwaɪnd	C	zurückspulen
Rhine	raɪn	C	Rhein
rhyme	raɪm	B	Reim; reimen
rhythm	rɪðm	C	Rhythmus
rib	rɪb	C	Rippe
ribbon	rɪb(ə)n	B	Band, Farbband
rice	raɪs	A	Reis
rich	rɪtʃ	A	reich; üppig
riches	ˈrɪtʃɪz	C	Reichtümer
get rid of	ˈrɪd	B	loswerden
riddle	rɪdl	B	Rätsel
ride	raɪd	A	reiten, fahren;
rode	rəʊd		Ritt, Fahrt
ridden	rɪdn		
riding	ˈraɪdɪŋ	B	Reiten, Pferdesport
ridiculous	rɪˈdɪkjʊləs	B	lächerlich
rifle	raɪfl	B	Gewehr, Flinte
right	raɪt	A	Recht; richtig
all right		A	in Ordnung, okay
right away	ˌəˈweɪ	B	sofort
right now	ˌnaʊ	B	jetzt gleich
be right		A	recht haben
on (= to) the right		A	rechts
right of way		B	Vorfahrt
ring	rɪŋ	A	Ring; läuten
rang	ræŋ		
rung	rʌŋ		

risky	ˈrɪskɪ	C	gefährlich, riskant
rival	ˈraɪvəl	B	Rivale, -in; rivalisieren C
rivalry	ˈraɪvlrɪ	C	Rivalität
river	ˈrɪvə	A	Fluß, Strom
riverside	ˈrɪvəsaɪd	C	Flußufer, Fluß-
road	rəʊd	A	Straße, Weg
roadside	ˈrəʊdsaɪd	C	Straßenrand; Straßen-
roam	rəʊm	C	(herum)wandern
roar	rɔ:	C	brüllen; Getöse
roast	rəʊst	A	braten, rösten
roast beef	ˌbi:f	A	Roastbeef, Rinderbraten
rob	rɒb	A	(be)rauben
robber	ˈrɒbə	A	Räuber
robbery	ˈrɒbərɪ	B	Raub
robe	rəʊb	C	Robe; Talar
robin	ˈrɒbɪn	C	Rotkehlchen
robot	ˈrəʊbɒt	B	Roboter
rock	rɒk	B	Felsen; schaukeln
rock music		B	Rockmusik
on the rocks (US)		C	mit Eis
rocky	ˈrɒkɪ	C	felsig
rocket	ˈrɒkɪt	A	Rakete
rod	rɒd	C	Rute, Stab
rodeo	ˈrəʊdɪəʊ	C	Rodeo, Cowboywettstreit
role	rəʊl	B	Rolle

roll	rəʊl A	Rolle; Semmel; rollen	
rollerskates	'rəʊləskeɪts B	Rollschuhe	
roller-skating	ˌskeɪtɪŋ B	Rollschuhfahren	
Roman	'rəʊmən B	römisch; Römer	
Rome	rəʊm B	Rom	
romantic	rə'mæntɪk C	romantisch	
roof,s	ruːf,fs A	Dach	
room	rʊm A	Zimmer; Platz	
root	ruːt B	Wurzel	
rope	rəʊp B	Seil, Tau	
rose	rəʊz A	Rose	
rosebush	'rəʊzbʊʃ C	Rosenstrauch	
rosy	'rəʊzɪ C	rosig	
rough	rʌf A	rauh, grob	
roughly	'rʌflɪ B	ungefähr	
round	raʊnd A	rund; (um...) herum; Runde C	
round off	C	(ab)runden	
all the year round	A	das ganze Jahr hindurch	
round the clock	B	rund um die Uhr	
roundabout	'raʊndəbaʊt A	Karussell; Kreisverkehr	
route	ruːt B	Route	
row	rəʊ A	Reihe; rudern	
rowing boat	'rəʊɪŋbəʊt C	Ruderboot	
row	raʊ C	Streit, Schlägerei	
rowdy	'raʊdɪ C	Raufbold	
royal	'rɔɪəl B	königlich	
royalty	'rɔɪəltɪ C	königl. Familie; Königswürde	
rub	rʌb A	reiben	
rub out/off	A	ausradieren, (ab)wischen	
rubber	'rʌbə A	(Radier-)Gummi	
rubbish	'rʌbɪʃ B	Müll; Unsinn	
rucksack	'rʌksæk C	Rucksack	
rude	ruːd B	unhöflich	
rudeness	'ruːdnəs C	Unhöflichkeit	
rug	rʌg B	Läufer, Teppich	
rugby	'rʌgbɪ A	Rugby	
ruin	'ruːɪn A	Ruine; ruinieren	
rule	ruːl A	Regel; Herrschaft; Lineal; herrschen B	
as a rule	A	in der Regel	
rule out	C	ausschließen	
ruler	'ruːlə B	Herrscher; Lineal	
Rumania	ruː'meɪnjə C	Rumänien	
rumour	'ruːmə B	Gerücht	
run	rʌn A	rennen, laufen	
ran	ræn		
run	rʌn		
in the long run (= term)	C	auf die Dauer	
run across (= run into) sb	B	jd. zufällig begegnen	
run for	C	(US) kandidieren für	
run out of	C	ausgehen, zu Ende gehen	
run over	B	überfahren	
run a business	W	ein Geschäft führen	
runaway	'rʌnəweɪ C	Ausreißer(in)	
runner	'rʌnə B	Läufer(in)	
runway	'rʌnweɪ B	Start-, Landebahn	
rural	'rʊərəl C	ländlich	
rush	rʌʃ B	Eile; Andrang; eilen; drängen	
rush hour	ˌaʊə A	Hauptverkehrszeit	
Russia	'rʌʃə B	Rußland	
Russian	'rʌʃn B	russisch; Russe, -in	
rust	rʌst C	Rost; rosten	
rusty	'rʌstɪ C	rostig	
ruthless	'ruːθləs C	rücksichtslos, skrupellos	
rye	raɪ C	Roggen	

the sales

roofrack
Dachständer

S

s	es A	s	
sack	sæk C	Sack; entlassen	
sacred	'seɪkrɪd C	heilig	
sacrifice	'sækrɪfaɪs B	Opfer; opfern	
sad	sæd A	traurig	
sadness	'sædnəs B	Traurigkeit	
saddle	sædl B	Sattel; satteln	
safe (from)	seɪf A	sicher (vor); Safe	
to be on the safe side	C	um sicherzugehen	
safety	'seɪftɪ B	Sicherheit	
safety belt	ˌbelt B	Sicherheitsgurt	
safety pin	ˌpɪn C	Sicherheitsnadel	
sail	seɪl A	Segel; segeln; fahren (per Schiff)	
sailing boat	'seɪlɪŋbəʊt C	Segelboot	
sailor	'seɪlə B	Seemann, Matrose	
saint	seɪnt B	heilig; Heilige(r)	
for the sake of	fəˌðəˈseɪkˌəv B	um... willen	
for heaven's sake	fəˌhevnzˈseɪk C	um Himmels willen	
salad	'sæləd A	Salat	
salary	'sælərɪ A	Gehalt	
sale	seɪl A	Verkauf	
for sale	A	zu verkaufen	
the sales	A	Schlußverkauf	

salesman

salesman	'seɪlzmən	B	Verkäufer
sales manager	'.....	W	Verkaufsleiter
salmon	'sæmən	C	Lachs
salt	sɒlt, sɔ:lt	A	Salz; salzen
the same	seɪm	A	der-, die-, dasselbe

The same material

all the same		B	trotzdem
sample	sɑ:mpl	B	Muster, Probe
sand	sænd	A	Sand
sandy	'sændɪ	C	sandig
sandal	'sændəl	C	Sandale
sandwich	'sæn(d)wɪdʒ	A	belegtes Brot, Sandwich
sane	seɪn	B	geistig gesund; vernünftig
sardine	sɑ:'di:n	C	Sardine
satchel	'sætʃl	B	Schultasche, Schulmappe
satellite	'sætəlaɪt	A	Satellit
satisfy	'sætɪsfaɪ	B	befriedigen, zufriedenstellen
satisfied	'sætɪsfaɪd	B	zufrieden
satisfaction	sætɪs'fækʃn	B	Befriedigung, Zufriedenheit
satisfactory	sætɪs'fæktrɪ	B	zufriedenstellend
Saturday	'sætədɪ,eɪ	A	Samstag
sauce	sɔ:s	A	Soße
saucepan	'sɔ:spən	B	Stieltopf, Kasserolle
saucer	'sɔ:sə	A	Untertasse
flying saucer	'flaɪɪŋ'sɔ:sə	C	fliegende Untertasse
sauna	'sɔ:nə	C	Sauna
sausage	'sɒsɪdʒ	A	Wurst, Würstchen
savage	'sævɪdʒ	C	wild; Wilde(r)
save	seɪv	A	retten; sparen
savings	'seɪvɪŋz	B	Ersparnisse
savings bank	'..bæŋk	C	Sparkasse
savings book	'..bʊk	C	Sparbuch
saw	sɔ:	B	Säge; sägen
sawed	sɔ:d		
sawn, sawed	sɔ:n		
sawdust	'sɔ:dʌst	C	Sägemehl
Saxon	'sæksən	C	sächsisch
saxophone	'sæksəfəʊn	C	Saxophon
say	seɪ	A	sagen
said	sed		
said			
have a say (in)		C	etw. zu sagen haben (bei)
is said to		B	soll (angeblich)
it goes without saying		C	selbstverständlich
saying	'seɪɪŋ	C	Redensart
scaffold	'skæfəld	C	(Bau-)Gerüst
scale	skeɪl	B	Maßstab; Ausmaß; Tonleiter C

The scales

a pair of scales	peər‿əv‿'skeɪlz	B	eine Waage
scandal	skændl	C	Skandal; Klatsch
scandalous	'skændələs	C	skandalös
Scandinavia	skændɪ'neɪvɪə	C	Skandinavien
scar	skɑ:	C	Narbe
scarce	skeəs	B	knapp, selten
scarcely	'skeəslɪ	B	kaum, schwerlich
scare	skeə	C	erschrecken
be scared	skeəd	B	Angst haben
scarf, ves	skɑ:f,vz	A	Halstuch, Schal
scatter	'skætə	B	verstreuen; s. zerstreuen
scene	si:n	A	Schauplatz; Szene
scenery	'si:nərɪ	A	Landschaft, Szenerie
schedule	'ʃedju:l (US) 'skedʒʊl	B	Tabelle; Fahr-, Stundenplan
according to schedule		C	(fahr)planmäßig
scheme	ski:m	B	Plan, Projekt
scholar	'skɒlə	B	Gelehrte(r)
scholarship	'skɒləʃɪp	B	Stipendium
school	sku:l	A	Schule
schoolbag	'sku:lbæg	A	Schultasche
schoolboy, -girl	'sku:lbɔɪ,'..gɜ:l	A	Schulbub, -mädchen
schooling	'sku:lɪŋ	C	Schulbildung, schulische Erziehung

schoolmaster	ˈskuːlmɑːstə	A	Lehrer
schoolmistress	ˌmɪstrəs	A	Lehrerin
science	ˈsaɪəns	A	(Natur-)Wissenschaft
science fiction	ˈsaɪənsˈfɪkʃn	B	Science-fiction, Zukunftsroman
scientific	saɪənˈtɪfɪk	B	wissenschaftlich
scientist	ˈsaɪəntɪst	B	Wissenschaftler(in)
scissors	ˈsɪzəz	A	Schere
scold	skəʊld	C	schelten
scooter	ˈskuːtə	C	Roller
scope	skəʊp	C	Bereich, Rahmen
score	skɔː	B	Punktzahl; Punkte machen, Tor(e) schießen
scores of	ˈskɔːzˌəv	C	eine große Anzahl von
Scot(sman)	ˈskɒt(smən)	A	Schotte
Scotland	ˈskɒtlənd	A	Schottland
Scottish	ˈskɒtɪʃ	A	schottisch; Schotte(-in)
Scotch (whisky)	skɒtʃ	B	(schott.) Whisky
scout	skaʊt	A	Pfadfinder
scrambled eggs	ˈskræmbld	B	Rührei
scrape	skreɪp	C	kratzen, schaben
scratch	skrætʃ	C	(zer)kratzen; Kratzer
from scratch	frəmˈskrætʃ	C	von Grund auf
scream	skriːm	B	schreien, kreischen
screen	skriːn	A	(Bild-)Schirm, Projektionswand
screw	skruː	B	(Holz-)Schraube
screwdriver	ˈskruːdraɪvə	B	Schraubenzieher
script	skrɪpt	C	Manuskript, Text
scrub	skrʌb	B	schrubben
scrum	skrʌm	C	Gedränge (Rugby)
sculpture	ˈskʌlptʃə	C	Skulptur
sea	siː	A	Meer, die See
at sea	əˈtsiː	A	auf/zur See
by sea	baɪˈsiː	B	auf dem Seeweg, per Schiff
seagull	ˈsiːgʌl	C	Möwe
seaman	ˈsiːmən	C	Seemann
seaport	ˈsiːpɔːt	C	Seehafen; Hafenstadt
seashore	ˈsiːʃɔː	C	Küste(nland)
seasick	ˈsiːsɪk	B	seekrank
seaside	ˈsiːsaɪd	A	Badeküste
seal	siːl	B	Siegel; versiegeln; Robbe, Seehund
search (for)	sɜːtʃ	B	suchen; forschen (nach); durchsuchen
in search of	ɪnˈsɜːtʃˌəv	C	auf der Suche nach
season	siːzn	A	Jahreszeit, Saison; würzen; ablagern C
season ticket	ˌtɪkɪt	B	Zeitkarte
seat	siːt	A	Sitz, Platz
take a seat		A	Platz nehmen
be seated	ˈsiːtɪd	C	sitzen
seatbelt	ˈsiːtbelt	B	Sitzgurt
seating-plan	ˈsiːtɪŋplæn	B	Sitzplan
second	ˈsekənd	A	zweite(r,s); Sekunde
second-hand	ˌhænd	A	aus zweiter Hand
second-rate	ˌreɪt	C	zweitklassig
secondary school		A	weiterführende Schule
	ˈsekəndrɪ		
secondly	ˈsekəndlɪ	B	zweitens
secret	ˈsiːkrət	A	Geheimnis; geheim

A secret

Scotland Yard Londoner Polizeizentrale

secret service	ˌsɜːvɪs	C	Geheimdienst
secretary	ˈsekrɪtrɪ	A	Sekretär(in)
section	sekʃn	B	Abschnitt; Abteilung
secure	sɪˈkjʊə	B	sicher; sichern
security	sɪˈkjʊərətɪ	B	Sicherheit
Security Council		C	Sicherheitsrat
see	siː	A	sehen
saw	sɔː		
seen	siːn		
see sb off/out		B	jd. weg-, hinausbegleiten
see to it		C	dafür sorgen
see you tomorrow		A	bis morgen!
I see		B	ich verstehe! aha!
seed	siːd	B	Same(n), Saat
seek	siːk	B	suchen
sought	sɔːt		
sought			
seem	siːm	A	scheinen
seemingly	ˈsiːmɪŋlɪ	C	sichtlich
segregation	segrɪˈgeɪʃn	C	(Rassen-)Trennung
seize	siːz	B	ergreifen; beschlagnahmen

seldom	ˈseldəm	A	selten
select	sɪˈlekt	B	auswählen
selection	sɪˈlekʃn	B	Auswahl, Auslese
self	self	A	selbst
self-confidence	ˌkɒnfɪdəns	B	Selbstvertrauen
self-confident	ˌkɒnfɪdənt	C	selbstbewußt
self-conscious	ˌkɒnʃəs	C	unsicher, gehemmt
self-control	ˌkənˈtrəʊl	A	Selbstbeherrschung
self-defence	ˌdɪˈfens	C	Selbstverteidigung
self-determination	ˌdɪtɜːmɪˈneɪʃn	C	Selbstbestimmung
self-discipline	ˌdɪsɪplɪn	C	Selbstdisziplin
self-respect	ˌrɪˈspekt	C	Selbstachtung
self-service	ˌsɜːvɪs	A	Selbstbedienung
selfish	ˈselfɪʃ	C	egoistisch
selfishness	ˈselfɪʃnəs	C	Selbstsucht
sell	sel	A	verkaufen
sold	səʊld		
sold			

To sell   *Sold*

seller	ˈselə	B	Verkäufer(in)
best seller	bestˌselə	B	Bestseller
semi-final	semɪˈfaɪnl	C	Halbfinale
semi-detached house (=semi)		A	Doppelhaus(hälfte)
semicolon	semɪˈkəʊlən	B	Strichpunkt
Senate	ˈsenɪt	B	Senat
Senator	ˈsenətə	B	Senator
send	send	A	senden, schicken
sent	sent		
sent			
send for		B	holen lassen
sender	ˈsendə	C	(Ab-)Sender(in)
senior	ˈsiːnɪə	B	älter; Ober-
senior high school		B	US: Oberschule
sensation	senˈseɪʃn	C	Empfindung; Sensation
sensational	senˈseɪʃnəl	B	sensationell, aufsehenerregend
sense	sens	A	Sinn; Verstand
make sense		C	einen Sinn ergeben; vernünftig sein
sense of humour	ˌəvˈhjuːmə	A	(Sinn für) Humor
sensible	ˈsensəbl	B	vernünftig
sensitive	ˈsensɪtɪv	B	empfindlich, sensibel
senseless	ˈsensləs	C	sinnlos, unsinnig
sentence	ˈsentəns	A	Satz; Urteil, verurteilen C
sentimental	sentɪˈmentl	C	sentimental, Gefühls-
separate	ˈsepəreɪt	B	(s.) trennen
	ˈseprət	B	getrennt
separation	sepəˈreɪʃn	B	Trennung
separatism	ˈseprətɪzm	C	Separatismus
September	sepˈtembə	A	September
sergeant	ˈsɑːdʒnt	B	Feldwebel; Wachtmeister
series	ˈsɪəriːz	B	Serie(n)
serious	ˈsɪərɪəs	A	ernst, ernsthaft
sermon	ˈsɜːmən	C	Predigt
serpent	ˈsɜːpənt	C	Schlange
servant	ˈsɜːvənt	B	Diener; Dienstbote
civil servant	ˈsɪvlˌsɜːvənt	B	Beamter, -in
serve	sɜːv	A	(be)dienen; servieren
service	ˈsɜːvɪs	A	Dienst; Bedienung
civil service		B	öffentl. Dienst
session	seʃn	C	Sitzung
set	set	B	setzen, festsetzen; Satz, Garnitur
have one's hair set		C	s. das Haar legen lassen
set homework		B	Hausaufgabe geben
set free	ˌfriː	C	befreien
set light (=fire) to		C	anzünden
set off (=out) for		C	s. auf den Weg machen nach
setback	ˈsetbæk	C	Rückschlag
settee	seˈtiː	C	Sofa
setting	ˈsetɪŋ	B	Schauplatz, Rahmen
settle	setl	A	s. niederlassen; besiedeln; regeln
settle down	setlˈdaʊn	A	zur Ruhe kommen; heiraten
settlement	ˈsetlmənt	B	(Be-)Siedlung; Regelung
settler	ˈsetlə	B	Siedler
seven	sevn	A	sieben
seventeen	sevnˈtiːn	A	siebzehn
seventy	ˈsevntɪ	A	siebzig
several	ˈsevrəl	A	mehrere; verschiedene

severe	sɪˈvɪə B	streng; heftig	
severity	sɪˈverɪtɪ C	Strenge; Heftigkeit	
sew	səʊ B	nähen	
sewed	səʊd		
sewn, sewed	səʊn,d		
sewing-machine	B	Nähmaschine	
ˈsəʊɪŋməˈʃiːn			
sex	seks A	Geschlecht	
sexual	ˈsekʃʊəl C	geschlechtlich, Geschlechts-	
shabby	ˈʃæbɪ B	schäbig	
shade	ʃeɪd B	Schatten; Schattierung	
shadow	ˈʃædəʊ B	Schatten	
shake	ʃeɪk A	schütteln; zittern	
shook	ʃʊk		
shaken	ˈʃeɪkən		
shake hands	A	s. die Hand geben	

To shake hands

shall	ʃæl,ʃl A	soll(en); werde(n)
shallow	ˈʃæləʊ B	seicht
shame	ʃeɪm B	Schande, Scham
what a shame!	B	wie schade!
shameful	ˈʃeɪmfl C	schmachvoll, schändlich
shameless	ˈʃeɪmləs C	schamlos, unverschämt
shampoo	ʃæmˈpuː C	Haarwaschmittel
shamrock	ˈʃæmrɒk C	irischer Klee
shanty	ˈʃæntɪ C	Seemannslied
shape	ʃeɪp A	Gestalt, Form; gestalten
take shape	C	Gestalt annehmen
out of shape	B	aus der Form
share	ʃeə A	teilen; teilhaben (an) Anteil; Aktie W
shareholder	ˈʃeəhəʊldə W	Aktionär
shark	ʃaːk C	Hai
sharp	ʃaːp A	scharf; genau
sharpen	ˈʃaːpən B	schärfen
(pencil) sharpener	B	Bleistiftspitzer
ˈʃaːpənə		
shatter	ˈʃætə C	zerschmettern

shave	ʃeɪv A	(s.) rasieren; Rasur
shaver	ˈʃeɪvə C	Rasierer
shaving cream	C	Rasiercreme
ˈʃeɪvɪŋ kriːm		
she	ʃiː,ʃɪ A	sie
shed	ʃed B	Schuppen;
shed	ʃed	vergießen
shed		
sheep	ʃiːp A	Schaf(e)
sheepish	ˈʃiːpɪʃ C	schüchtern, kleinlaut
sheet	ʃiːt A	Blatt (Papier); Laken
shelf, ves	ʃelf,vz A	(Wand-)Brett; Regal
shell	ʃel B	Schale; Muschel; Granate
shelter	ˈʃeltə B	Schutz; Obdach; beschützen
shepherd	ˈʃepəd C	Schäfer, Hirte
sheriff	ˈʃerɪf C	Sheriff
sherry	ˈʃerɪ C	Sherry(wein)
shield	ʃiːld C	(der) Schild; beschirmen
shift	ʃɪft C	verschieben; Verschiebung; Schicht B
shilling	ˈʃɪlɪŋ C	Schilling
shine	ʃaɪn A	scheinen, glänzen;
shone	ʃɒn	Schein
shone		
shiny	ˈʃaɪnɪ B	glänzend
ship	ʃɪp A	Schiff; versenden W
shipment	ˈʃɪpmənt W	Versand, Sendung
shipwreck	ˈʃɪprek C	Schiffbruch
shipyard	ˈʃɪpjaːd C	Werft
shirt	ʃɜːt A	Hemd; Hemdbluse
shiver	ˈʃɪvə B	zittern
shock	ʃɒk A	Schlag, Stoß; erschüttern
be shocked	ʃɒkt A	empört sein
shocking	ˈʃɒkɪŋ B	anstößig, empörend
shoe	ʃuː A	Schuh
shoemaker	ˈʃuːmeɪkə B	Schuhmacher
shoot	ʃuːt A	schießen;
shot	ʃɒt	(Film) drehen
shot		
shop	ʃɒp A	Laden; einkaufen B
shop window	ˈwɪndəʊ B	Schaufenster
shop assistant	A	Verkäufer(in)
shopkeeper	ˈʃɒpkiːpə B	Ladeninhaber
shoplifting	ˈʃɒplɪftɪŋ C	Ladendiebstahl
shopping	ˈʃɒpɪŋ A	Einkauf(en)
go shopping	A	Einkaufen gehen
shopping list	B	Einkaufsliste
shopping bag	B	Einkaufstasche
shopping centre	B	Einkaufszentrum

shopping centre

shore

shore	ʃɔː	B	Ufer, Küste
offshore	ɒfˈʃɔː	C	vor der Küste (liegend)
short	ʃɔːt	A	kurz, klein
short of	ˈʃɔːt‿əv	B	knapp an
short-sighted	ˌʃɔːtˈsaɪtɪd	C	kurzsichtig
in short	ɪnˈʃɔːt	B	kurzum
run short	rʌnˈʃɔːt	C	knapp werden
short-term	ˌtɜːm	C	kurzfristig
shortwave	ˈʃɔːt‿weɪv	C	Kurzwelle
shortage	ˈʃɔːtɪdʒ	C	Knappheit
short circuit	ˌsɜːkɪt	C	Kurzschluß
shortcut	ˈʃɔːtˈkʌt	C	Abkürzung
shorten	ˈʃɔːtn	B	kürzen
shorthand	ˈʃɔːthænd	A	Kurzschrift
shorthand typist	ˌtaɪpɪst	W	Stenotypistin
shortly	ˈʃɔːtlɪ	B	in Kürze, bald
shorts	ʃɔːts	A	Shorts, kurze Hose
shot	ʃɒt	C	Schuß
should	ʃʊd, ʃəd	A	sollte, würde
shoulder	ˈʃəʊldə	A	Schulter; schultern C
shoulder-bag		B	Schultertasche
shout	ʃaʊt	A	laut schreien; Schrei
shovel	ˈʃʌvl	C	Schaufel
show	ʃəʊ	A	Schau; Vorstellung; zeigen
showed	ʃəʊd		
shown	ʃəʊn		
show off		B	angeben, prahlen
show round		B	herumführen
show business	ˈbɪznɪs	C	Showgeschäft
shower	ˈʃaʊə	A	Dusche; Regenguß
have a shower		A	sich duschen
shriek	ʃriːk	C	Schrei; kreischen
shrimps	ʃrɪmps	B	Muscheln
shrink	ʃrɪŋk	B	schrumpfen
shrank, shrunk			
shrunk	ʃræŋk, ʃrʌŋk		
shrub	ʃrʌb	C	Strauch
shrug (one's shoulders)	ʃrʌg	B	(die Achseln) zucken
shut	ʃʌt	A	(ver)schließen, zumachen
shut			
shut			
shut down		C	stillegen
shut off		C	absperren (Licht, Wasser)
shut up	ʃʌtˈʌp	B	halt den Mund!
shutter	ˈʃʌtə	B	Fensterladen; (Foto:) Verschluß C
shutter speed	ˌspiːd	C	Belichtungszeit
shy	ʃaɪ	B	schüchtern
sick	sɪk	A	krank; unwohl
be sick of		B	etw. satt haben
sickness	ˈsɪknɪs	C	Krankheit; Übelkeit

To feel sick

side	saɪd	A	Seite
side by side	ˈsaɪd‿baɪ‿saɪd	A	nebeneinander
take sides		A	Partei ergreifen
side street	ˌ	B	Seitenstraße
sideboard	ˈsaɪdbɔːd	B	Kommode
sidewalk (US)	ˈsaɪdwɔːk	C	Gehsteig
sideways	ˈsaɪdweɪz	C	seitwärts, seitlich
sigh	saɪ	B	Seufzer; seufzen
sight	saɪt	A	Anblick; Sehenswürdigkeit
at first sight		A	auf den ersten Blick
catch sight of		B	erblicken
in/out of sight		A	in/außer Sicht
sightseeing	ˈsaɪtsiːɪŋ	A	Anschauen von Sehenswürdigkeiten
sightseeing tour	ˈ…‿ˌ	A	(Stadt-)Rundfahrt
sign	saɪn	A	Zeichen; Schild; unterzeichnen
signal	ˈsɪgnəl	A	Signal; signalisieren B
signature	ˈsɪgnɪtʃə	B	Unterschrift
significance	sɪgˈnɪfɪkəns	C	Bedeutung; Bedeutsamkeit
significant	sɪgˈnɪfɪkənt	B	bedeutsam, bezeichnend
signify	ˈsɪgnɪfaɪ		bedeuten
signpost	ˈsaɪnpəʊst	B	Wegweiser; beschildern
silence	ˈsaɪləns	A	Stille; Schweigen
silent	ˈsaɪlənt	A	still; schweigsam
silk	sɪlk	A	Seide
silly	ˈsɪlɪ	A	dumm, albern
silver	ˈsɪlvə	A	Silber; silbern
silvery	ˈsɪlvərɪ	C	silbrig glänzend
similar (to)	ˈsɪmɪlə	B	ähnlich (wie)
similarity	sɪmɪˈlærətɪ	B	Ähnlichkeit
similarly	ˈsɪmɪləlɪ	C	in ähnlicher Weise
simple	ˈsɪmpl	A	einfach
simply	ˈsɪmplɪ	A	einfach; bloß, nur

simplicity	sɪm'plɪsətɪ B	Einfachheit; Schlichtheit
simplify	'sɪmplɪfaɪ B	vereinfachen
simultaneous	C	gleichzeitig
	sɪməl'teɪnɪəs	
sin	sɪn C	Sünde; sündigen
since	sɪns A	seit, seitdem; da
ever since	A	seitdem
sincere	sɪn'sɪə B	aufrichtig
Yours sincerely	B	Mit freundlichen
	'jɔːz sɪn'sɪəlɪ	Grüßen
sincerity	sɪn'serətɪ C	Aufrichtigkeit
sing	sɪŋ A	singen
sang	sæŋ	
sung	sʌŋ	
singer	'sɪŋə A	Sänger(in)
single	'sɪŋgl A	einzeln; ledig; Single; einfache (Fahr-)Karte
single room	A	Einzelzimmer
singular	'sɪŋgjʊlə B	Einzahl
sink	sɪŋk B	sinken; Spülbecken
sank	sæŋk	
sunk	sʌŋk	
sip	sɪp B	nippen; kleiner Schluck
sir	sɜː A	mein Herr
Sir ...	sɜː B	Sir (Adelstitel)
sister	'sɪstə A	Schwester
sister-in-law	'...ˌlɔː B	Schwägerin
sit	sɪt A	sitzen
sat	sæt	
sat		
sit down	sɪt ˌdaʊn A	s. setzen

To sit down

site	saɪt C	Lage, Platz
sitting-room	'sɪtɪŋrʊm A	Wohnzimmer
situated	'sɪtjʊeɪtɪd A	gelegen, liegend
situation	sɪtjʊ'eɪʃn A	Lage, Situation
six	sɪks A	sechs
sixteen	sɪks'tiːn A	sechzehn
sixty	'sɪkstɪ A	sechzig
size	saɪz A	Größe, Format
what size is it?	A	wie groß ist es?
skate	skeɪt B	Schlittschuh; Schlittschuh laufen
skateboard	'skeɪtbɔːd B	Rollbrett; Rollbrettlaufen
skating rink	C	Eislaufstadion
	'skeɪtɪŋ ˌrɪŋk	
sketch	sketʃ B	Skizze; skizzieren
ski	skiː A	Ski; Skilaufen
go skiing	gəʊ ˌskiːɪŋ A	zum Skilaufen fahren, Skifahren
skid	skɪd C	ausrutschen, schliddern
skill	skɪl B	Geschick; Fertigkeit
skilled	skɪld B	geschickt; ausgebildet
skilled worker	ˌwɜːkə C	Facharbeiter
skilful	'skɪlfl B	geschickt, gewandt
skin	skɪn A	Haut, Fell; schälen C
skip	skɪp B	überspringen
skirt	skɜːt A	(Damen-)Rock
sky	skaɪ A	Himmel
skyline	'skaɪlaɪn B	Silhouette
skyscraper	'skaɪskreɪpə B	Wolkenkratzer
slalom	'slɑːləm C	Slalom
slacks	slæks B	(Damen-)Hosen
slam	slæm C	zuschlagen, zuknallen
slang	slæŋ B	lässige Umgangssprache
slapstick	'slæpstɪk C	Klamauk
slave	sleɪv C	Sklave, -in
slavery	'sleɪvərɪ C	Sklaverei
sledge	sledʒ C	Schlitten
sleep	sliːp A	schlafen; Schlaf
slept	slept	
slept		
sleeping bag	B	Schlafsack
	'sliːpɪŋ ˌbæg	
sleeping pill	'...ˌpɪl C	Schlaftablette
sleepy	'sliːpɪ A	schläfrig
sleeve	sliːv B	Ärmel
sleigh	sleɪ C	Schlitten
slender	'slendə B	schlank
slice	slaɪs A	Scheibe, Schnitte
slide	slaɪd B	gleiten, rutschen; Dia(positiv)
slid	slɪd	
slid		
slight	slaɪt B	leicht, schwach
slightly	'slaɪtlɪ B	etwas, ein bißchen
slim	slɪm A	schlank; abnehmen
slip	slɪp B	schlüpfen; Fehler; Zettel
I'll slip up (down)	C	ich geh mal nach oben (unten)

I'll slip up

slippery							
slippery	ˈslɪpərɪ	C	rutschig	snowflake	ˈsnəʊfleɪk	C	Schneeflocke
slippers	ˈslɪpəz	C	Pantoffeln	snowman	ˈsnəʊmæn	C	Schneemann
slit	slɪt	C	(auf-)schlitzen;	so	səʊ	A	so; also; daher
slit			Schlitz, Riß	so as to	ˈsəʊ ˌəz tə	B	um... zu
slit				so far	ˈsəʊ ˌfɑ:	B	bis jetzt, bisher
slogan	ˈsləʊgən	C	Slogan, Werbespruch	so long as	səʊ ˈlɒŋ ˌəz	B	solange wie
slope	sləʊp	B	Abhang	so that	ˈsəʊ ˌðt	B	damit
slot	slɒt	B	Schlitz	so am I/so do I		B	ich auch
slot machine	ˈˌməʃi:n	B	Automat	and so on	ənd ˈsəʊ ˌɒn	A	und so weiter
slow	sləʊ	A	langsam	even so	i:vn ˈsəʊ	B	dennoch
slow down	sləʊ ˈdaʊn	B	langsamer fahren	if so	ɪf ˈsəʊ	A	wenn ja
slum	slʌm	C	Slum, Elendsviertel	quite so	kwaɪt ˈsəʊ	B	ganz recht
small	smɔ:l	A	klein, gering	I hope so	aɪ ˈhəʊp ˌsəʊ	B	ich hoffe es
smallpox	ˈsmɔ:lpɒks	C	Pocken	soap	səʊp	A	Seife
smart	smɑ:t	A	forsch, schick	soap-box	ˈsəʊpbɒks	C	Seifenkiste
smash	smæʃ	B	zertrümmern	sob	sɒb	B	schluchzen
smashing	ˈsmæʃɪŋ	C	toll, dufte	sober	ˈsəʊbə	B	nüchtern
smell	smel	A	Geruch; riechen	so-called	ˈsəʊkɔ:ld	A	sogenannt
smile	smaɪl	A	lächeln; Lächeln	soccer	ˈsɒkə	B	Fußball
smog	smɒg	C	Smog, verschmutzte Luft	social	ˈsəʊʃl	A	sozial; gesellschaftlich
smoke	sməʊk	A	Rauch; rauchen	socialism	ˈsəʊʃlɪzm	C	Sozialismus
				socialist	ˈsəʊʃlɪst	A	Sozialist
				social studies	..ˈstʌdɪz	C	Sozialkunde
				social worker		A	Sozialarbeiter
				society	səˈsaɪətɪ	B	Gesellschaft; Verein
				sock(s)	sɒk(s)	A	Socke(n)
				socket	ˈsɒkɪt	C	Fassung; Steckdose
				soda	ˈsəʊdə	C	Sodawasser
				sofa	ˈsəʊfə	A	Sofa
				soft	sɒft	A	weich, sanft
				soft drink	ˌdrɪŋk	B	alkoholfreies Getränk
				software	ˈsɒftweə	C	Software (= Programme)
				soil	sɔɪl	C	(Erd-)Boden
				solar	ˈsəʊlə	B	Sonnen-
				solar system	..ˈsɪstəm	B	Sonnensystem
				solar energy	..ˈenədʒɪ	B	Sonnenenergie
				solarium	səʊˈleərɪəm	C	Solarium
				soldier	ˈsəʊldʒə	A	Soldat
				sole	səʊl	C	Sohle; Seezunge; einzig

No smoking

smoked	sməʊkt	C	geräuchert	sole agent	..ˈeɪdʒənt	W	Alleinvertreter
smooth	smu:ð	B	glatt; glätten	solemn	ˈsɒləm	C	feierlich, ernst
smuggle	ˈsmʌgl	C	schmuggeln	solicitor	səˈlɪsɪtə	C	Anwalt
smuggler	ˈsmʌglə	C	Schmuggler	solid	ˈsɒlɪd	C	fest, solid
snack	snæk	A	Imbiß	solution	səˈlu:ʃn	C	Lösung
snack bar	ˈsnækbɑ:	B	Imbißstube	solve	sɒlv	A	lösen
snail	sneɪl	C	Schnecke	some	sʌm, səm, sm	A	einige; irgendein, -etwas
snake	sneɪk	B	Schlange	some day		B	eines Tages
snap	snæp	B	schnappen	somebody	ˈsʌmbədɪ	A	jemand
snapshot	ˈsnæpʃɒt	B	Schnappschuß	somehow	ˈsʌmhaʊ	B	irgendwie
snatch	snætʃ	B	schnappen, packen	someone	ˈsʌmwʌn	A	(irgend-)jemand
sneeze	sni:z	C	niesen	something	ˈsʌmθɪŋ	A	(irgend-)etwas
snob	snɒb	C	Snob	sometime	ˈsʌmtaɪm	B	einmal
snobbery	ˈsnɒbərɪ	C	Snobismus	sometime or other		B	irgendwann
snobbish	ˈsnɒbɪʃ	C	snobistisch				
snore	snɔ:	C	schnarchen				
snow	snəʊ	A	Schnee; schneien				
snowball	ˈsnəʊbɔ:l	B	Schneeball				
snowdrop	ˈsnəʊdrɒp	C	Schneeglöckchen				

sometimes	ˈsʌmtaɪmz	A	manchmal
somewhat	ˈsʌmwɒt	B	etwas, ein wenig
somewhere	ˈsʌmweə	A	irgendwo
son	sʌn	A	Sohn
song	sɒŋ	A	Lied
soon	suːn	A	bald; früh
as soon as	əsˈsuːnˌəz	A	sobald (wie)
no sooner... than	nəuˈsuːnə ðən	B	kaum... als
sooner or later		B	früher oder später
soothe	suːð	B	besänftigen
sophomore (US)	ˈsɒfəmɔː	C	Schüler(in) oder Student(in) im 2. Studienjahr
sore	sɔː	B	weh, entzündet
sorrow	ˈsɒrəʊ	B	Sorge, Kummer
sorry	ˈsɒrɪ	A	betrübt; Verzeihung!
I'm sorry		A	es tut mir leid
I'm so sorry		A	es tut mir so leid
I'm very sorry indeed		B	es tut mir wirklich sehr leid
sort	sɔːt	A	Sorte, Art
sort out	sɔːtˈaʊt	C	aussortieren
soul	səʊl	B	Seele
sound	saʊnd	A	Ton, Klang; klingen; gesund
soup	suːp	A	Suppe
sour	ˈsaʊə	A	sauer
source	sɔːs	B	Quelle, Ursprung
south	saʊθ	A	süden; südlich
southern	ˈsʌðən	A	südlich
southward(s)	ˈsaʊθwəd(z)	B	nach Süden
souvenir	suːvəˈnɪə	A	Souvenir
sovereign	ˈsɒvrɪn	C	Souverän, Landesherr(in)
Soviet Union	ˈsəʊvɪət ˈsɒv-	B	Sowjetunion
sow	səʊ	C	säen
sowed	səʊd		
sown	səʊn		
space	speɪs	A	Raum; Platz
spacecraft	ˈspeɪskrɑːft	B	Raumschiff
spaceship	ˈspeɪsʃɪp	B	Raumschiff
space shuttle	ʃʌtl	C	Raumfähre
spade	speɪd	B	Spaten
Spain	speɪn	B	Spanien
Spaniard	ˈspænjəd	B	Spanier(in)
Spanish	ˈspænɪʃ	B	spanisch
spanner	ˈspænə	C	Schraubenschlüssel
spare	speə	B	übrighaben
spare part	ˌpɑːt	C	Ersatzteil
spare room	ˌrʊm	C	Gästezimmer
spare time	ˌtaɪm	A	Freizeit
spare wheel	ˌwiːl	C	Reserverad
spark	spɑːk	B	Funke
spark plug	ˌplʌg	C	Zündkerze
sparkle	ˈspɑːkl	B	funkeln
sparrow	ˈspærəʊ	C	Spatz, Sperling
speak	spiːk	A	sprechen
spoke	spəʊk		
spoken	ˈspəʊkən		
speak up		C	lauter sprechen
generally speaking		C	im großen und ganzen
strictly speaking		C	genaugenommen
speaker	ˈspiːkə	B	Sprecher(in)
special	speʃl	A	besondere(r,s); Sonder-
special delivery		W	Eilzustellung
specialist	ˈspeʃəlɪst	A	Fachmann
speciality	speʃɪˈælətɪ	C	Spezialität
specialise(-ize)	ˈspeʃəlaɪz	C	s. spezialisieren
specific	spəˈsɪfɪk	B	besondere(r,s), spezifisch
specify	ˈspesɪfaɪ	C	detaillieren
specimen	ˈspesɪmən	B	Muster
spectacle	ˈspektəkl	B	Schauspiel
spectacles	ˈspektəklz	B	Brille
spectacular	spekˈtækjʊlə	C	aufsehenerregend
spectator	spekˈteɪtə	A	Zuschauer
speech	spiːtʃ	B	Sprache; Rede
speechless	ˈspiːtʃləs	C	sprachlos

speaker Lautsprecher

speed	speed sped, speeded sped, speeded	spi:d	B	Geschwindigkeit; rasch fahren
	speed limit	ˈ‿lɪmɪt	B	Geschwindigkeits- begrenzung
	speed up	spi:d ‿ʌp	B	beschleunigen
	speedometer	spiˈ:dɒmɪtə	C	Tacho
	speedy	ˈspi:dɪ	C	rasch, geschwind
	spell spelt, spelled spelt, spelled	spel	A	buchstabieren; schreiben
	spelling	ˈspelɪŋ	A	Rechtschreibung
	spend spent spent	spend spent	A	ausgeben; verbringen
	spice	spaɪs	B	Gewürz
	spider	ˈspaɪdə	C	Spinne
	spill spilt, spilled spilt, spilled	spɪl	C	verschütten
	spin spun spun	spɪn spʌn	C	spinnen; s. drehen
	spiral	ˈspaɪərəl	C	Spirale
	spiral staircase	..‿ˈsteəkeɪs	C	Wendeltreppe
	spire	ˈspaɪə	C	(Turm-)Spitze
	spirit	ˈspɪrɪt	B	Geist; Gespenst
	spirits	ˈspɪrɪts	C	Spirituosen
	in high spirits		C	in gehobener Stimmung
	spiritual	ˈspɪrɪtjʊəl	B	geistlich; Spiritual
	spit spat spat	spɪt spæt	B	spucken
	in spite of	ɪn‿ˈspaɪt‿əv	A	trotz
	splendid	ˈsplendɪd	B	glänzend, prächtig
	splendour	ˈsplendə	C	Glanz, Pracht
	split split split	splɪt	B	spalten; aufteilen
	spoil spoilt, spoiled spoilt, spoiled	spɔɪl spɔɪlt	B	verwöhnen; verderben
	spokesman	ˈspəʊksmən	C	Sprecher
	sponge	spʌndʒ	B	Schwamm
	spoon	spu:n	A	Löffel
	spoonful	ˈspu:nfəl	C	ein Löffel voll
	sporran	ˈspɒrən	C	schottische Felltasche
	sport	spɔ:t	A	Sport, Sportart
	spot	spɒt	A	Fleck; Stelle; herausfinden B
	on the spot		C	auf der Stelle
	spotlight	ˈspɒtlaɪt	C	Rampenlicht
	spray	spreɪ	B	sprühen; spritzen; Sprühdose

The sports page

spread spread spread	spred	B	(s.) ausbreiten
spring sprang sprung	sprɪŋ spræŋ sprʌŋ	B	springen; Früh- ling A; Feder C
(brussels) sprouts	spraʊts	C	Rosenkohl
spy	spaɪ	B	Spion; spionieren
square	skweə	A	Quadrat; Platz
squash	skwɒʃ	C	(zer)quetschen; Squash; Fruchtsaft
squeeze	skwi:z	B	pressen, (aus-) quetschen
squirrel	ˈskwɪrəl	B	Eichhörnchen
St. (Paul's)	snt	B	Sankt...
stable	steɪbl	B	Stall; stabil
stability	stəˈbɪlɪtɪ	C	Stabilität
stadium	ˈsteɪdjəm	B	Stadion
staff	stɑ:f	B	Personal, Lehrkörper
staff room	ˈ‿rʊm	B	Lehrerzimmer
stage	steɪdʒ	A	Bühne; Stadium; inszenieren C
at this stage		C	in diesem Stadium
stain	steɪn	C	Fleck(en); beflecken
stainless steel	ˈsteɪnlɪs ˈsti:l	C	rostfreier Stahl
stair	steə	B	Stufe
stairs, staircase	steəz, ˈsteəkeɪs	A	Treppe
stale	steɪl	C	abgestanden, schal
stall	stɔ:l	B	Stand
stalls	stɔ:lz	B	Parkett (Theat.)
stammer	ˈstæmə	C	stammeln, stottern
stamp	stæmp	A	Stempel; Brief- marke; stem- peln C
stand stood stood	stænd stʊd	A	stehen; aushalten; Ständer

stand for		C	stehen für, kandidieren für (GB)
stand up	ˌʌp	A	stehen; aufstehen (v. Stuhl)
stand up for	ˌʌp fɔ:	C	s. einsetzen, eintreten für
standard	ˈstændəd	B	Standard; Maßstab
standard of living		B	Lebensstandard
	ˌəvˈlivɪŋ		
standard lamp	ˌlæmp	C	Stehlampe
standpoint	ˈstændpɔɪnt	B	Standpunkt
standstill	ˈstændstɪl	B	Stillstand
star	stɑ:	A	Stern; Star
starling	ˈstɑ:lɪŋ	C	Star (Vogel)
Stars and Stripes		C	Sternenbanner
ˈstɑ:zˌəndˈstraɪps			
stare	steə	B	(an)starren; Starren
start	stɑ:t	A	anfangen; Anfang
starter	ˈstɑ:tə	C	Vorspeise
start for		B	aufbrechen nach
starter motor		C	Anlasser
ˈstɑ:tə məʊtə			
starting point		C	Ausgangspunkt
ˈstɑ:tɪŋ pɔɪnt			
startle	ˈstɑ:tl	B	erschrecken
starve	stɑ:v	B	großen Hunger haben, hungern
starve to death		C	verhungern
state	steɪt	A	Zustand; Staat; feststellen; erklären C
state of affairs		C	Sachlage
statement	ˈsteɪtmənt	A	Darstellung, Erklärung
statesman	ˈsteɪtsmən	C	Staatsmann
station	ˈsteɪʃn	A	Bahnhof; Station; stationieren C
stationary	ˈsteɪʃnəri	B	fest(stehend)
stationer('s)	ˈsteɪʃnə(z)	B	Schreibwarenhändler
(=stationery shop)			
stationery	ˈsteɪʃnəri	B	Schreibwaren, -papier
stationmaster		C	Bahnhofsvorsteher
ˈsteɪʃnmɑ:stə			
statistics	stəˈtɪstɪks	C	Statistik
statue	ˈstætju:	B	Statue
status	ˈsteɪtəs	C	Status, Stand
status symbol		C	Statussymbol
ˈsteɪtəsˌsɪmbəl			
stay	steɪ	A	Aufenthalt; s. aufhalten, bleiben
steady	ˈstedɪ	B	fest; stetig
steak	steɪk	A	Steak
steal	sti:l	A	stehlen
stole	stəʊl		
stolen	ˈstəʊlən		
steam	sti:m	B	Dampf
steam engine	ˌendʒɪn	B	Dampfmaschine
steamer	ˈsti:mə	B	Dampfer
steel	sti:l	B	Stahl
steelworks	ˈsti:lwɜ:ks	C	Stahlwerk
steep	sti:p	B	steil
steer	stɪə	A	lenken
steering wheel		A	Lenkrad
stem (from)	stem	B	stammen; Stamm
step	step	A	Schritt; Stufe; treten
take steps		C	Maßnahmen ergreifen
stepmother	ˈstepmʌðə	C	Stiefmutter
stereo	ˈsterɪəʊ	B	Stereo
sterling	ˈstɜ:lɪŋ	C	engl. Währung
stew	stju:	C	schmoren
steward	ˈstju:əd	A	Steward
shop steward	ʃɒpˌ..	C	Vertrauensmann der Gewerkschaft
stewardess		A	Stewardeß
stju:əˈdes,ˈstju:ədɪs			
stewed fruit	ˈstju:dˈfru:t	C	Kompott
stick	stɪk	B	stecken, befestigen; Stock
stuck	stʌk		
stuck			
stick to		C	bei etw. bleiben
sticky	ˈstɪkɪ	C	klebrig
stiff	stɪf	B	steif
still	stɪl	A	(immer) noch; dennoch
sit still	sɪtˌ.	B	still sitzen
stimulating		C	anregend
ˈstɪmjʊleɪtɪŋ			
sting	stɪŋ	C	stechen; Stich
stung	stʌŋ		
stung			
stir	stɜ:	C	(s.) rühren
stock	stɒk	C	Vorrat; Aktien; lagern, führen
in stock	ɪnˌ.	W	auf Lager, vorrätig
out of stock	aʊtˌəvˌ.	W	vergriffen, nicht vorrätig
Stock Exchange		C	Börse
ˈstɒk ɪksˈtʃeɪndʒ			

sticker
Aufkleber

Stony

stockbroker		stockbroker	ˈstɒkbrəʊkə	W	Börsenmakler	stretch	stretʃ	B	(aus)strecken; s. erstrecken
		stocking	ˈstɒkɪŋ	A	Strumpf	strict	strɪkt	B	streng, genau
		stomach	ˈstʌmək	A	Magen, Bauch	strictly speaking	ˈ..ˌ..	C	genaugenommen
		stone	stəʊn	A	Stein; (Obst-)Kern	strike	straɪk	A	schlagen; auffallen; Streik, streiken
		stony	ˈstəʊnɪ	B	steinig	struck	strʌk		
		stop	stɒp	A	anhalten; aufhören	struck			
		bus stop	ˈbʌsˌ.	A	Bushaltestelle	go on strike	ˈgəʊˌɒnˌ.	A	in Streik treten
		full stop	fʊlˌ.	A	Punkt	striking	ˈstraɪkɪŋ	C	auffallend
		store	stɔː	B	Lager; Geschäft; aufbewahren	string	strɪŋ	B	Schnur, Bindfaden
						string instrument		C	Streichinstrument
		in store	ɪnˌ.	W	vorrätig	strip	strɪp	B	Streifen
		storeroom	ˈstɔːrʊm	C	Lagerraum	stripe	straɪp	A	Streifen
		stor(e)y	ˈstɔːrɪ	B	Stockwerk	striped	straɪpt	A	gestreift
		storm	stɔːm	A	Sturm; stürmen	stroke	strəʊk	B	Schlag; Strich; streicheln
		story	ˈstɔːrɪ	A	Geschichte				
		stove	stəʊv	B	Ofen	a stroke of luck		C	ein Glücksfall
		straight	streɪt	A	gerade, unmittelbar; (US) pur	stroll	strəʊl	B	schlendern; Bummel
		straight ahead	ˌəˈhed	A	geradeaus	strong	strɒŋ	A	stark, kräftig
		straight away	ˌəˈweɪ	A	sofort	structure	ˈstrʌktʃə	B	Struktur, Aufbau
		straightforward		C	offen, ehrlich	struggle	strʌgl	B	Kampf; Anstrengung; kämpfen
			streɪtˈfɔːwəd						
		straight on	ˌɒn	A	geradeaus	stubborn	ˈstʌbən	B	stur, hartnäckig
		strain	streɪn	C	Belastung, Streß	student	ˈstjuːdnt	A	Student(in)
		strange	streɪndʒ	A	fremd; sonderbar	student card	ˈ..ˌkɑːd	C	Studenten-, Schülerausweis
		strangely enough		C	eigenartigerweise				
		stranger	ˈstreɪndʒə	A	Fremde(r)	studio	ˈstjuːdɪəʊ	C	Studio; Atelier
						study	ˈstʌdɪ	A	studieren; Arbeitszimmer
						studies		B	Studium
						stuff	stʌf	B	Zeug; (voll)stopfen
						stuffy	ˈstʌfɪ	C	muffig, stickig
						stumble	stʌmbl	B	stolpern
						stupid	ˈstjuːpɪd	A	dumm
						style	staɪl	B	Stil
						subcontinent		C	Subkontinent
							sʌbˈkɒntɪnənt		
						subject	ˈsʌbdʒekt	B	Gegenstand; Fach; Subjekt; Untertan
						subject to		C	vorbehaltlich
						submarine	sʌbməˈriːn	B	U-Boot
						submit	səbˈmɪt	C	vorlegen, unterbreiten
						subordinate clause		C	Nebensatz
							səbˈɔːdɪnət ˈklɔːz		
		straw	strɔː	B	Stroh	subscribe (to)		C	abonnieren
		strawberry	ˈstrɔːbərɪ	B	Erdbeere		səbˈskraɪb		
		stream	striːm	B	Bach				
		streamlined		C	stromlinienförmig	subscription		C	Abonnement
			ˈstriːmlaɪnd				səbˈskrɪpʃn		
		street	striːt	A	Straße	subsequent	ˈsʌbsɪkwənt	C	folgend
		streetcar (US)	ˈstriːtkɑː	C	Tram	subsequently		C	nachher
		strength	streŋθ	B	Stärke, Kraft	subsidiary	sʌbˈsɪdjərɪ	C	Filiale; Tochtergesellschaft W
		on the strength of		C	auf Grund				
			ɒnˌðəˌ.ˌəv			subsidy	ˈsʌbsɪdɪ	W	Zuschuß
		strengthen	ˈstreŋθən	B	(be)stärken; erstarken	subsidise(-ize)		W	subventionieren
							ˈsʌbsɪdaɪz		
		strenuous	ˈstrenjʊəs	C	anstrengend				
		stress	stres	B	Druck; Betonung	substance	ˈsʌbstəns	C	Stoff, Substanz

Stuart Age
Stuartzeit
(alter)
1603-1714

A stranger in London

substantial	səb'stænʃl	C	wesentlich, ausgiebig
substitute	'sʌbstɪtjuːt	C	einsetzen für; Ersatz
subtle	sʌtl	B	fein, delikat
subtract	səb'trækt	C	abziehen
subtraction	səb'trækʃn	C	Subtraktion
suburb	'sʌbɜːb	A	Vorstadt
suburban	sə'bɜːbən	C	vorstädtisch
subway	'sʌbweɪ	C	Unterführung; (US)U-Bahn
succeed (in)	sək'siːd	A	Erfolg haben
success	sək'ses	A	Erfolg
successful	sək'sesfəl	A	erfolgreich
successor	sək'sesə	B	Nachfolger
such	sʌtʃ,sətʃ	A	solch(e,-er,-es)
such a	'‿ə	A	so ein(e,r)
such as	'‿əz	A	wie z.B.
suck	sʌk	C	saugen
sudden(ly)	'sʌdn(li)	A	plötzlich
all of a sudden		C	ganz plötzlich
suffer (from)	'sʌfə	A	leiden (unter)
sufficient	sə'fɪʃnt	A	genügend, ausreichend
suffix	'sʌfɪks	C	Suffix, Nachsilbe
sugar	'ʃʊgə	A	Zucker
suggest	sə'dʒest	A	vorschlagen; andeuten
suggestion	sə'dʒestʃn	A	Vorschlag; Andeutung
suicide	'suːɪsaɪd	B	Selbstmord
suit	suːt	A	Anzug; passen
suited	'suːtɪd	C	geeignet
suitable	'suːtəbl	B	geeignet, passend
suitcase	'suːtkeɪs	A	Koffer
sum	sʌm	A	Summe; Betrag
sum up	‿ʌp	B	zusammenzählen; zusammenfassen
summarise(-ize)	'sʌməraɪz	C	zusammenfassen
summary	'sʌməri	C	Zusammenfassung
summer	'sʌmə	A	Sommer
summit	'sʌmɪt	C	Gipfel

The summit

sun	sʌn	A	Sonne
sunbathe	'sʌnbeɪð	B	sonnenbaden
sunburn	'sʌnbɜːn	C	Sonnenbrand
Sunday	'sʌndɪ,eɪ	A	Sonntag
sunny	'sʌnɪ	A	sonnig
sunrise	'sʌnraɪz	B	Sonnenaufgang
sunset	'sʌnset	B	Sonnenuntergang
sunshine	'sʌnʃaɪn	A	Sonnenschein
super	'suːpə	A	toll, herrlich
superficial	suːpə'fɪʃl	C	oberflächlich
superfluous	suː'pɜːfluəs	C	überflüssig
superior	suː'pɪərɪə	C	Vorgesetzte(r); überlegen
superlative	suː'pɜːlətɪv	C	Superlativ
supermarket	'suːpəmɑːkɪt	A	Supermarkt
supersonic	suːpə'sɒnɪk	B	Überschall-
superstition	suːpə'stɪʃn	C	Aberglaube(n)
superstitious	suːpə'stɪʃəs	C	abergläubisch
supervise	'suːpəvaɪz	C	beaufsichtigen
supervision	suːpə'vɪʒn	C	Aufsicht, Überwachung
supervisor	'suːpəvaɪzə	B	Aufseher(in)
supper	'sʌpə	A	Abendessen
supplement	'sʌplɪmənt	C	Ergänzung; ergänzen
supplementary	sʌplɪ'mentərɪ	C	ergänzend
supplier	sə'plaɪə	C	Lieferant
supply	sə'plaɪ	B	Versorgung; Vorrat; versorgen; liefern
support	sə'pɔːt	A	unterstützen; Unterstützung
supporter	sə'pɔːtə	B	Anhänger, Fan
suppose	sə'pəʊz	A	vermuten, annehmen
be supposed to		A	sollen
supreme	suː'priːm	C	höchste(r,s)
Supreme Court		C	(US) Bundesgericht
sure	ʃʊə,ʃɔː	A	sicher, gewiß
make sure	meɪk ‿	B	s. vergewissern, dafür sorgen
surely	'ʃʊəlɪ,'ʃɔːlɪ	B	sicherlich, bestimmt
surface	'sɜːfɪs	B	Oberfläche
surfing	'sɜːfɪŋ	C	Wellenreiten
surgeon	'sɜːdʒən	C	Chirurg
surgery	'sɜːdʒərɪ	C	Chirurgie; Praxis
surname	'sɜːneɪm	A	Familien-, Nachname
surpass	sə'pɑːs	C	übertreffen
surplus	'sɜːpləs	C	Überfluß
surprise	sə'praɪz	A	überraschen; Überraschung
surrender	sə'rendə	B	s. ergeben; übergeben
surround	sə'raʊnd	B	umgeben

surroundings	səˈraʊndɪŋz	B	Umgebung
survey	ˈsɜːveɪ	B	Umfrage
survive	səˈvaɪv	B	überleben
survival	səˈvaɪvəl	B	Überleben
survivor	səˈvaɪvə	C	Überlebende(r)
suspect	səˈspekt	C	verdächtigen
suspense	səˈspens	C	Spannung
suspension bridge	səˈspenʃn	C	Hängebrücke
suspicion	səˈspɪʃn	B	Verdacht
suspicious	səˈspɪʃəs	C	verdächtig
swallow	ˈswɒləʊ	B	schlucken; Schwalbe
swan	swɒn	C	Schwan
swear	sweə	B	schwören; fluchen
swore	swɔː		
sworn	swɔːn		
sweat	swet	C	Schweiß; schwitzen
sweater	ˈswetə	A	Pullover
Swede	swiːd	B	Schwede, -in
Sweden	ˈswiːdn	B	Schweden
Swedish	ˈswiːdɪʃ	B	schwedisch
sweep	swiːp	B	kehren
swept	swept		
swept			
sweepstakes	ˈswiːpsteɪks	C	Pferdetoto
chimneysweep	ˈtʃɪmnɪswiːp	B	Kaminkehrer
sweet	swiːt	A	süß; Süßigkeit
sweetheart	ˈswiːthɑːt	B	Liebling, Schatz
swift	swɪft	B	schnell, flink
swim	swɪm	A	schwimmen
swam	swæm		
swum	swʌm		
go for a swim		B	schwimmen gehen
swimmer	ˈswɪmə	B	Schwimmer(in)
swimming pool	ˈswɪmɪŋˌpuːl	A	Schwimmbecken
swimsuit	ˈswɪmsuːt	B	Badeanzug
swing	swɪŋ	B	schwingen, schaukeln
swung	swʌŋ		
swung			
in full swing	ɪnˌfʊlˈ.	C	in vollem Gange
Swiss	swɪs	A	schweizerisch; Schweizer(in)
switch	swɪtʃ	B	Schalter
switch on/off		A	ein-/ausschalten
switchboard	ˈswɪtʃbɔːd	C	Schalttafel; Vermittlung
Switzerland	ˈswɪtsələnd	A	Schweiz
swollen	ˈswəʊlen	C	(an)geschwollen
swop	swɒp	B	(aus)tauschen
sword	sɔːd	C	Schwert; Säbel
syllable	ˈsɪləbl	B	Silbe
syllabus	ˈsɪləbəs	C	Stoff-, Lehrplan
symbol	ˈsɪmbl	B	Symbol
symbolic	sɪmˈbɒlɪk	B	symbolisch
symbolise(-ize)	ˈsɪmbəlaɪz	C	symbolisieren, darstellen
sympathy	ˈsɪmpəθɪ	B	Mitgefühl
symphony	ˈsɪmfənɪ	C	Symphonie
synonym	ˈsɪnənɪm	B	Synonym, Wort mit ähnlicher Bedeutung
system	ˈsɪstəm	B	System
systematic	sɪstɪˈmætɪk	B	systematisch

To swop

T

t	tiː	A	t
table	teɪbl	A	Tisch; Tabelle
table of contents	ˌ..əvˈkɒntənts	C	Inhaltsverzeichnis
table tennis	ˈ..tenɪs	B	Tischtennis
tablecloth	ˈ..klɒθ	B	Tischdecke
tablet	ˈtæblət	A	Tablette
tackle	tækl	B	anpacken
tact	tækt	B	Takt(gefühl)
tactful	ˈtæktfʊl	B	taktvoll
tactless	ˈtæktlɪs	B	taktlos
tag	tæg	C	Anhänger; Anhängsel
question tag	ˈkwestʃənˌ.	C	Frageanhängsel
tail	teɪl	B	Schwanz
tailor	ˈteɪlə	A	Schneider; schneidern C
take	teɪk	A	nehmen; (Zeit) brauchen; (hin)bringen
took	tʊk		
taken	ˈteɪkən		
take after		C	geraten nach
take away		A	wegnehmen
take back		A	zurückbringen, -nehmen
take care		A	Obacht geben
take for		B	halten für

take off		A	starten; ausziehen
take-off	ˈteɪk ˌɒf	A	Start
take on		B	übernehmen
take one's time		C	s. Zeit lassen
take part	teɪkˈpɑːt	A	teilnehmen
take place	teɪkˈpleɪs	A	stattfinden
take to		C	die Gewohnheit annehmen
take up		A	s. befassen mit
I take it (that)		C	ich gehe davon aus, daß
tale	teɪl	B	Erzählung
talent	ˈtælənt	B	Begabung
talented	ˈtæləntɪd	B	begabt
talk	tɔːk	A	reden; Gespräch
have a talk		A	s. unterhalten
talk sth over		B	etw. besprechen
talkative	ˈtɔːkətɪv	C	schwatzhaft
tall	tɔːl	A	groß, hoch
tame	teɪm	C	zahm; zähmen
tangerine	tændʒəˈriːn	C	Mandarine
tank	tæŋk	B	Tank; Panzer
tanker	ˈtæŋkə	C	Tanker
tap	tæp	C	Klopfen; klopfen; (Wasser-)Hahn
tape	teɪp	A	(Ton-; Klebe-)Band; aufnehmen
tape recorder	ˈ...rɪkɔːdə	A	Tonbandgerät
tapestry	ˈtæpɪstrɪ	B	Wandteppich
target	ˈtɑːgɪt	C	Ziel
tariff	ˈtærɪf	W	Tarif
tart	tɑːt	B	(Obst-)Torte
tartan	ˈtɑːtən	B	Schottenmuster; -stoff
task	tɑːsk	B	Aufgabe
taste	teɪst	A	Geschmack; kosten; schmecken
tasteful	ˈteɪstfʊl	B	geschmackvoll
tasteless	ˈteɪstlɪs	B	geschmacklos
tasty	ˈteɪstɪ	C	gut schmeckend
tax	tæks	A	Steuer; besteuern C
taxi	ˈtæksɪ	A	Taxi
tea	tiː	A	Tee
teapot	ˈtiːpɒt	A	Teekanne
teach	tiːtʃ	A	lehren, unterrichten
taught	tɔːt		
taught			
teacher	ˈtiːtʃə	A	Lehrer(in)
tea-time	ˈtiːˌtaɪm	B	Teezeit, -stunde
team	tiːm	A	Team, Mannschaft
tear	teə	A	(zer)reißen
tore	tɔː		
torn	tɔːn		
tear	tɪə	B	Träne
tease	tiːz	B	ärgern, hänseln
technical	ˈteknɪkl	B	technisch; fachlich
technician	tekˈnɪʃn	C	Techniker

Tea-time

technique	tekˈniːk	C	Methode, Verfahren
technology	tekˈnɒlədʒɪ	C	Technik, Technologie
teenage ...	ˈtiːneɪdʒ	A	Teenager-
teenager	ˈtiːneɪdʒə	A	Teenager
telegram	ˈtelɪgræm	B	Telegramm
telegraph	ˈtelɪgrɑːf	C	Telegraph; telegraphieren
telephone	ˈtelɪfəʊn	A	Telefon; telefonieren
telephone box	ˈ...ˌbɒks	A	Telefonzelle
telephone booth	ˌbuːð		
(telephone) call	ˈ...ˌkɔːl	A	Anruf
telephone number		A	Telefonnummer
televise	ˈtelɪvaɪz	C	im Fernsehen übertragen
television	ˈtelɪvɪʒn,...	A	Fernsehen, -seher
television set	ˈ.....ˌset	A	Fernseher
tele, telly	ˈtelɪ	A	Fernseher
telex	ˈteleks	W	Fernschreiben
tell	tel	A	erzählen, sagen
told	təʊld		
told			
tell off	telˈɒf	C	tadeln, schimpfen
temper	ˈtempə	B	Stimmung, Laune
lose one's temper		B	wütend werden
good-tempered	ˌgʊdˈtempəd	B	gutgelaunt
bad-tempered	ˌbædˈtempəd	B	schlechtgelaunt
temperature	ˈtemprətʃə	A	Temperatur
have a temperature		B	Fieber haben
temple	templ	C	Tempel
temporary	ˈtemprərɪ	C	vorübergehend, zeitweilig
tempt	tem(p)t	C	versuchen, verlocken
temptation	tem(p)ˈteɪʃn	C	Versuchung
ten	ten	A	zehn
tend (to)	tend	B	neigen (zu)
tendency	ˈtendənsɪ	B	Tendenz
tender	ˈtendə	C	zärtlich; zart

tee-shirt
(= T-shirt)
T-shirt

tenderness				

tenderness	ˈtendənɪs C	Zärtlichkeit	
tennis	ˈtenɪs A	Tennis	
tennis court	ˌ…ˈkɔːt C	Tennisplatz	
tense	tens B	Zeitform; (an)gespannt C	
tension	ˈtenʃn B	Spannung, Streß	
tent	tent A	Zelt	
term	tɜːm C	Trimester; Ausdruck	
terminal	ˈtɜːmɪnəl B	Anschluß, Pol	
terms	tɜːmz W	Bedingungen	
come to terms	C	s. einigen	
in terms of	ɪnˈtɜːmzˌəv C	von... her betrachtet	
terrace	ˈterəs B	Terrasse	
terraced house	terəstˌhaʊs B	Reihenhaus	
terrible	ˈterəbl A	schrecklich	
terrific	təˈrɪfɪk B	toll, herrlich	
terrify	ˈterɪfaɪ C	erschrecken	
territory	ˈterɪtrɪ B	Gebiet	
terror	ˈterə C	Schrecken; Terror	
terrorism	ˈterərɪzm B	Terrorismus	
terrorist	ˈterərɪst B	Terrorist	
test	test A	Test, Probe; prüfen, testen	
test paper	ˌ…ˈpeɪpə B	Schulaufgabe	
text	tekst A	Text	
textbook	ˈtekstbʊk A	Lehrbuch	
textiles	ˈtekstaɪlz A	Textilien	
Thames	temz A	Themse	
than	ðæn, ðən, ðn A	als (bei Steigerung)	
thank	θæŋk A	danken	
thank goodness (=thank God)	ˌˈɡʊdnəs C	Gott sei Dank	
thank you	ˈθæŋkjʊ A	danke	

Thank you

thank you very/so much	A	vielen Dank
thank you very much indeed	A	vielen herzlichen Dank
thank you all the same	B	trotzdem vielen Dank
thankful	ˈθæŋkfəl B	dankbar

thanks	θæŋks A	Dank; danke
thanks very much	A	vielen Dank
thanks a lot	ˌəˈlɒt A	vielen Dank
that	ðæt, ðət A	jener,e,es; daß; der, die, das
(not) that much	C	(nicht) so viel/sehr
so (...) that	ˈsəʊˌ B	so (...), daß
in order that	ɪnˈɔːdəˌ C	so daß, damit
thatched	ˈθætʃt B	strohgedeckt
thaw	θɔː C	Tauwetter; tauen
the	ðə, ðɪ A	der, die, das
the... the...	B	je... desto...
theatre	ˈθɪətə A	Theater
thee	ðiː C	dich (dir, deiner) (archaisch)
theft	θeft C	Diebstahl
then	ðen A	dann, damals; damalig
by then	baɪˈðen A	bis dann, bis damals
(every) now and then	A	hin und wieder
theory	ˈθɪərɪ C	Theorie
theoretical	θɪəˈretɪkl C	theoretisch
there	ðeə A	da, dort; dorthin
there is/are	A	es gibt; es sind
thereby	ˈðeəbaɪ C	dadurch, damit
therefore	ˈðeəfɔː A	daher, deshalb
these	ðiːz A	diese
these days	A	heutzutage
they; their(s)	ðeɪ, ðeə(z) A	sie; ihr(e)
thick	θɪk A	dick; dicht; dumm
thickness	ˈθɪknəs C	Dicke; Dichte
thief,ves	θiːf,vz A	Dieb(in)
thigh	θaɪ C	Oberschenkel
thin	θɪn A	dünn
thing	θɪŋ A	Ding, Sache
the thing is...	C	die Sache ist die...
think thought thought	θɪŋk A θɔːt	denken; meinen; glauben
think sth over	B	etw. überlegen
third	θɜːd A	dritte(r,s); Drittel
thirst	θɜːst A	Durst
thirsty	ˈθɜːstɪ A	durstig
be thirsty	A	Durst haben
thirteen	θɜːˈtiːn A	dreizehn
thirty	ˈθɜːtɪ A	dreißig
this	ðɪs A	diese(r,s)
this time	A	diesmal
thistle	θɪsl C	Distel
thorn	θɔːn C	Dorn, Stachel
thorough	ˈθʌrə B	gründlich
thoroughness	ˈθʌrənɪs C	Gründlichkeit
those	ðəʊz A	jene
though	ðəʊ A	obgleich; zwar
as though	əzˈðəʊ B	als ob
even though	ˈiːvnˌðəʊ B	obwohl

thought	θɔ:t	B	Gedanke
on second thoughts		C	bei nochmaligem Nachdenken
thoughtful	'θɔ:tfʊl	C	nachdenklich; rücksichtsvoll
thousand	'θaʊzənd	A	tausend
thread	θred	C	Faden, Zwirn
threat	θret	C	Drohung
threaten	'θretən	C	(be-, an)drohen
three	θri:	A	drei
threshold	'θreʃ(h)əʊld	C	Schwelle
thrifty	'θrɪftɪ	C	sparsam
thrill	θrɪl	C	begeistern; Spannung
thriller	'θrɪlə	B	spannender Roman oder Film
thrilling	'θrɪlɪŋ	B	spannend
throat	θrəʊt	B	Hals, Kehle
throne	θrəʊn	B	Thron
through	θru:	A	durch
throughout	θru:'aʊt	B	während, hindurch; in ganz...
throw	θrəʊ	A	werfen; Wurf
threw	θru:		
thrown	θrəʊn		
thrush	θrʌʃ	C	Drossel
thrust	θrʌst	C	stoßen, stechen;
thrust			Stoß, Stich
thrust			
thumb	θʌm	B	Daumen
thunder	'θʌndə	B	Donner; donnern
thunderstorm	'θʌndəstɔ:m	A	Gewitter
Thursday	'θɜ:zdɪ, eɪ	A	Donnerstag
thus	ðʌs	B	so, auf diese Weise
tick off	tɪk 'ɒf	C	abhaken
ticket	'tɪkɪt	A	Fahr-, Eintrittskarte
ticket office	'...'ɒfɪs	B	Kartenschalter
single ticket	'sɪŋgl ...	A	einfache Karte
one-way ticket (US)	'wɒnweɪ ...		
return ticket	rɪ'tɜ:n ...	A	Rückfahrkarte
round-trip ticket (US)	'raʊnd ˌtrɪp ...		
tide(s)	taɪd	B	Gezeit(en)
high tide	haɪ 'taɪd	B	Flut
low tide	ləʊ 'taɪd	B	Ebbe
tidy	'taɪdɪ	A	sauber; aufräumen
tie	taɪ	A	Krawatte; binden; Bindung B; Unentschieden C
tiger	'taɪgə	B	Tiger
tight	taɪt	B	dicht; fest; knapp
hold tight	həʊld 'taɪt	C	festhalten
tights	taɪts	B	Strumpfhose
tile	taɪl	C	Dachziegel, Fliese
till	tɪl	A	bis
not till	'nɒt ˌtɪl	A	nicht vor, erst

To hold tight

timber	'tɪmbə	C	Bauholz
time	taɪm	A	Zeit; Mal
all the time	ɔ:l ðə 'taɪm	A	die ganze Zeit
by the time	baɪ ðə 'taɪm	B	bis, sobald
for the time being		C	vorläufig, einstweilen
from time to time		B	von Zeit zu Zeit
in (good) time		B	beizeiten
in no time		C	im Nu
in time for		B	rechtzeitig für
on time		B	pünktlich

On time

have a good time		A	s. gut unterhalten
3 times 4		B	3 mal 4
at times	ət 'taɪmz	B	manchmal, zeitweise
timetable	'taɪmteɪbl	A	Stundenplan
timid	'tɪmɪd	C	ängstlich, schüchtern
tin	tɪn	C	Zinn; Konservendose
tin-opener	'tɪnəʊpnə	C	Dosenöffner
tiny	'taɪnɪ	B	winzig
tip	tɪp	A	Spitze; Trinkgeld; Tip; Tip geben; Trinkgeld geben

tire			
tire (US)	ˈtaɪə	C	(Rad-)Reifen
tired	ˈtaɪəd	A	müde
be tired of		B	überdrüssig sein
tiring	ˈtaɪrɪŋ	C	ermüdend, anstrengend
tissue	ˈtɪʃuː	B	Gewebe; Papiertaschentuch
tit for tat	ˈtɪt fə ˈtæt	C	wie du mir, so ich dir
title	taɪtl	B	Titel
to	tuː, tʊ, tə	A	zu, an, auf
to and fro	tuː ənd ˈfrəʊ	C	hin und her
toast	təʊst	A	Toast; toasten
toaster	ˈtəʊstə	C	Toaströster
tobacco	təˈbækəʊ	A	Tabak
tobacconist	təˈbækənɪst	C	Tabakwarenhändler
toboggan	təˈbɒgən	C	Rodelschlitten
today	təˈdeɪ	A	heute
today week (= a week today)	...wiːk	C	(heute) in einer Woche
toe	təʊ	B	Zehe
toffee	ˈtɒfɪ	C	Sahnebonbon
together	təˈgeðə	A	zusammen, zugleich
toilet	ˈtɔɪlət	B	Toilette
tolerant	ˈtɒlərənt	B	tolerant
tolerance	ˈtɒlərəns	B	Toleranz
tolerate	ˈtɒləreɪt	C	tolerieren
toll	təʊl	C	Maut
tomato, es (US)	təˈmɑːtəʊ,z təˈmeɪtəʊ,z	A	Tomate
tomb	tuːm	C	Grab(mal)
tomorrow	təˈmɒrəʊ	A	morgen
ton	tʌn	B	Tonne (Gewicht)
tone	təʊn	C	Ton, Klang
tongue	tʌŋ	A	Zunge
mother tongue	ˈmʌðə..	A	Muttersprache
tongue in cheek	ɪn ˈtʃiːk	C	nicht ganz ernst (gemeint)
tonight	təˈnaɪt	A	heute abend
tonsillitis	tɒnsɪˈlaɪtɪs	B	Mandelentzündung
too	tuː	A	auch; allzu
tool	tuːl	A	Werkzeug
toolbag	ˈtuːlbæg	C	Werkzeugtasche
tooth, teeth	tuːθ, tiːθ	A	Zahn
toothache	ˈtuːθeɪk	A	Zahnweh
toothbrush	ˈtuːθbrʌʃ	A	Zahnbürste
toothpaste	ˈtuːθpeɪst	A	Zahnpasta
top	tɒp	A	Gipfel, Spitze
on top (of)	ɒn ˈtɒp	A	obenauf
on top of that		C	außerdem
topic	ˈtɒpɪk	C	Thema
topical	ˈtɒpɪkl	C	aktuell
torch	tɔːtʃ	C	Taschenlampe; Fackel
tornado	tɔːˈneɪdəʊ	C	Wirbelsturm
tortoise	ˈtɔːtəs	C	(Land-)Schildkröte
torture	ˈtɔːtʃə	C	Folter; foltern

Tory	ˈtɔːrɪ	C	(GB) Konservative(r)
toss	tɒs	C	werfen, schleudern
total	ˈtəʊtl	A	ganz; Gesamtbetrag
touch	tʌtʃ	A	berühren; Berührung
get in touch with		A	s. in Verbindung setzen mit
keep in touch with		A	in Verbindung bleiben mit
be out of touch		C	keine Verbindung haben
touch wood!	tʌtʃ ˈwʊd	B	unberufen!
tough	tʌf	B	zäh; hartnäckig
tour	tʊə	A	Tour, Reise; reisen
tourism	ˈtʊərɪzm	B	Fremdenverkehr
tourist	ˈtʊərɪst	A	Tourist
tourist board	...	C	Fremdenverkehrsamt
tow (off)	təʊ	C	(ab)schleppen
towards	təˈwɔːdz	A	auf... zu; gegen
towel	ˈtaʊəl	A	Handtuch
towel rack	..ræk	C	Handtuchhalter
tower	ˈtaʊə	A	Turm, Wolkenkratzer
town	taʊn	A	Stadt
in town	ɪn ˈtaʊn	A	in der Stadt
town council	..ˈkaʊnsɪl	C	Stadtrat
town hall	..ˈhɔːl	C	Rathaus
toy	tɔɪ	A	Spielzeug
trace	treɪs	C	Spur; nachspüren
track	træk	C	Spur(en); Geleise
tractor	ˈtræktə	B	Traktor
trade	treɪd	B	Handel
trade in		C	in Zahlung geben
trade union US: labour union	..ˈjuːnjən	B	Gewerkschaft
tradition	trəˈdɪʃn	A	Tradition, Überlieferung
traditional	trəˈdɪʃnəl	A	traditionell, herkömmlich
traffic	ˈtræfɪk	A	Verkehr
traffic jam	..dʒæm	B	Verkehrsstau
traffic lights	..laɪts	A	Ampel
traffic sign	..saɪn	A	Verkehrsschild
tragedy	ˈtrædʒədɪ	C	Tragödie
tragic	ˈtrædʒɪk	C	tragisch
trailer	ˈtreɪlə	C	Anhänger; (US) Campingbus
train	treɪn	A	Zug; trainieren; ausbilden
train station (US)	..ˈsteɪʃn	C	Bahnhof
trainee	treɪˈniː	C	Praktikant(in)
training	ˈtreɪnɪŋ	A	Training; Ausbildung
traitor	ˈtreɪtə	C	Verräter

tram	træm	A	Straßenbahn
transfer		C	übertragen;
	tra:ns'fɜ:, træns-		Übertragung,
	'tra:nsfɜ:, træns-		Transfer
transform	tra:ns'fɔ:m	C	umformen
transistor	tra:n'zɪstə	C	Transistorradio
translate	tra:ns'leɪt	A	übersetzen
translation	tra:ns'leɪʃn	A	Übersetzung
translator	tra:ns'leɪtə	B	Übersetzer(in)
transparency		C	Folie; Dia
	tra:n'spærənsɪ		
transplant	tra:ns'pla:nt	C	verpflanzen
transport	tra:n'spɔ:t	A	befördern, transportieren
transport	'tra:nspɔ:t	A	Beförderung, Transport
public transport		B	öffentliche Verkehrsmittel
trap	træp	C	Falle; fangen

The trap

trashcan (US)	'træʃkæn	C	Mülleimer
travel	trævl	A	Reise; reisen
travel agency		B	Reisebüro
	..'eɪdʒənsɪ		
traveller	'trævələ	B	Reisende(r)
traveller's cheque		C	Reisescheck
	...tʃek		
trawler	'trɔ:lə	C	Fischfangboot
tray	treɪ	B	Tablett
treacherous	'tretʃərəs	C	verräterisch, trügerisch
tread	tred	C	treten, schreiten
trod	trɒd		
trodden	trɒdn		
treason	tri:zn	C	Verrat
treasure	'treʒə	B	Schatz
treat	tri:t	A	behandeln; bewirten C
treatment	'tri:tmənt	B	Behandlung
under treatment		C	in Behandlung
treaty	'tri:tɪ	C	Vertrag
tree	tri:	A	Baum
tremble	trembl	C	zittern

tremendous	trɪ'mendəs	C	ungeheuer, riesig
trend	trend	C	Trend, Tendenz
trespass	'trespəs	C	Übertretung; übertreten
no trespassing		C	(Unbefugten) Betreten verboten!
trial	'traɪəl	B	Versuch; Prozeß
on trial		B	auf Probe; angeklagt
triangle	'traɪæŋgl	C	Dreieck
tribe	traɪb	B	Stamm, Sippe
tributary	'trɪbjʊtərɪ	C	Nebenfluß
trick	trɪk	B	Trick; Streich
tricky	'trɪkɪ	C	verzwickt, tückisch
trifle	traɪfl	C	Biskuitdessert
a trifle	traɪfl	C	ein wenig
trim	trɪm	C	(zurecht-)schneiden, stutzen
trip	trɪp	A	Reise; Ausflug; stolpern C
triumph	'traɪəmf	C	Triumph; triumphieren
trolley	'trɒlɪ	A	Teewagen; Kuli; Einkaufswagen
trombone	trɒm'bəʊn	C	Posaune
troops	tru:ps	C	Truppen
Trooping the Colour		C	Fahnenparade
tropical	'trɒpɪkl	C	tropisch
the tropics	'trɒpɪks	C	die Tropen
trouble	trʌbl	A	Unruhe; Schwierigkeit; beunruhigen; stören
be in trouble		A	in Schwierigkeiten sein
take (= go to) the trouble		B	s. die Mühe machen
it's no trouble		A	es macht keine Mühe
troublesome	'trʌblsəm	C	störend, lästig
trousers	'traʊzəz	A	lange Hose
trouser suit		B	Hosenanzug
	'traʊzə‿su:t		
trout	traʊt	B	Forelle(n)
truck	trʌk	A	Lastwagen
true	tru:	A	wahr, echt; treu
come true		C	wahr werden
truly	'tru:lɪ	B	wirklich, echt
Yours truly	jɔ:z‿..	B	Hochachtungsvoll
trumpet	'trʌmpɪt	A	Trompete
trunk	trʌŋk	B	Baumstamm; (US) Kofferraum C
trunk-call	'..kɔ:l	C	Ferngespräch
trust	trʌst	A	vertrauen; Vertrauen C
trustworthy	'trʌstwɜ:ðɪ	C	zuverlässig
truth	tru:θ	A	Wahrheit
truthful	'tru:θfʊl	C	wahr

truthful

try

To try out

try	traɪ	A	versuchen; Versuch; vor Gericht stellen C
try on/out		A	an-/ausprobieren
T-shirt	ˈtiːˌʃɜːt	B	T-Shirt
tube	tjuːb	A	Röhre, Schlauch; (Londoner) U-Bahn B
Tuesday	ˈtjuːzdɪ,eɪ	A	Dienstag
tuition	tjuːˈɪʃn	C	Unterricht
tulip	ˈtjuːlɪp	A	Tulpe
tune	tjuːn	C	Melodie; (ab)stimmen
tune in		C	(Sender) einstellen
tunnel	ˈtʌnəl	A	Tunnel
turbine	ˈtɜːbaɪn	C	Turbine
Turk	tɜːk	C	Türke, -in
Turkey	ˈtɜːkɪ	C	Türkei
turkey	ˈtɜːkɪ	A	Truthahn
Turkish	ˈtɜːkɪʃ	C	türkisch
turn	tɜːn	A	drehen, (um)wenden; abbiegen; Drehung, Wendung
turn down		A	ablehnen; leiser stellen
turn into		C	(s.)verwandeln in
turn off/on		A	aus-, einschalten
turn over		B	umdrehen
turn round		A	wenden
turn upside down		B	auf den Kopf stellen
in turn		C	der Reihe nach; wiederum
whose turn is it?		A	wer ist an der Reihe?
it's my turn		A	ich bin dran
turn up		A	auftauchen, vorkommen
turning point		C	Wendepunkt
turning	ˈtɜːnɪŋ	A	Abzweigung, Seitenstraße

Tudor Age Tudorzeit (alter) 1485-1603

turnip	ˈtɜːnɪp	C	Rübe
turnover	ˈtɜːnəʊvə	W	Umsatz
turnpike (US)	ˈtɜːnpaɪk	C	Schnellstraße
turtle	ˈtɜːtl	C	Schildkröte
tutor	ˈtjuːtə	C	Betreuungslehrer
TV	ˈtiːˈviː	A	Fernsehen
tweed	twiːd	B	Tweed (Wollstoff)
twelve	twelv	A	zwölf
twelfth	twelfθ	A	zwölfte,r,s
twenty	ˈtwentɪ	A	zwanzig
twentieth	ˈtwentɪəθ	A	zwanzigste,r,s
twice	twaɪs	A	zweimal
twig	twɪg	C	Zweig
twilight	ˈtwaɪlaɪt	C	Zwielicht, Dämmerung
twin	twɪn	B	Zwilling

Twins

twin-set	ˈtwɪnset	B	Twinset
twin town		C	Partnerstadt
twinkle	ˈtwɪŋkl	C	zwinkern; blinken
twist	twɪst	C	(s.) drehen, winden
two	tuː	A	zwei
type	taɪp	A	Typ(e); Art; tippen
typewriter	ˈtaɪpraɪtə	A	Schreibmaschine
typical (of)	ˈtɪpɪkl	A	typisch (für)
typist	ˈtaɪpɪst	A	Maschinenschreiber(in)
tyre (US tire)	taɪə	A	(Rad-)Reifen
Tyrol	ˈtɪrəl	B	Tirol
Tyrolean	tɪrəˈliːən	B	tirolerisch

U

u	juː	A	u
ugly	ˈʌglɪ	A	häßlich
ugliness	ˈʌglɪnəs	C	Häßlichkeit
ultimately	ˈʌltɪmətlɪ	B	schließlich
umbrella	ʌmˈbrelə	A	Regenschirm
umpire	ˈʌmpaɪə	C	Schiedsrichter (Kricket)
unable	ʌnˈeɪbl	A	unfähig, außerstande
unavoidable	ʌnəˈvɔɪdəbl	B	unvermeidbar
unbearable	ʌnˈbeərəbl	C	unerträglich
uncle	ʌŋkl	A	Onkel
uncomfortable	ʌnˈkʌmfətəbl	B	unbequem
unconscious	ʌnˈkɒnʃəs	B	bewußtlos; unbewußt
undecided	ʌndɪˈsaɪdɪd	B	unentschlossen
under	ˈʌndə	A	unter; unten
under repair	ˈʌndə rɪˈpeə	C	in Reparatur
underdeveloped	ʌndədɪˈveləpt	B	unterentwickelt
undergraduate	ʌndəˈgrædjʊət	C	Student(in)
underground	ˈʌndəgraʊnd	A	Untergrund; U-Bahn
underline	ʌndəˈlaɪn	A	unterstreichen
underneath	ʌndəˈniːθ	B	unten; unterhalb
undershirt	ˈʌndəʃɜːt	C	(US) Unterhemd
understand	ʌndəˈstænd	A	verstehen; begreifen
understood	ʌndəˈstʊd		
understood			
understandable		C	verständlich
understanding	ʌndəˈstændɪŋ	B	Verständnis; Abmachung; verständnisvoll
undertake	ʌndəˈteɪk	C	unternehmen
undertaking		C	Unternehmung
underwear	ˈʌndəweə	A	Unterwäsche
undoubtedly	ʌnˈdaʊtɪdlɪ	B	zweifellos
undress	ʌnˈdres	A	(s.) ausziehen
unfair	ʌnˈfeə	A	ungerecht, unfair
unfaithful	ʌnˈfeɪθfəl	C	untreu
uneasy	ʌnˈiːzɪ	C	unbehaglich; ängstlich
uneducated	ʌnˈedjʊkeɪtɪd	B	ungebildet
unemployed	ʌnɪmˈplɔɪd	A	arbeitslos
unemployment	ʌnɪmˈplɔɪmənt	A	Arbeitslosigkeit
un-English	ʌnˈɪŋglɪʃ	C	unenglisch
unexpected	ʌnɪkˈspektɪd	B	unerwartet
unfavourable	ʌnˈfeɪvərəbl	B	ungünstig
unfit	ʌnˈfɪt	C	ungeeignet
unforgettable	ʌnfəˈgetəbl	C	unvergeßlich
unfortunate(ly)	ʌnˈfɔːtʃnət(lɪ)	A	unglücklich(erweise)
unfriendly	ʌnˈfrendlɪ	A	unfreundlich
unhappy	ʌnˈhæpɪ	A	unglücklich
uniform	ˈjuːnɪfɔːm	A	Uniform; gleichförmig C
union	ˈjuːnjən	B	Vereinigung; Gewerkschaft
Union Jack		C	britische Flagge
unique	juːˈniːk	C	einzigartig
unit	ˈjuːnɪt	B	Einheit
unite	juːˈnaɪt	A	(s.) vereinigen
United Kingdom (U.K.)	juːˈnaɪtɪd ˈkɪŋdəm	A	Vereinigtes Königreich
United Nations (U.N.)		A	Vereinte Nationen
United States (U.S.)	…ˈsteɪts	A	Vereinigte Staaten
unity	ˈjuːnətɪ	B	Einheit; Einigkeit
universal	juːnɪˈvɜːsl	C	allgemein, Universal-
universe	ˈjuːnɪvɜːs	B	Weltall
university	juːnɪˈvɜːsətɪ	A	Universität
unkind	ʌnˈkaɪnd	B	unfreundlich
unjust	ʌnˈdʒʌst	C	ungerecht
unknown	ʌnˈnəʊn	B	unbekannt
unless	ʌnˈles	A	wenn nicht, außer
unlike	ʌnˈlaɪk	B	anders als
unlikely	ʌnˈlaɪklɪ	B	unwahrscheinlich
unlimited	ʌnˈlɪmɪtɪd	C	unbegrenzt
unload	ʌnˈləʊd	C	ab-, entladen
unlucky	ʌnˈlʌkɪ	A	unglücklich
be unlucky		A	Pech haben
unnecessary	ʌnˈnesəsrɪ	A	unnötig
unpack	ʌnˈpæk	C	auspacken
unpleasant	ʌnˈpleznt	A	unangenehm
unpopular	ʌnˈpɒpjʊlə	B	unbeliebt
unreliable	ʌnrɪˈlaɪəbl	B	unzuverlässlich
unskilled	ʌnˈskɪld	C	ungelernt
until	ʌnˈtɪl	A	bis
untiring	ʌnˈtaɪrɪŋ	C	unermüdlich
unusual	ʌnˈjuːʒəl	A	ungewöhnlich
unwilling	ʌnˈwɪlɪŋ	B	nicht willens
be unwilling		B	nicht wollen
unwise	ʌnˈwaɪz	B	unklug, unvernünftig
up	ʌp	A	auf; hinauf; oben
up and down		B	auf und ab
up to	ˈʌp tə	A	bis zu
up-to-date	ʌp tə ˈdeɪt	A	modern, zeitgemäß
it's up to you		B	es hängt von dir ab
what's up?		C	was ist los?
uphill	ʌpˈhɪl	C	bergauf
upon	əˈpɒn	A	auf

upon

once upon a time

once upon a time		C	es war einmal
upper	ˈʌpə	A	obere(r,s)
upright	ˈʌpraɪt	C	aufrecht, gerade
uprising	ˈʌpraɪzɪŋ	C	Revolte, Aufstand
upset	ʌpˈset	B	in Unordnung bringen
upset			
be upset		B	bestürzt sein
get upset		B	s. aufregen
upside down		B	auf dem Kopf
upstairs	ʌpˈsteəz	A	(nach) oben (1. Stock)

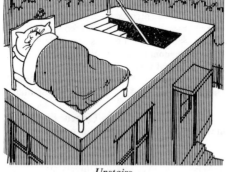

Upstairs

upward(s)	ˈʌpwəd(z)	B	aufwärts, nach oben
uranium	juːˈreɪnjəm	C	Uran
urban	ˈɜːbən	C	städtisch
urgent	ˈɜːdʒənt	B	dringend, eilig
urgency	ˈɜːdʒənsɪ	B	Dringlichkeit, Eile
urge	ɜːdʒ	C	drängen; Drang
us	ʌs, əs	A	uns
use	juːz	A	benutzen, verwenden
use up	juːz ˈʌp	C	aufbrauchen
used to	ˈjuːstə	A	pflegte zu
be used to	ˈjʊstə	A	gewöhnt sein
get used to		B	s. gewöhnen an
use	juːs	A	Nutzen, Gebrauch
make use of		C	Gebrauch machen von
it's no use		A	es nützt nichts
used car (US)	juːzd	B	Gebrauchtwagen
useful	ˈjuːsfəl	A	nützlich
useless	ˈjuːsləs	A	nutzlos, sinnlos
usual	ˈjuːʒʊəl	A	gewöhnlich, üblich
as usual	əz ˈjuːʒʊəl	A	wie gewöhnlich
usually	ˈjuːʒʊəlɪ	A	gewöhnlich, normalerweise
utilise(-ize)	ˈjuːtɪlaɪz	C	nützen; Gebrauch machen von
utmost	ˈʌtməʊst	C	äußerst, höchst
utterly	ˈʌtəlɪ	C	äußerst, überaus
U-turn	ˈjuːˌtɜːn	C	Kehrtwendung

vandal
Vandale,
Gewalttäter

vandalism
Vandalismus,
Zerstörungs-
wut

V

v	viː	A	v
vacant	ˈveɪkənt	B	frei, nicht besetzt
vacancy	ˈveɪkənsɪ	B	freie Stelle; freies Zimmer
vacation	vəˈkeɪʃn; (US) veɪ-	B	Ferien; Urlaub
vacuum cleaner	ˈvækjʊəmkliːnə	B	Staubsauger
vague	veɪg	C	vage, unbestimmt
vain	veɪn	B	eitel
vanity	ˈvænətɪ	C	Eitelkeit
in vain	ɪnˈveɪn	B	vergebens, umsonst
valid	ˈvælɪd	B	gültig
valley	ˈvælɪ	A	Tal
value	ˈvæljuː	B	Wert
valuable	ˈvæljʊəbl	B	wertvoll
valve	vælv	C	Ventil
van	væn	A	Lieferwagen
vanish	ˈvænɪʃ	C	verschwinden
variation	veərɪˈeɪʃn	C	Variation, Abwandlung
variety	vəˈraɪətɪ	B	Vielfalt
various	ˈveərɪəs	A	verschiedene
vary	ˈveərɪ	B	s. verändern; (ab)wechseln
varnish	ˈvɑːnɪʃ	C	Lack; lackieren
vase	vɑːz	A	Vase
vast	vɑːst	A	weit, riesig
veal	viːl	C	Kalbfleisch
vegetable	ˈvedʒtəbl	A	Gemüse; pflanzlich

Vegetables

vehicle	ˈviːɪkl, ˈvɪəkl	A	Fahrzeug
veil	veɪl	C	Schleier
velvet	ˈvelvɪt	A	Samt
venture	ˈventʃə	C	wagen; Wagnis
verb	vɜːb	B	Verb(um)
verify	ˈverɪfaɪ	C	prüfen
verse	vɜːs	B	Vers, Strophe
version	ˈvɜːʃn	B	Version, Fassung
vertical	ˈvɜːtɪkl	C	senkrecht

very	ˈverɪ	A	sehr
vessel	vesl	B	Gefäß; Schiff
vest	vest	C	Unterhemd
vet(erinary surgeon)	ˈvet(ərɪnərɪ ˈsɜːdʒn)	C	Tierarzt
via	ˈvaɪə	B	über, via
Vice-President	ˈvaɪsˌprezɪdənt	B	Vizepräsident
vice versa	ˈvaɪsɪˈvɜːsə	C	umgekehrt
victim	ˈvɪktɪm	B	Opfer
victorious	vɪkˈtɔːrɪəs	C	siegreich
victory	ˈvɪktərɪ	A	Sieg
video recorder	ˈvɪdɪəʊ rɪˈkɔːdə	A	Videorecorder
view	vjuː	A	Aus-, Ansicht; betrachten C
in view of	ɪnˈvjuːəv	B	im Hinblick auf
village	ˈvɪlɪdʒ	A	Dorf
vinegar	ˈvɪnɪɡə	B	Essig
violence	ˈvaɪələns	B	Heftigkeit; Gewalt (tätigkeit)
violent	ˈvaɪələnt	B	heftig; gewalttätig
violet	ˈvaɪələt	C	Veilchen; violett
viola	vɪˈəʊlə	C	Viola, Bratsche
violin	vaɪəˈlɪn	A	Geige
virgin	ˈvɜːdʒɪn	C	Jungfrau
virtue	ˈvɜːtjuː	C	Tugend
visa	ˈviːzə	B	Visum
visible	ˈvɪzəbl	B	sichtbar
visibility	vɪzɪˈbɪlɪtɪ	C	Sicht(weite)
vision	ˈvɪʒn	B	Vision; Weitblick
visit	ˈvɪzɪt	A	Besuch; besuchen
pay a visit		B	einen Besuch abstatten
visitor	ˈvɪzɪtə	A	Besucher, Gast
visual	ˈvɪʒʊəl	C	visuell, Sicht-
vital	ˈvaɪtl	B	lebenswichtig; wesentlich
vitamin	ˈvɪtəmɪn	C	Vitamin
vivid	ˈvɪvɪd	C	lebhaft, lebendig
vocabulary	vəˈkæbjʊlərɪ	B	Wortschatz, Wörterverzeichnis
vocational	vəʊˈkeɪʃnl	C	beruflich
vocational school		C	Berufsschule
voice	vɔɪs	A	Stimme
voiced	vɔɪst	C	stimmhaft
voiceless	ˈvɔɪsləs	C	stimmlos
volleyball	ˈvɒlɪbɔːl	C	Volleyball
volume	ˈvɒljuːm	B	Lautstärke; Band
voluntary	ˈvɒləntrɪ	A	freiwillig
volunteer	vɒlənˈtɪə	B	Freiwillige(r); s. melden C
vote	vəʊt	A	Stimme; abstimmen
voter	ˈvəʊtə	C	Wähler
voucher	ˈvaʊtʃə	C	Gutschein
vowel	ˈvaʊəl	B	Vokal
voyage	ˈvɔɪɪdʒ	C	Seereise
vulgar	ˈvʌlɡə	C	gewöhnlich; vulgär

W

w	ˈdʌbljuː	A	w
wag	wæɡ	C	wedeln
wage(s)	weɪdʒ(ɪz)	A	Lohn
wage-earner	ˈweɪdʒɜːnə	C	Lohnempfänger
wag(g)on	ˈwæɡən	B	Waggon
waist	weɪst	B	Taille
waistcoat	ˈweɪskəʊt	C	(Anzug-)Weste
wait (for)	weɪt	A	warten (auf)
wait on		C	bedienen
waiter, waitress	ˈweɪtə, -trɪs	A	Kellner(in)
waiting room	ˈweɪtɪŋruːm	B	Warteraum
wake (up) woke/waked woken/waked	weɪk əʊ, eɪ əʊ, eɪ	A	aufwecken, aufwachen
Wales	weɪlz	A	Wales, Walisien
walk	wɔːk	A	Spaziergang; (spazieren) gehen
go for (=take) a walk		A	einen Spaziergang machen
walk of life		C	soziale Schicht
wall	wɔːl	A	Wand, Mauer
wallet	ˈwɒlɪt	A	Brieftasche
wallpaper	ˈwɔːlpeɪpə	C	Tapete

Wallpaper

walnut	ˈwɔːlnʌt	C	Walnuß
waltz	wɔːl(t)s	C	Walzer; Walzer tanzen
wander	ˈwɒndə	C	wandern
want	wɒnt	A	wünschen, haben wollen
want to	wɒntˌtə	A	wollen
want + -ing		C	nötig haben
wanna (US slang)	ˈwɒnə	C	wollen
war	wɔː	A	Krieg
warden	wɔːdn	B	Aufseher, Herbergswirt

warden

to wait and see abwarten

traffic warden			
	traffic warden	B	Verkehrsaufseher, Politesse
	ˈtræfɪk ˈwɔːdn		
	warder	ˈwɔːdə C	Wächter, Wärter
	wardrobe	ˈwɔːdrəʊb A	Kleiderschrank
	warehouse	ˈweəhaʊs W	Lager
	warm	wɔːm A	warm; (s.) wärmen
	warmth	wɔːmθ B	Wärme
	warn	wɔːn A	warnen
	warning	ˈwɔːnɪŋ B	Warnung
	wash	wɒʃ A	(s.) waschen
	wash up	wɒʃ ˈʌp A	abspülen
	washbasin	ˈwɒʃbeɪsn B	Waschbecken
	washing machine	B	Waschmaschine
	ˈwɒʃɪŋ məˈʃiːn		
	wasp	wɒsp C	Wespe
on the way unterwegs	waste	weɪst B	Verschwendung; Abfall; vergeuden
	waste-paper basket	B	Papierkorb
	ˈweɪstpeɪpə ˈbɑːskɪt		
	watch	wɒtʃ A	(Taschen-, Armband-)Uhr; beobachten; zuschauen
	watch out	wɒtʃ ˈaʊt B	aufpassen
	watchmaker	A	Uhrmacher
	ˈwɒtʃmeɪkə		
	water	ˈwɔːtə A	Wasser; begießen C
	water colour	ˈwɔːtəkʌlə C	Aquarell
	waterfall	ˈwɔːtəfɔːl C	Wasserfall
	waterproof	ˈwɔːtəpruːf C	wasserdicht
	wave	weɪv B	Welle; winken
	wax	wæks C	Wachs; wachsen
	waxworks	ˈwækswɜːks C	Wachsfigurenkabinett
	way	weɪ A	Weg; Art
	by the way	baɪ ðə ˈweɪ A	übrigens
	in a way	ɪn ə ˈweɪ B	in gewisser Hinsicht
	this way	ˈðɪs weɪ B	hier entlang
	way in	A	Eingang
wedding ring Ehering	way out	A	Ausgang
	way of life	weɪ əv ˈlaɪf A	Lebensart, -stil
	W. C.	ˈdʌbljuː ˈsiː C	WC
	we	wiː, wɪ A	wir
to weld schweißen	weak	wiːk A	schwach
	weakness	ˈwiːknəs B	Schwäche
	weaken	ˈwiːk(ə)n B	schwächen; schwächer werden
Wembley (Londoner Fußballstadion)	wealth	welθ B	Reichtum, Wohlstand
	wealthy	ˈwelθɪ B	reich, wohlhabend
	weapon	ˈwepən B	Waffe
	wear	weə A	tragen;
	wore	wɔː	(s.) abnutzen;
	worn	wɔːn	Abnutzung C
	weary	ˈwɪərɪ C	müde
	weather	ˈweðə A	Wetter

weather satellite	C	Wettersatellit
ˈ.. sætəlaɪt		
weave	wiːv C	weben
wove	wəʊv	
woven	ˈwəʊvən	
wedel	weɪdl C	wedeln
wedding	ˈwedɪŋ A	Hochzeit
Wednesday	A	Mittwoch
ˈwenz-, ˈwednzdɪ		
weed	wiːd C	Unkraut; jäten
week	wiːk A	Woche
weekday	ˈwiːkdeɪ B	Werktag
weekend	wiːkˈend A	Wochenende
weekly	ˈwiːklɪ B	wöchentlich; Wochenblatt C
weep	wiːp B	weinen
wept	wept	
wept		
weigh	weɪ A	wiegen; abwägen
weight	weɪt B	Gewicht
welcome (to)	ˈwelkəm A	willkommen (in); begrüßen
you're welcome	A	bitte sehr, gern geschehen
welfare	ˈwelfeə B	Wohlfahrt, -ergehen
well	wel A	wohl; gut; nun!
be well	A	gut gehen, gesund sein
as well as	əz ˈwel əz A	sowie
as well	əzˈwel A	auch
well-known	ˈwelˈnəʊn B	berühmt
well-to-do	ˈwel tə ˈduː C	wohlhabend
Welsh	welʃ A	walisisch
Welshman	ˈwelʃmən B	Waliser
west	west A	(nach) West(en); westlich
western	ˈwestən A	westlich; Western
westward(s)	B	westwärts
wet	wet A	naß; feucht
wet paint	wet ˈpeɪnt C	frisch gestrichen!
what	wɒt A	was, was für (ein)
what a...!	ˈwɒt ə A	was für ein...!
what about...?	A	wie steht es...?

Wet paint

what else	wɒtˈels A	was noch	
what's on (at)...?	B	was gibt's (im)...?	
	wɒtsˈɒn		
what... for	B	wozu	
what's it like?	A	wie ist es?	
what time...?	A	wann...? um wieviel Uhr...?	
whatever	wɒtˈevə B	was auch (immer)	
whatsoever	wɒtsəʊˈevə B	was auch immer	
wheat	wiːt A	Weizen	
wheel	wiːl A	Rad	
wheelbarrow	C	Schubkarren	
	ˈwiːlbærəʊ		
when	wen A	wann; wenn, als; während	
whenever	wenˈevə A	wann auch immer	
where	weə A	wo, wohin	
whereas	ˈweərəz A	während, wogegen	
wherever	weərˈevə A	wo auch immer	
whether	ˈweðə A	ob	

Which of you was it?

which	wɪtʃ A	welche(r,s); der, die, das
whichever	wɪtʃˈevə B	welch auch immer
while	waɪl A	während; Weile
whilst	waɪlst B	während
whip	wɪp C	Peitsche; peitschen
whipped cream	C	Schlagrahm
	wɪptˈkriːm	
whirlpool	ˈwɜːlpuːl C	Stromschnelle
whisky, -ey	ˈwɪskɪ A	Whisky
whisper	ˈwɪspə B	flüstern; Geflüster
whistle	ˈwɪsl B	Pfeife; Pfiff; pfeifen
white	waɪt A	weiß
Whitsun	ˈwɪtsn A	Pfingsten
who	huː A	wer; der, die, das
whodunit	huːˈdʌnɪt C	Kriminalroman
whoever	huːˈevə A	wer auch immer
whole	həʊl A	ganz
on the whole	A	im ganzen
	ɒnðəˈhəʊl	
whole-hearted	C	aus vollem Herzen
	həʊlˈhɑːtɪd	
wholly	ˈhəʊllɪ B	gänzlich

wholesale	ˈhəʊlseɪl W	Großhandel
wholesaler	ˈhəʊlseɪlə W	Großhändler
whom	huːm, hʊm A	wen; den, die, das
whose	huːz A	wessen; dessen, deren
why	waɪ A	warum? nanu! nun
wicked	ˈwɪkɪd C	böse
wide	waɪd A	weit, breit
far and wide	C	weit und breit
width	wɪdθ B	Weite, Breite
widely	ˈwaɪdlɪ B	weitgehend, häufig, stark
widen	ˈwaɪdən C	erweitern
widespread	ˈwaɪdspred C	weitverbreitet
widow, -er	ˈwɪdəʊ(ə) B	Witwe, Witwer
wife, wives	waɪf, vz A	Ehefrau
wig	wɪg C	Perücke
wild	waɪld A	wild
wilderness	ˈwɪldənəs C	Wildnis
wildlife	ˈwaɪldlaɪf C	Tierwelt, Tierbestand
will	wɪl A	werden; wollen; Wille; Testament C
willing	ˈwɪlɪŋ B	willens; willig
be willing to	B	gewillt sein, wollen
willingly	ˈwɪlɪŋlɪ C	gerne, bereitwillig
win	wɪn A	gewinnen; erlangen
won	wʌn	
won		
wind	wɪnd A	Wind
windy	ˈwɪndɪ A	windig
wind (up)	waɪnd A	aufziehen
wound	waʊnd	
wound		
window	ˈwɪndəʊ A	Fenster
window-shop	...ʃɒp B	Schaufenster anschauen
windscreen	ˈwɪndskriːn C	Windschutzscheibe
windshield (US)		
	ˈwɪndʃiːld	
windscreen wipers	C	Scheibenwischer
wine	waɪn A	Wein
wing	wɪŋ B	Flügel; Tragfläche
winner	ˈwɪnə B	Gewinner(in), Sieger(in)
winning	ˈwɪnɪŋ C	gewinnend, siegreich
winter	ˈwɪntə A	Winter
wipe	waɪp B	(ab)wischen
wire	ˈwaɪə B	Draht; Telegramm C; telegraphieren C
wise	waɪz B	klug, weise
wisdom	ˈwɪzdəm C	Weisheit, Klugheit
wish	wɪʃ A	wünschen; wollen; Wunsch

wish

windsurfing
Windsurfen

best wishes

best wishes		A	viele Grüße
with	wɪð	A	mit, bei
I'm (not) with you		B	ich verstehe (nicht)
withdraw	wɪð'drɔ:	C	(s.) zurückziehen;
withdrew	wɪð'dru:		(vom Konto)
withdrawn	wɪð'drɔ:n		abheben
withdrawal	wɪð'drɔ:l	C	Rückzug
within	wɪð'ɪn	B	innerhalb; drin
without (+ing)	wɪð'aʊt	A	ohne, (ohne zu)
witness	'wɪtnɪs	C	Zeuge, -in
witty	'wɪtɪ	C	witzig
wolf, ves	wʊlf, vz	B	Wolf
woman, women	'wʊmən, 'wɪmɪn	A	Frau
wonder	'wʌndə	A	s. wundern; wissen wollen; Wunder
wonderful	'wʌndəfəl	A	wunderbar
wood	wʊd	A	Wald; Holz
wooden	wʊdn	B	hölzern; Holz-
woodwind instrument	'wʊdwɪnd	C	Holzblasinstument
woodwork	'wʊdwɜ:k	B	Werken
wool	wʊl	A	Wolle
woollen	'wʊlən	A	wollen, aus Wolle
woollens	'wʊlənz	B	Wollsachen
word	wɜ:d	A	Wort
have a word with		C	sprechen mit
word order	'..ɔ:də	C	Wortstellung
work	wɜ:k	A	Arbeit; Werk; arbeiten; funktionieren
work away		C	drauflosarbeiten
be at work		A	arbeiten
work out		B	ausrechnen
be in work		A	Arbeit haben
be out of work		A	arbeitslos sein
worker	'wɜ:kə	A	Arbeiter
worker control	..ˌkɒn'trəʊl	C	Mitbestimmung
working class		C	Arbeiterklasse, Arbeiter-

It's getting worse and worse

working conditions		B	Arbeitsbedingungen
work(ing)-day		C	Werktag
working hours		B	Arbeitszeit
works	wɜ:ks	C	Werk; Fabrik
workshop	'wɜ:kʃɒp	C	Werkstatt
world	wɜ:ld	A	Welt, Erde
world-wide		B	weltweit, international
worm	wɜ:m	B	Wurm
worn	wɔ:n	B	abgetragen, abgenutzt
worn out	..ˈaʊt	C	erschöpft
worry	'wʌrɪ	A	s. sorgen; Sorge
worse, worst	wɜ:s, wɜ:st	A	schlimmer, am schlimmsten
worship	'wɜ:ʃɪp	C	anbeten; verehren
worsted	'wʊstɪd	C	Kammgarn
worth	wɜ:θ	A	Wert; wert
it's worth it		A	es lohnt sich
worthwhile	wɜ:θ'waɪl	A	lohnend
worthless	'wɜ:θləs	A	wertlos; nichtsnutzig
worthy	'wɜ:ðɪ	B	wertvoll
would	wʊd	A	würde; pflegte zu C
would like (to)		A	möchte, würde gerne
wound	wu:nd	B	Wunde; verwunden
wrap	ræp	B	einwickeln
wreck	rek	C	Wrack; Schiffbruch
wretched	'retʃɪd	C	elend; gemein
wrist	rɪst	C	Handgelenk
wrist-watch		A	Armbanduhr
write	raɪt	A	schreiben
wrote	rəʊt		
written	rɪtn		
writing paper		B	Schreibpapier
in writing		B	schriftlich
writer	'raɪtə	B	Schriftsteller
wrong	rɒŋ	A	falsch
be wrong		A	unrecht haben
the wrong way		C	verkehrt; in die falsche Richtung
the wrong way round		C	(seiten)verkehrt

X

x	eks	A	x
Xmas = Christmas	'krɪsməs	A	Weihnachten
X-ray	'eksreɪ	C	Röntgenstrahl
x-ray		C	durchleuchten

<u>word processor</u> Wortprozessor

<u>the words</u> Liedtext

<u>World Cup</u> Fußball-Weltmeisterschaft

<u>would-be</u> zukünftig

Y

y	waɪ	A	y
yacht	jɒt	C	Jacht, Segelboot
yard	jɑːd	A	Hof; Yard (91,4 cm)
yarn	jɑːn	C	Garn, Faden
yawn	jɔːn	B	gähnen

To yawn

year	jɪə	A	Jahr
yearly	ˈjɪəlɪ	B	jährlich
yeast	jiːst	C	Hefe
yell	jel	B	brüllen, schreien
yellow	ˈjeləʊ	A	gelb
yes	jes	A	ja
yesterday	ˈjestədɪ,eɪ	A	gestern
the day before yesterday		A	vorgestern
yet	jet	A	schon; jedoch
as yet	əzˈjet	B	bis jetzt
not yet	nɒtˈjet	A	noch nicht
yield	jiːld	C	nachgeben; einbringen; Ertrag
yodel	ˈjəʊdl	C	jodeln
yoga	ˈjəʊgə	C	Yoga
yoghurt	ˈjɒgət	B	Joghurt
you	juː, jʊ	A	du; ihr; Sie; man
young	jʌŋ	A	jung
youngster	ˈjʌŋstə	C	Jugendlicher
your	jɔː, jʊə	A	dein(e), euer(e), Ihr(e)
yours	jɔːz, jʊəz	A	der (die, das) deinige(n), eure(n), Ihre(n)
youth	juːθ	A	Jugend; Jugendlicher
youthful	ˈjuːθfʊl	C	jugendlich
youth hostel	ˈ.hɒstl	A	Jugendherberge
Yugoslav	juːgəˈslɑːv	C	jugoslawisch; Jugoslawe(in)
Yugoslavia	juːgəˈslɑːvjə	C	Jugoslawien

Z

z	zed, (US) ziː	A	z
zebra	ˈzebrə, ˈziːbrə	B	Zebra
zebra crossing	ˈzebrəˈkrɒsɪŋ	A	Zebrastreifen
zero	ˈzɪərəʊ	B	Null
zigzag	ˈzɪgzæg	B	zickzack
zip	zɪp	B	Reißverschluß
zip code (US)		B	Postleitzahl
zither	ˈzɪðə	C	Zither
zodiac	ˈzəʊdɪæk	C	Tierkreis
sign of the zodiac		C	Tierkreiszeichen
zone	zəʊn	B	Zone
zoo	zuː	A	Zoo
zoom	zuːm	C	Zoom, Varioobjektiv

ABBREVIATIONS

AA	Automobile Association (GB)
ABC	American Broadcasting Company
ac	alternating current
a/c	account
AD	after the birth of Christ (= anno domini)
AFN	American Forces Network
A-level	Advanced Level (GCE Exam)
a.m.	before midday (= ante meridiem)
AM	amplitude modulation
AP	Associated Press
Av(e)	Avenue
b	born
BA	Bachelor of Arts; British Airways
B & B	bed and breakfast
BBC	British Broadcasting Corporation
BC	before Christ
B/E	bill of exchange (Wechsel)
B/L	bill of lading (Seefrachtbrief)
BR	British Rail
Bro(s)	Brother(s)
BS	Bachelor of Science (US)
BSc	Bachelor of Science (GB)
BST	British Summer Time
C	Centigrade
c	cent; copyright
CBS	Columbia Broadcasting System
cc	cubic centimetre
CET	Central European Time
cf	compare with
CIA	Central Intelligence Agency (US)
CID	Criminal Investigation Department (GB)
c.i.f.	cost, insurance, freight
Co	company
c/o	care of, at the address of
c.o.d.	cash on delivery (US: collect on delivery)
Con	Conservative (Party)
contd	continued
cwt	hundredweight (= Zentner)
CSE	Certificate of Secondary Education
d	died
dc	direct current
DC	District of Columbia
Dept	department
Dip	diploma
Dip Ed	Diploma of Education
DJ	disc-jockey
doz	dozen
Dr	Doctor
EDP	Electronic Data Processing
EEC	European Economic Community
e.g.	for example (= exempli gratia)
enc(l)	enclosure
ER II	Queen Elizabeth II (= Elizabeth Regina)
Esq	Esquire (in an address after the name instead of 'Mr')
etc	et cetera, and so on
F	Fahrenheit
FA	Football Association
f.a.s.	free alongside ship
FBI	Federal Bureau of Investigation (US)
FM	frequency modulation
f.o.b.	free on board
f.o.r.	free on rail
GB	Great Britain
GCE	General Certificate of Education
GI	American soldier (= Government Issue)
GMT	Greenwich Mean Time
GNP	Gross National Product
G.O.P.	Grand Old Party (= Republican Party, US)
GP	General Practitioner (doctor, GB)
GPO	General Post Office
h & c	hot and cold water
hi-fi	high-fidelity
HM	His/Her Majesty
HMS	His/Her Majesty's Ship
hp	horsepower
HP	hire-purchase
HQ	headquarters
IBM	International Business Machines
ICE	in-car entertainment
ICI	Imperial Chemical Industries
in(s)	inch(es)
Inc	Incorporated
incl	including
IOU	I owe you (Schuldschein)
IQ	intelligence quotient
IRA	Irish Republican Army
ITV	Independent Television

Abbreviations

IYHF	International Youth Hostels Federation	PhD	Doctor of Philosophy
		PM	Prime Minister
		p.m.	after noon (= post meridiem)
J	joule	P.O. Box	Post Office Box
		PR	Public Relations
kg	kilogram	PS	postscript
km	kilometre(s)	p.t.o.	please turn over
kph	kilometres per hour		
kw	kilowatt	RAC	Royal Automobile Club
		RAF	Royal Air Force
l	left; line	Rd	Road
Lab	Labour (Party)	Rev	Reverend
lb	pound (454 grams)	rpm	revolutions per minute
Lib	Liberal (Party)	RSVP	please reply (= répondez s'il vous plaît)
LP	long-playing record		
Ltd	Limited		
		SALT	Strategic Arms Limitation Talks
m	male; married; metre; mile; million	SDP	Social Democratic Party
		Sq	Square
M	Mach number; motorway	SS	Steamship
MA	Master of Arts	St	Saint; Street
MP	Member of Parliament; Military Police	START	Strategic Arms Reduction Talks
mpg	miles per gallon		
Mr	Mister	t	time; ton(s)
Mrs	(married woman)	TUC	Trades Union Congress
Ms	(married or unmarried woman)	TV	television
ms(s)	manuscript(s)		
MS	Master of Science (US)	UFO	unidentified flying object
MSc	Master of Science (GB)	UHF	ultra-high frequency
		UK	United Kingdom
NASA	National Aeronautics and Space Administration	UN(O)	United Nations (Organisation)
		UNESCO	United Nations Educational, Scientific and Cultural Organisation
NATO	North Atlantic Treaty Organisation		
NBC	National Broadcasting Company (US)	UNICEF	United Nations International Children's Emergency Fund
NHS	National Health Service	UPI	United Press International
no(s)	number(s)	U.S.	United States
NY(C)	New York (City)	U.S.A.	United States of America
O-level	Ordinary Level (GCE Exam)	v, vs	against (= versus)
OPEC	Organisation of Petroleum Exporting Countries	VAT	value added tax (Mehrwertsteuer)
opp	opposite	VHF	very high frequency
OXFAM	Oxford Committee for Famine Relief	VIP	very important person
		vol	volume
oz	ounce(s) (28.35 grams)		
		WC	water closet
p	page; pence		
pa	per annum, per year	YHA	Youth Hostels Association
PC	Police Constable	YMCA	Young Men's Christian Association
PEN	International Association of Poets, Playwrights, Editors, Essayists and Novelists	YWCA	Young Women's Christian Association

HOMOPHONES

air	heir	him	hymn	red	read
allowed	aloud	hole	whole	right	write
alter	altar	holy	wholly	road	rode; rowed
are	r	hour	our	roam	Rome
band	banned	I	i; eye	role	roll
bare	bear	I'll	isle; aisle	rose	rows
base	bass	idle	idol	root	route
be	b; bee	in	inn	sail	sale
bean	been	its	it's	sauce	source
beat	beet	key	quay	scene	seen
beetle	Beatle	knew	new	sea	c; see
berry	bury	know	no	seam	seem
bill	Bill	knows	nose	seas	sees; seize
blue	blew	lain	lane	sell	cell
board	bored	lead	led	sent	cent; scent
born	borne	lessen	lesson	sew	so; sow
bow /aʊ/	bough	made	maid	side	sighed
bread	bred	mail	male	sighs	size
break	brake	manner	manor	sight	site
Britain	Briton	march	March	sole	soul
by	bye; buy	mark	Mark	some	sum
capital	Capitol	may	May	son	sun
caught	court	meat	meet	sort	sought
cell	sell	meter	metre	stair	stare
cellar	seller	mind	mined	steak	stake
cent	sent	miner	minor	stationary	stationery
course	coarse	miss	Miss	steal	steel
current	currant	mist	missed	suite	sweet
dam	damn	morning	mourning	sword	sawed; soared
dear	deer	new	knew	tea	t
desert /ˈ./	dessert	no	know	tale	tail
dew	due	none	nun	taxes	taxis
die	dye	nose	knows	their	there
draft	draught	oh	o; owe	threw	through
eaten	Eton	one	won	throne	thrown
fare	fair	or	ore; oar	tide	tied
father	farther	pact	packed	toe	tow
feet	feat	pail	pale	too	two
find	fined	pain	pane	turkey	Turkey
flee	flea	pair	pear	vain	vein; vane
flower	flour	passed	past	waist	waste
flew	flu	pause	paws; pours	wait	weight
formerly	formally	pea	p	Wales	whales
four	for	peer	pier	war	wore
fourth	forth	piece	peace	warn	worn
fur	fir	plane	plain	way	weigh
groan	grown	pole	Pole; poll	wear	where
guest	guessed	practice	practise	weather	whether
gym	Jim	praise	prays	week	weak
hair	hare	principle	principal	which	witch
hear	here	profit	prophet	whole	hole
heard	herd	quay	key	wholly	holy
heel	heal; he'll	queue	q	why	y
heir	air	rain	reign; rein	wood	would
higher	hire	raise	rays	you	u; yew; ewe

HOMONYMS

arms	Arme; Waffen	might	Macht, Gewalt; wird vielleicht
ball	Ball (zum Spielen); Ball (Tanz)	mine	Bergwerk; (der, die, das) meine
bank	Bank; Ufer	net	Netz; Netto
blow	blasen, wehen; Schlag	page	Seite; Page
board	Bord (Schiff); Brett; Ausschuß	park	Park; parken
boot	Stiefel; Kofferraum	pipe	Pfeife; Röhre
bore	bohren; trug; langweilen, langweiliger Mensch	plain	Ebene; einfach
		plane	Flugzeug; Hobel, hobeln
bowl	Schüssel; Holzkugel; werfen (Kricket)	plant	Pflanze, pflanzen; Werk
		porter	Gepäckträger; Portier
can	können; Dose	post	Post, aufgeben; Posten; Pfosten
cape	Kap; Umhang	present	Geschenk; anwesend; Gegenwart, gegenwärtig
capital	Kapital; Hauptstadt		
case	Koffer, Kasten; Fall, Sache	punch	Faustschlag; lochen; Punsch
chips	Pommes frites; Computerelemente	race	Rasse; Rennen, rennen
		record	Schallplatte; Rekord
coach	Kutsche; Reisebus; Trainer	rest	Rest; Rast, rasten, ausruhen
count	zählen; Graf	ring	Ring; läuten; anrufen
customs	Bräuche; Zoll	rock	Felsen; Rock(musik)
face	Gesicht; Zifferblatt	rose	Rose; stand auf
fair	Messe; gerecht; blond	row	Reihe; rudern
figure	Figur; Zahl	ruler	Lineal; Herrscher
file	Feile; Ordner	scale	Waagschale; Skala; Maßstab
fine	schön; Geldbuße	seal	Seehund; Siegel; abdichten
fit	passen, passend; Anfall	second	zweite(r,s); Sekunde
flight	Flug; Flucht	sentence	Satz; Urteil
form	Form; Klasse	sound	gesund; klingen, Klang, Laut
found	gründen; fand	soil	Erdboden; beschmutzen
general	allgemein; General	spell	buchstabieren; Zeitraum; Zauberbann
grave	Grab; ernst, würdig		
ground	Grund, Boden; mahlte	spring	Frühling; Feder; springen
hand	Hand; Zeiger; reichen	stable	stabil; Pferdestall
just	gerade; gerecht	stage	Stadium; Bühne; inszenieren
kind	freundlich; Art	stamp	Briefmarke; Stempel; stampfen
key	Schlüssel; Taste	state	Staat; Zustand; sagen
last	(zu)letzt; dauern	step	Stufe; Schritt, schreiten; Stiefkleben, heften; Stock
lean	(s.) anlehnen; mager	stick	
leave	verlassen; Urlaub	story	Geschichte; Stockwerk
left	link(s); verließ	strike	schlagen; Streik, streiken
letter	Brief; Buchstabe	succeed	Erfolg haben; nachfolgen
lie	liegen; Lüge, lügen	swallow	Schwalbe; schlucken
light	leicht; hell; Licht; anzünden	table	Tisch; Tabelle
lighter	leichter; Feuerzeug	term	Ausdruck; Zeitraum; Schuljahrdrittel
like	wie; mögen, gern haben		
love	Liebe, lieben; Null (in Tennis)	tip	Trinkgeld; Tip; Spitze
mass	Masse; Messe (Kirche)	tire	ermüden; Radreifen (US)
match	passen zu; Streichholz; Wettspiel	vice	Laster, Fehler; Vize-; Schraubstock
mean	bedeuten, meinen; geizig; gemein	watch	beobachten; Uhr
		well	wohl(auf); gut; Brunnen
means	Mittel; (es) bedeutet, (er) meint	yard	Yard (=3 Fuß); Hof

SYNONYMS

A

to abandon	to give up, to leave
to abbreviate	to shorten
able (to)	capable (of)
about	approximately; concerning, regarding
above	over
to accept	to agree to
to accommodate	to put up
to accompany	to go with
on no account	by no means
accurate	exact, precise
to accuse of	to charge with
accustomed to	used to
acquainted with	familiar with
actual(ly)	real(ly)
adult	grown-up
to advise	to recommend
affair	matter
afraid	frightened, scared
I'm afraid (that)	I'm sorry (that)
afterwards	later
again	once more
age (Zeitalter)	time, period
to agree to	to accept
agreeable	pleasant
aim	goal, target, purpose
air-hostess	stewardess
alien	foreign, foreigner
all right	okay, O.K.
all the time	always
to allow	to permit
almost	nearly
also	too, as well
to alter	to change
alternative	choice
although	(even) though
altitude	height
always	all the time
amazed	surprised, astonished
amount	sum
to amuse	to entertain
amusing	funny, entertaining
ancestor	forefather
and so on	etc (et cetera)
and yet	nevertheless, even so
angry	cross
annual	yearly
(to) answer	(to) reply
anxious	worried
anxious to	keen to, eager to
anyhow	anyway, at any rate, in any case
apart	separate
apart from	except, aside from (US)
to apologise	to be sorry
apparent	evident, clear
to appear	to seem
approximately	about
area	region, zone
argument	quarrel, dispute
arms	weapons
to arrange	to organise
to arrive at/in	to get to
as well	also, too
aside from (US)	apart from, except
to ask for	to request
ass	donkey
to assassinate	to kill, to murder
to assist	to help
assistance	help, aid
astonished	amazed, surprised
at once	immediately
to attempt	to try
to attend	to go to
attractive	good-looking
automobile	car
average	usual, normal
awful	dreadful, terrible

B

bad	evil
to be	to exist
can't bear	can't stand
to beat	to hit, to strike; to defeat
beautiful	wonderful, fine
because of	owing to
before	in front of; previously, earlier
behaviour	conduct
to begin	to start
belief	faith, conviction
below	under(neath)
beside	next to
besides	moreover
big	large
a bit	a little
bloke	chap, guy, fellow
bold	daring
border	frontier
bowl	dish
brave	courageous
break	interval
to break up	to divide; to separate
brief	short
bright	light
to bring about	to cause
broad	wide
to build	to construct
burial	funeral
to be busy	not to be free, to have no time
to buy	to purchase

C

to calculate	to work out
to call on	to visit
caller	visitor
calm	quiet, peaceful
capable (of)	able (to)
car	automobile
careless	negligent
to carry on	to continue, to keep on, to go on
in any case	at any rate, anyway
cause	reason
to cause	to bring about
to cease	to stop, to finish, to end
centre	middle
chance	opportunity
to change	to alter
chap	guy, bloke, fellow

Synonyms

to charge with	to accuse of	crowd	multitude	dove	pigeon
cheap	inexpensive	crowded	full, packed	a dozen	twelve
cheerful	happy	cruel	heartless, ruthless	dramatist	playwright
chief	main, principal			dreadful	terrible, horrible, awful
china	porcelain	to cry	to weep; to shout		
choice	selection; alternative			dreary	gloomy, dull
		curious	strange; inquisitive	driver	motorist
to choose	to select; to elect			dull	boring, uninteresting
circular	round				
clever	smart, intelligent	**D**			
to close	to shut	damage	harm	**E**	
close	near	to damage	to harm, to injure		
to collect	to gather			each	every (one of)
to come across	to meet; to find, to discover	damp	moist	eager (to)	keen (to)
		daring	bold, brave	earnest	serious
		decent	respectable	easy	simple
to come back	to return	to decide	to make up one's mind	eatable	edible
command	order			to educate	to bring up
common	usual, ordinary			effect	consequence, result
competition	rivalry; contest	to decline	to refuse, to reject		
competitor	rival				
complete	total, entire, whole	to defeat	to beat	egg-shaped	oval
		delicate	gentle; weak	to elect	to choose, to select
to comprehend	to understand, to grasp	delicious	tasty		
		delight	pleasure, joy	emblem	symbol
concerning	about, regarding	to deliver	to supply	to emigrate	to leave one's country
		(to) demand	(to) claim		
conduct	behaviour	dense	thick	to enable	to make possible
to connect	to join (together)	to depart	to leave, to go away		
				in the end	eventually, finally
consequence	result, effect	to depend on	to rely on		
to consider	to regard (as)	dependable	reliable	energetic	vigorous
considerate	kind, thoughtful	to desert	to leave, to run away from	enormous	huge, immense
				enough	sufficient
constant	steady, continuous	desire	wish	to ensure	to make certain
		despite	in spite of	to entertain	to amuse
to construct	to build	to detest	to hate	entertaining	amusing
to consult	to ask	different	various	entire	complete, whole
to continue	to carry on, to go on, to keep on	difficult	hard		
		to disappear	to vanish	to entitle	to authorise
		disc, disk	record	entrance	way in, entry
contrary	opposite	to discover	to find, to come across	entry	entrance, way in
convenient	suitable				
conventional	traditional	to discuss	to talk about	environment	surroundings
conviction	belief	disease	illness	to erase	to rub out
to co-operate	to work together	disgrace	shame	error	mistake, fault
		dish	bowl	to escape	to get away
to cope (with)	to manage	to display	to show	especially	particularly
correct	right; proper	dispute	quarrel, argument	essential	necessary, vital
countless	innumerable			to establish	to found
cost(s)	expense(s)	distant	remote	etc (et cetera)	and so on
courageous	brave, bold	distinct	clear	even so	nevertheless, and yet
courteous	polite	to distribute	to give out		
courtesy	politeness	district	region, area	event	happening
crazy	mad	to divide	to break up	eventually	in the end, finally, ultimately
crop	harvest	doctor	physician		
cross	angry, annoyed	donkey	ass		

111

Synonyms

every	each	to find out	to guess	to go on	to continue, to carry on, to proceed
everything	all	fine	good; beautiful		
evident	apparent, clear	to finish	to end, to stop		
evil	bad	to fix	to arrange; to repair, to mend	to go to	to attend
exact	accurate, precise			to go with	to accompany
				goal	aim, target
example	instance	folk	people	goodbye	farewell
excellent	superb	to follow	to pursue	good-looking	handsome, attractive
except	apart from, aside from (US)	follower	supporter		
		to be fond of	to like	gorgeous	beautiful, marvellous
		foolish	silly		
to exchange	to swop	forefather	ancestor	to grab	to snatch
excursion	outing, trip	foreign(er)	alien	gradually	slowly, step by step
to execute	to carry out; to put to death	not to forget	to remember		
		to forgive	to pardon	to grasp	to seize; to understand, to comprehend
to exhibit	to show, to display	fortnight	two weeks		
		fortunate	lucky		
to exist	to be	to found	to establish	grateful	obliged
exit	way out	freedom	liberty	grave	serious; tomb
to expect	to foresee; to wait for	frequently	often	to grow	to increase
		frightened	afraid, scared	grown-up	adult
expense(s)	cost(s)	frontier	border		
expensive	dear	full	crowded		
expert	specialist	funeral	burial		
to extend	to lengthen	funny	humorous, amusing	**H**	
exterior	outer				
to extinguish	to put out	furthermore	moreover, besides	handsome	good-looking
				to happen	to occur, to take place
				happening	event
F		**G**		happy	cheerful
				hard	difficult
to facilitate	to make easier			hardship	difficulty; poverty
factory	plant, works	to gather	to collect		
faint	weak, feeble	gentle	kind, friendly	hard-working	industrious
fair	just; honest	to get	to obtain, to receive; to become	harm	damage
faith	belief, trust			harsh	rough
faithful	loyal			harvest	crop
false	wrong	to get away	to escape	to hate	to detest
familiar with	acquainted with	to get better	to improve, to recover	to have	to own, to possess; to eat, to drink
famous	well-known	to get to	to arrive at/in	heap	pile
fantastic	marvellous, super	gift	present; talent	height	altitude
		gigantic	huge, enormous, immense, vast	to help	to assist
farewell	goodbye			help	assistance
fast	quick, rapid			historic	famous, important
fault	error, mistake				
feeble	weak, faint	to give back	to return		
to feed	to nourish	to give out	to distribute, to hand out	historical	real, not fiction
fellow	chap, bloke, guy			to hit	to beat, to strike
		to give up	to abandon, to stop		
fierce	violent, wild			holy	sacred
to fight	to oppose; to struggle	to glance	to look	horrible	terrible, dreadful
		glasses	spectacles		
finally	in the end, eventually	gloomy	dark, dreary	huge	immense, vast, enormous
		to go away	to leave, to depart		
to find	to come across, to discover				
		to go back	to return		

Synonyms

I

idea	thought
ideal	perfect
if	whether
illness	disease
immediately	at once
immense	enormous, huge, vast
impolite	rude
important	major
imposing	impressive
to improve	to make/to get better
to increase	to grow; to raise
incredible	unbelievable
to indicate	to show, to point out
industrious	hard-working
inevitable	unavoidable
inexpensive	cheap
to inhabit	to live in
to injure	to hurt, to damage
innumerable	countless
inquisitive	curious
in spite of	despite
instance	example
instant	moment; immediate
instead of	in place of, rather than
to instruct	to teach
instructor	teacher, trainer
to insult	to offend
intelligent	bright, clever
intention	plan, aim
intentionally	on purpose
interval	break
inverted commas	quotation marks
to irritate	to annoy
issue	matter, problem

J

jail	prison
jewel	precious stone
jobless	unemployed, out of work
to join (together)	to connect, to link
journey	trip
joy	delight, pleasure
just	fair

K

keen (to)	eager (to)
to keep	to maintain
to kill	to murder, to assassinate
kind (of)	type (of), sort (of)

L

large	big, major
largely	mainly, chiefly
later	afterwards
to learn (by heart)	to memorise
to leave	to depart, to go away, to abandon, to desert
to leave out	to omit, to drop
leisure (time)	spare (= free) time
to lengthen	to extend
to liberate	to set free, to release
liberty	freedom
to lift	to raise
to like	to be fond of
likely	probable
a little	a bit, somewhat
to live in	to inhabit
lobby	pressure group
to look	to glance
to look for	to search for, to seek
to look like	to resemble
a lot (of), lots of	many, much
loyal	faithful, true
lucky	fortunate

M

mad	crazy
magnificent	wonderful, splendid
mail	post
main	chief, principal
mainly	mostly
to maintain	to keep; to state
major	important, large
to make	to produce, to manufacture
to make better	to improve
to make sure	to ensure
to make dirty	to pollute
to make easier	to facilitate
to make longer	to prolong
to make up one's mind	to decide
to manage	to cope
to manage to	to succeed in
to manufacture	to make, to produce
many	a lot, lots of
many a	some, quite a few
marvellous	fantastic, wonderful
matter	affair
means	way, method
by no means	on no account
melody	tune
memorial	monument
memorise	to learn (by heart)
to mend	to repair, to fix
method	means, way
middle	centre
mighty	powerful
minor	small, unimportant
mistake	error, fault
moist	damp
moment	instant
monument	memorial
moreover	besides
mostly	mainly
motion	movement
motorist	driver
movement	motion
multitude	crowd
to murder	to kill, to assassinate

N

naked	nude
nasty	unpleasant
near	close
nearly	almost
necessary	essential, vital
to need	to require
negligent	careless
nevertheless	even so, and yet
next to	beside
nice	pleasant, pretty

Synonyms

nonsense	rubbish
noon	midday
normal	average, usual
to nourish	to feed
nude	naked
a number of	several, some, a few, a couple of

O

obligation	duty
obliged	grateful
to observe	to watch
to obtain	to get, to receive
obvious	clear, evident
occupied	busy
to occur	to happen
ocean	sea
odd	unusual, strange
odour	smell
to offend	to insult
often	frequently
okay, O.K.	all right
old-fashioned	out-of-date
to omit	to leave out
once more	(once) again
opportunity	chance
to oppose	to be against, to fight
opposite	contrary
orator	public speaker
to orbit	to move round
order	command
ordinary	usual, plain, common, regular
to organise	to arrange
origin	beginning, start
out-of-date	old-fashioned, outdated
outcome	result, consequence
outer	exterior
outing	excursion, trip
output	production
oval	egg-shaped
over	above
to overdo	to exaggerate
owing to	because of
to own	to have, to possess
owner	proprietor

P

painting	picture
to pardon	to forgive
to participate	to take part
particular	special
particularly	especially
peaceful	quiet, calm
perfect	ideal
period	age, time, epoch
to permit	to allow
physician	doctor
picture	painting; photo
pile	heap
in place of	instead of
plain	ordinary
plan	project, scheme
plant	factory, works
playwright	dramatist
pleasant	nice, agreeable
pleasure	delight
to point out	to indicate
polite	courteous
politeness	courtesy
to pollute	to make dirty
to possess	to own, to have
post	mail
poverty	hardship
powerful	mighty
precious	valuable
precious stone	jewel
to prefer	to like better
present	gift
pressure group	lobby
pretty	attractive
to prevent (from)	to stop (from)
previous	former, earlier
previously	before
principal	chief, main
prison	jail
probable	likely
to proceed	to go on, to go ahead
to produce	to make, to manufacture
production	output
project	plan, scheme
to prolong	to extend
prompt(ly)	punctual(ly)
proper	correct, suitable
proposal	suggestion
to propose	to suggest
proprietor	owner
prosperous	well-to-do, wealthy
to provide	to supply
punctual(ly)	prompt(ly)
pupil	schoolboy, schoolgirl
to purchase	to buy
pure	clear
purpose	intention, aim
on purpose	intentionally
to pursue	to follow
to put out	to extinguish
to put up	to accommodate
to put up with	to tolerate

Q

quarrel	argument, dispute
quick	fast, rapid
quiet	peaceful, calm
to quit	to stop, to leave

R

to raise	to lift
rapid	fast, quick
at any rate	in any case, anyway
rarely	seldom
rather than	instead of
real(ly)	actual(ly)
reason	cause
reasonable	sensible
to recall	to remember
recently	lately
to recommend	to advise
record	disc, disk
to recover	to get better
to reduce	to cut, to decrease
to refuse	to reject, to decline
to regard (as)	to consider
regarding	concerning
region	area, district
to regret	to be sorry for
to reject	to refuse, to decline
to release	to set free, to bring out
reliable	dependable
to rely on	to depend on
to remain	to stay
to remember	not to forget, to recall

Synonyms

remote	far away, distant	selection	choice	sufficient	enough	
to repair	to fix, to mend	sensible	reasonable, intelligent	to suggest	to propose	
to replace	to substitute	separate	apart	suggestion	proposal	
replacement	substitute	separation	segregation	suitable	convenient, proper	
to reply	to answer	serious	earnest	sum	amount	
reputation	name	to set free	to release, to liberate	superb	excellent	
to request	to ask for			superior (to)	better (than)	
to require	to need	several	a number of, various	to supply	to provide	
to rescue	to save			supporter	follower	
to resemble	to look like	shame	disgrace	supreme	highest, greatest	
respectable	decent	ship	boat			
result	outcome, consequence	to shorten	to abbreviate	surprised	astonished, amazed	
		to shout	to cry (out)			
to retire	to withdraw	to show	to display, to exhibit	surroundings	environment	
to return	to go back, to come back; to give back			to survive	to stay alive; to outlive	
		to shut	to close			
		silly	foolish, stupid	to swop	to exchange	
to reveal	to show	similar	alike	symbol	emblem	
rich	wealthy, well-to-do	simultaneously	at the same time			
ridiculous	laughable, ludicrous	slowly	gradually, step by step	**T**		
rival	competitor	smart	bright, clever; fashionable	to take part	to participate	
rivalry	competition			talent	gift	
rough	harsh	smell	odour	to talk	to speak	
round	circular	to snatch	to grab	to talk about	to discuss	
to rub out	to erase	some	several, a number of	target	aim, goal	
rubbish	nonsense			task	job, duty	
rude	impolite	to be sorry	to regret, to apologise	tasty	delicious	
ruthless	cruel, harsh			to teach	to instruct	
		I'm sorry (that)	I'm afraid (that)	teacher	instructor, trainer	
		sort	kind, type			
		special	particular	to tend to	to be inclined to	
		specialist	expert			
S		spectacles	glasses	tender	gentle, delicate	
sacred	holy	in spite of	despite	terrible	dreadful, awful	
sailor	seaman	splendid	magnificent	thankful	grateful, obliged	
savage	wild	can't stand	can't bear			
to save	to rescue	to start	to begin	thick	dense	
scarcely	hardly	to stay	to remain	thorough	efficient	
scared	frightened, afraid	steady	constant, continuous	though	although, even though	
schedule	plan, timetable					
scheme	plan, project	step by step	slowly, gradually	thought	idea	
schoolboy	pupil			thoughtful	kind, considerate	
schoolgirl	pupil	stewardess	air-hostess			
sea journey	voyage	to stop	to finish, to end, to quit	tidy	clean, orderly	
seaman	sailor			time	era, period, epoch	
to search for	to look for	to stop (from)	to prevent (from)			
secure	safe			tired	weary	
to seek	to look for	strange	unusual, curious, odd	to tolerate	to put up with	
to seem	to appear			tomb	grave	
segregation	separation	to strike	to hit, to beat	too	also, as well	
to seize	to grasp, to grab	strong	vigorous, powerful	topic	subject	
				Tory	Conservative	
seldom	rarely	(to) struggle	(to) fight	traditional	conventional	
to select	to choose, to pick out	stupid	foolish	trainer	instructor, coach	
		to succeed in	to manage to			

Synonyms

tremendous	enormous, immense, huge; marvellous	usual	ordinary, common, normal, average	weary	tired
				to weep	to cry
				well-known	famous
trip	journey, excursion, outing	usually	normally, generally, as a rule	well-to-do	rich, wealthy
				whereas	while
true	correct; loyal, faithful			whether	if
				while	as; whereas
trust	faith, confidence	**V**		whole	complete, total, entire
(to) try	(to) attempt	vacant	empty, unoccupied	wide	broad
tune	melody			wild	fierce
twelve	a dozen	in vain	unsuccessfully	wish	desire
		valuable	precious	to withdraw	to retire, to pull out
U		to vanish	to disappear		
		various	different, several	wonderful	beautiful, marvellous
unable	incapable				
unavoidable	inevitable	vast	immense, huge	to work together	to co-operate
under(neath)	below	vigorous	energetic, strong		
to understand	to grasp, to comprehend			works	plant, factory
		violent	fierce	worried	anxious
unemployed	jobless	to visit	to call on	wrong	incorrect, false
to unite	to join (together)	visitor	guest, caller		
		vital	essential, necessary	**Y**	
unless	if not				
unpleasant	nasty	voyage	sea journey	yearly	annual
unusual	odd, strange				
used	second-hand, old	**W**		**Z**	
used to	accustomed to	way	method, means		
useful	helpful, valuable	weak	feeble, faint	zone	area, district
		wealthy	rich, well-to-do		

OPPOSITES

A

able	unable, incapable
above	below
absence	presence
absent	present
abstract	concrete
to accelerate	to slow down, to brake
to accept	to refuse
acceptance	refusal
accurate	inaccurate
to add	to subtract
to admit	to deny
adult	child
advantage	disadvantage
afraid	brave
after	before
against	for, in favour of
(old) age	youth
to agree	to disagree
agreeable	unpleasant
agreement	disagreement
ahead	behind
alike	different
alive	dead
all	nothing
to allow	to forbid
ally	enemy
already	not yet
always	never
amateur	professional
ancestor	descendant
anti-	pro-
apart	together
to appear	to disappear
appearance	disappearance
approval	disapproval
to approve	to reject
approximate(ly)	exact(ly)
arrival	departure
to arrive	to leave, to depart, to go away
artificial	natural
asleep	awake
to fall asleep	to wake (up)
to assemble	to take apart
at least	at most
to attack	to defend
awake	asleep
away from	toward(s)

B

bad	good
worse	better
worst	best
badly	well
bad luck	good luck
back	front
backward(s)	forward(s)
bare	covered
beautiful	ugly, plain
before	after
to behave	to misbehave
to begin	to end, to finish
beginning	end, finish
belief	disbelief
to believe	to doubt
below	above
best	worst
better	worse
big	small
birth	death
black	white
blunt	sharp
to boil	to freeze
boiling point	freezing point
bold	timid, shy
boring	dull, uninteresting
to be born	to die
bottom	top
to brake	to accelerate
brief	long
bright	dull, dark; stupid
broad	narrow
to buy	to sell

C

calm	nervous, upset
capable	incapable, unable
to capture	to escape
careful	careless
centre	edge
cheap	dear, expensive
chief	minor, unimportant
child	adult
chilly	warm
civilian	military
clean	dirty
clever	stupid
cold	hot
cold	heat
to collect	to distribute
to come	to go, to leave
common	rare, unusual
complete	incomplete
completely	partly, partially
complicated	simple
concrete	abstract
to connect	to disconnect, to cut off
cons	pros
consumer	producer
to continue	to discontinue, to stop
convenience	inconvenience
convenient	inconvenient
cooked	raw
cool	warm
crazy	sane, normal

D

damp	dry
dark	bright, light
darkness	light
dawn	dusk
day	night
dead	alive, live, living
death	birth, life
decent	indecent
deep	shallow
defeat	victory
to defend	to attack
demand	supply
to depart	to arrive, to come
dependence	independence
dependent	independent
descendant	ancestor
(to) despair	(to) hope
to die	to be born, to live
dirty	clean
to discourage	to encourage
(to) dislike	(to) like
to dismantle	to assemble
to dismiss	to appoint
distant	near(by)
to distribute	to collect
to divide	to multiply, to unite
domestic	international
down	up
downstairs	upstairs

Opposites

to dress	to undress
to drop	to lift, to raise
drunk	sober
dry	wet, damp
dull	interesting; bright
dusk	dawn

E

earlier	later
early	late
easy	difficult
economical	wasteful
edge	centre, middle
efficiency	inefficiency
efficient	inefficient
efficiency	inefficiency
emigration	immigration
employee	employer
empty	full
to empty	to fill
to encourage	to discourage
to end	to begin, to start
enemy	friend, ally
enormous	tiny
to enter	to go out, to leave
entirely	partly, partially
entrance	exit, way out
equal	unequal, different
equality	inequality
to escape	to capture
essential	inessential, superfluous, unnecessary
even	uneven
evening	morning
everybody	nobody
everything	nothing
everywhere	nowhere
evil	good
exact	inexact, inaccurate
excellent	poor, bad
except	including
to exclude	to include
exit	entrance, way in
expensive	cheap, inexpensive
(to) export	(to) import
to extinguish	to light
extraordinary	ordinary, normal

F

fact	fiction
to fail	to succeed; to pass
failure	success
to fall	to rise
to fall asleep	to wake (up)
false	true, genuine
famous	unknown
far away	near, close
fast	slow
fat	thin; lean
female	male
fertile	sterile, barren, infertile
fewer	more
fiction	fact
fierce	gentle
to fill	to empty
final	initial, first
to find	to lose
to finish	to begin, to start
firm	loose
first	last, final
flat	hilly; sharp (music)
to float	to sink
foolish	wise, clever
for	against
to forbid	to allow, to permit
to forget	to remember
(the) former	(the) latter
forward(s)	backward(s)
to freeze	to boil
freezing point	boiling point
frequent	infrequent, rare
frequently	rarely, seldom
friend	enemy
friendly	hostile, unfriendly
front	back
full	empty
funny	serious

G

to gain	to lose
gain	loss
generosity	meanness
generous	mean
gentle	rough, fierce
genuine	false
to get on (in)	to get off (out)
to get up	to go to bed
to give	to take
gloomy	bright
to go	to come
to go out	to come in, to enter
good	bad
good luck	bad luck
gorgeous	ugly, horrible
Government	Opposition
gradual	sudden
grateful	ungrateful
gratitude	ingratitude
guest	host
guilt	innocence
guilty	innocent

H

handsome	ugly, plain
happy	unhappy, sad
hard	soft
hardware	software
harsh	gentle
hate(=hatred)	love
to hate	to love
health	sickness
heat	cold
heaven	hell
heavy	light
hell	heaven
to hide	to show, to reveal
high	low
hilly	flat
honest(y)	dishonest(y)
honour	disgrace, shame
(to) hope	(to) despair
hopeful	hopeless
horizontal	vertical
horrible	lovely, beautiful
host	guest
hostile	friendly
hot	cold
huge	tiny
human	inhuman
humble	proud, arrogant
humorous	serious

I

to ignore	to pay attention to
ill	well
imaginary	real
immense	tiny

Opposites

immigration	emigration	to live	to die	**N**	
(to) import	(to) export	long	short, brief	narrow	broad
important	unimportant, insignificant	to look after	to neglect	nasty	nice, pleasant
to include	to exclude	loose	tight, firm	national	international, world-wide
including	excluding	to lose	to win, to gain	natural	unnatural, artificial
to increase	to decrease, to reduce	loss	profit	near	far (away)
increase	decrease, reduction	loud	quiet, soft, silent	necessary	unnecessary, superfluous
indoor	outdoor, open-air	(to) love	(to) hate	need not	must
industrious	lazy	low	high	negative	positive
inferior	superior	to lower	to raise, to lift	to neglect	to take care of, to look after
initial	final, last	lower	upper	nervous	calm
innocence	guilt			never	always
innocent	guilty			new	old; used, secondhand
intelligent	stupid	**M**		night	day
interesting	uninteresting, dull, boring	mad	sane, normal	nobody	everybody, somebody
international	national, domestic	main	minor	noise	silence
into	out of	major	minor, unimportant	noisy	quiet, silent
		majority	minority	non-smoker	smoker
		male	female	noon	midnight
		man-made	natural	normal	abnormal, unusual
J		manual	mental	not yet	already
to join	to separate, to leave	many	few	nothing	everything; something
joy	misery	masculine	feminine	nowhere	everywhere; somewhere
joyful	miserable, sad	maximum	minimum	numerous	few, not many
just	unjust	mean	generous		
justice	injustice	meanness	generosity	**O**	
		mental	manual, physical	obedience	disobedience
		merry	sad	to obey	to disobey
L		mess	order	obvious	obscure
large	small	messy	tidy	occupied	vacant, free
last	first, initial	midday	midnight	often	rarely, seldom
later	earlier, sooner	middle	edge	old	young; new
(the) latter	(the) former	midnight	midday, noon	old age	youth
lazy	hardworking, industrious	mild	severe	old-fashioned	modern, up-to-date
lean	fat	military	civilian	to open	to close
to leave	to arrive, to come	minimum	maximum	open-air	indoor
left	right	minor	major, significant, important	optimist(ic)	pessimist(ic)
legal	illegal	minority	majority	oral	written
to lend	to borrow	miserable	happy, joyful	order	mess
life	death	misery	happiness, joy	ordinary	unusual, strange
to lift	to drop, to lower	modern	old-fashioned, out-of-date	out of	into
light	dark; heavy	modest	immodest, arrogant	out-of-date	up-to-date, modern
(to) like	(to) dislike	moist	dry	outdoor	indoor
like	unlike	much	little	over	under
little	much, a lot	more	less		
less	more	most	least		
least	most	to multiply	to divide		
		must	need not		

Opposites

P

part	whole
partly	completely, wholly, entirely, totally
(to) pass	(to) fail
patience	impatience
patient	impatient
to pay attention to	to ignore
peace	war
to permit	to forbid
pessimist(ic)	optimist(ic)
physical	mental, spiritual
pleasant	unpleasant, nasty
polite(ness)	impolite(ness), rude(ness)
poor	rich, wealthy; excellent
positive	negative
possible	impossible
post-	pre-
post-war	pre-war
poverty	wealth
powerful	powerless
practice	theory
precious	worthless
precise	vague, inexact
predecessor	successor
presence	absence
present	absent
pre-	post-
pre-war	post-war
private	public
pro-	anti-
pros	cons
probable	improbable, unlikely
producer	consumer
professional	amateur
profit	loss
proud	humble, modest
public	private
to pull	to push
pure	impure, dirty
to push	to pull
to put on (clothes)	to take off
to put on (light)	to switch off, to put out

Q

quick	slow
quiet	loud, noisy

R

to raise	to lower
rapid	slow
rare	common, frequent
rarely	often, frequently
raw	cooked
ready	unprepared
real	imaginary
to reduce	to increase
to refuse	to accept
regular	irregular
to remember	to forget
responsibility	irresponsibility
responsible	irresponsible
responsibility	irresponsibility
retail	wholesale
to reveal	to conceal, to hide
rich	poor
right	left; wrong
to rise	to fall
rough	smooth; gentle
round	square

S

sad	happy, joyful, merry
safe	dangerous
sane	mad, crazy
second-hand	new
seldom	often, frequently
to sell	to buy
sensible	silly
to separate	to join
serious	funny, humorous
severe	mild
shallow	deep
sharp	blunt, flat (music)
short	long; tall
to shorten	to extend, to lengthen
to shout	to whisper
to show	to hide, to conceal
sick	well
sickness	health
silence	noise
silly	sensible
similar	dissimilar, unlike
simple	complicated
to sink	to float
slow	fast, rapid
to slow down	to accelerate
small	big, large
smoker	non-smoker
smooth	rough
sober	drunk
soft	hard
software	hardware
somebody	nobody
something	nothing
sometimes	never; always
somewhere	nowhere
sooner	later
sour	sweet
spring	autumn
square	round
to start	to finish
straight	bent, crooked
strength	weakness
strict	lenient
strong	weak
stupid	clever, intelligent
to subtract	to add
to succeed	to fail
success	failure
successor	predecessor
sudden	gradual, slow
summer	winter
sunrise	sunset
superfluous	essential, vital, necessary
superior	inferior
supply	demand
sweet	sour, bitter
swift	slow
to switch on	to switch off (out)

T

tactful	tactless
to take	to give
to take off (plane)	to land, to touch down
to take care of	to neglect
tame	wild
theory	practice
thin	thick, fat
tight	loose
timid	bold
tiny	huge, enormous, immense
together	apart

Opposites

tolerance	intolerance			well	badly; ill, sick
tolerant	intolerant	**V**		well-known	unknown
top	bottom	vacant	occupied	wet	dry
totally	partly, partially	vague	precise, exact	to whisper	to shout
tough	gentle; tender; weak	valid	invalid	white	black
		valuable	worthless	whole	part
toward(s)	away from	vertical	horizontal	wholly	partly, partially
true	false	victory	defeat	wholesale	retail
(to) trust	(to) distrust	violence	non-violence	wholesaler	retailer
		violent	non-violent, peaceful	wide	narrow
				wild	tame
U		visible	invisible	willing	unwilling
ugly	beautiful, handsome	vital	unnecessary, superfluous	to win	to lose
				win	defeat
under	over	voiced	unvoiced	winter	summer
to understand	to misunderstand			wise	foolish, silly
				with	without
understanding	misunderstanding	**W**		worse	better
				worst	best
unknown	well-known, famous	to wake up	to fall asleep	worthless	valuable
		warm	cool, chilly	written	oral
unlike	similar, like	to waste	to use	wrong	right
up	down	wasteful	economical		
upper	lower	way in	way out, exit		
upset	calm	way out	way in, entrance		
upstairs	downstairs			**Y**	
up-to-date	out-of-date, old-fashioned	weak	strong		
		weakness	strength	yes	no
to use	to waste	wealth	poverty	young	old
used	new	wealthy	poor	youth	(old) age
useful	useless				

121

PREFIXES AND SUFFIXES

Prefixes

anti-	against	anti-war, antisocial
bi-	two, twice	bi-monthly, bilingual
by-	secondary	by-product, by-election
co-	together	co-pilot, co-operate
dis-	not	dislike, disagree
en-	to give	encourage, enforce
ex-	out, from	export, excluding
	former	ex-consul, ex-chancellor
fore-	before	foreword, forecast
il-	not	illegal, illogical
im-	not	impolite, impossible
in-	not	indiscreet, indecent
ir-	not	irregular, irresponsible
inter-	between	international, Inter-City
micro-	small	microscope, microelectronics
mid-	middle	mid-winter, mid-August
mis-	wrong, bad	mistake, misunderstand
multi-	many	multi-national
neo-	new, again	neo-classical
non-	not	non-swimmer, nonstop
out-	out	outbreak, outsider
	to do better	outdo, outgrow
over-	above, too much	over-ambitious, overdo
post-	after	post-war, postpone
pre-	before	pre-war, prepare
pro-	for	pro-government, pro-EEC
re-	again, new	return, re-establish
self-	without help	self-service, self-opening
	on one's own	self-control, self-respect
semi-	half	semi-final, semi-detached
sub-	under	sub-teenage, sub-standard
super-	above, big	superpower, supervise
trans-	across	transatlantic, translate
un-	not	untrue, unsuccessful
under-	not enough	underestimate, underdeveloped
up-	on, up	uphill, upstairs
vice-	second in rank	vice-consul, vice-chancellor

Suffixes

NOUNS

-al	survival	-ator	dictator	-eer	engineer	-ity	reality
-an	electrician	-asion	invasion	-ence	difference	-let	leaflet
-ance	assistance	-burger	beefburger	-er	teacher	-ment	government
-ant	assistant	-cy	accuracy	-ery	snobbery	-ness	fairness
-ar	burglar	-dom	freedom	-ess	hostess	-off	kick-off
-ation	dictation	-ee	refugee	-hood	childhood	-or	sailor
				-ics	electronics	-ship	friendship
				-in	sit-in	-ision	television
				-ing	painting	-ition	recognition
				-ism	realism	-ure	failure
				-ist	realist		

ADJECTIVES

-able	bookable		-ical	critical
-al	personal		-ing	fascinating
-an	American		-ish	sevenish
-ant	tolerant		-ist	socialist
-ary	necessary		-ive	active
-ate	passionate		-less	careless
-ative	conservative		-like	childlike
-ed	pointed		-most	southernmost
-en	wooden		-ory	obligatory
-ent	different		-ous	famous
-ese	Japanese		-some	troublesome
-fold	threefold		-ward(s)	backward(s)
-ful	peaceful		-wise	money-wise
-ible	responsible		-y	sunny
-ic	dramatic			

VERBS

-ate	to separate		-ise	to organise
-en	to widen		-ize	to organize
-ify	to simplify		-ish	to astonish

GRAMMATICAL ENDINGS

-ed	(past tense)	asked, answered, stopped
	(past participle)	(have/had/is) asked
-er	(comparative)	greater, bigger, easier
-es	(plural)	dresses, watches, flies
	(third person)	(he/she/it) rushes, tries
-est	(superlative)	greatest, biggest, easiest
-ing	(present participle)	going, having, running
	(continuous form)	it is raining
	(gerund)	it has stopped raining
	(participle construction)	the man standing there
-ly	(adverb)	quickly, simply, happily
-s	(plural)	books, pupils, days
	(third person)	(he/she/it) works, plays

LIST OF "A" WORDS

a, an
able
to be able to
about
to be about to
how about …?
what about …?
above
above all
abroad
absent
to be absent
to accept
accident
to accompany
ache, to ache
acquaintance
across
to act
action
actor, actress
actually
to add
address
to admire
to admit
advantage
adventure
to advise
aeroplane, plane
to afford
to be afraid
after
after all
after that
afterwards
afternoon
again
again and again
against
age
agency
agent
ago
to agree
to agree to
to agree with
aim
air
open-air
in the open air
airline
airmail
airport
alarm clock, alarm
alive
all
all day
all right
to allow
to be allowed to
almost
alone
along
already
also
although
always
a. m.
America, American
ambulance

among
amount
to amount to
to amuse
and
and so on
angry
animal
another
one another
answer
to answer
any
not any
anybody, anyone
anything
anyway
anywhere
apart
apart from
apartment
to apologise (for)
to appear
apple
to apply for
to apply to
appointment
April
area
to argue
arm, armed, arms
armchair
around
to arrange
to arrest
to arrive
arrival
art
artist
as
as … as
as far as
as if, as though
as soon as
as well
as well as
to ask
to ask a question
to ask for
to ask the way
to be asleep
to fall asleep
assistant
to astonish
astonishing
astonished
astronaut
at
at the door
at the cinema
at three o'clock
at all, not at all
at first, at last
at least
at once
at the moment
atom
atomic
attack
to attack
to attend

to attend school
attention
to pay attention
attractive
August
aunt
Australia
Australian
Austria
Austrian
automatic
autumn
to avoid
to be awake
away
to go away
away from home
awful
awfully nice

baby
back
to come back
the back seat
background
backward, backwards
bacon
bad, worse, worst
bag
a paper bag
a leather bag
to bake
baker
at the baker's
ball
banana
band
bank
the left bank
bank note
bar
to bark
basket
bath, bathroom
to have a bath
bathing suit
Bavaria
Bavarian
to be
to be to
beach
bean
beard
beat; to beat
beautiful
because
because of
to become
bed
bedroom
beef
beer
before
I beg your pardon?
to begin
beginning
to behave
behind
to believe (in)

bell
to belong (to)
below
belt
beside
besides
better, best
had better
between
bicycle, bike
big
bill
biology
bird
birthday
a bit
a little bit
to bite
black
blackboard
blind
blouse
to blow
blue
board, on board
boat
body
to boil
book, to book
booking office
boot(s)
boring
to be born
to borrow
both
both … and
to bother
bottle
bottom
at the bottom of
box
to box
boy
brake, to brake
branch
bread
break
to break
breakdown
to break down
breakfast
to have breakfast
bridge
briefcase
to bring
Britain
British
broad
brother
brown
brush, to brush
to build
building
to burn
bus
to go by bus
bus stop
business
businessman
busy
to be busy

but
butcher
at the butcher's
butter
button
to buy
by
by the window
by car, by air
by Sunday
by listening
bye, bye-bye

café
cake
calculator
call
to call
to be called …
calm
camera
camp, camp site
to go camping
can, could
to cancel
cap
capital (city)
car
car park
card
care
to care
to care for
to take care (of)
careful
careless
career
carpet
to carry
to carry on
to carry on doing
case
in case
in this case
cassette
cassette recorder
castle
cat
to catch
to catch a cold
to catch a train
cathedral
cattle
ceiling
to celebrate
cellar
cent
central
centre
century
certain, certainly
certificate
chair
chance
by chance
change
to change
to charge
charming
to chat

cheap
to cheat
to check
to check in
cheerio
cheers
cheese
chemist
at the chemist's
cheque
cherry
chicken
child, children
chips
chocolate(s)
to choose
Christian name
Christmas
church
at church, to church
cigar, cigarette
cinema
city
class
classroom
clean
to clean
clear
to clear
clerk
clever
climate
to climb
clock, … o'clock
to close
close (to, by)
clothes
cloud
club
coach
coast
coat
coffee
cold
a cold
to collect
collection
colony
colour
what colour is …?
comb, to comb
to come
to come along
to come and see
comfortable
common
to compare
compartment
to complain (about)
complete, completely
computer
concerning
concert
condition
to congratulate
congratulations!
to conquer
conservative
Conservative Party
to consist of
contact, to contact

to contain	delighted	duck	every	it's my fault	four
continent	democracy	due to	everybody	favourite (subject)	fourteen
continental	democratic	dull	everyone	February	forty
to continue	dentist	during	every one of	to feel	France
to continue to do	at the dentist's	duty	everything	feeling	free
control, to control	department		everywhere	fence	to free
to convince	department store		exact	ferry	freedom
cook, to cook	to depend (on)	each	exactly	to fetch	to freeze
cool, to cool	that depends	each of	exam	few	French
corner	to describe	each other	examination	a few	fresh
correct	design	ear	to examine	quite a few	Friday
to correct	to design	early	example	field	fridge
to cost	desk	to earn	for example	five	friend
cough, to cough	dessert	earth	excellent	fifteen	friendly
to count	to destroy	east	except	fifty	friendship
country	detective	eastern	except that	fight, to fight	from
course	to develop	Easter	exception	to fill	front
of course	diary	easy	excited	filling station	in front of
cousin	dictionary	to eat	to get excited	film	frontier
to cover	to die	to educate	exciting	to film	fruit
cow	difference	education	excuse	final	fruit juice
crash	different (from)	effect	to excuse	finally	to fry
to crash	difficult	egg	excuse me	to find	full
crazy	difficulty	eight	exercise	to find out	fun
cream	to dig	eighteen	to exist	fine	it's fun
crew	dining-room	eighty	to expect	finger	funny
criminal	dinner	either	to expect sb to	to finish	furniture
cross, to cross	direction	not … either	expensive	fire	further
crossroads	dirt	either … or	experience	fireplace	future
crowd	dirty	elder, eldest	expert	firm	in future
crowded	disadvantage	to elect	to explain	a firm	
crown	to disagree	election	explanation	first	
to crown	to disappoint	electric(al)	to explore	first of all	to gain
to cry	disco, discotheque	electricity	export	at first	gallery
cup	to discover	elegant	to export	first name	game
a cup of …	to discuss	eleven	express	fish	garage
cupboard	discussion	… else	express train	fit	garden
curtain	dish, dishes	or else	by express post	to fit	gardener
customer	to dislike	what else?	to express	flat	gardening
customs	district	who else?	extra	a flat	gas
cut, to cut	to disturb	elsewhere	extreme	flight	gate
cycle	to dive	to employ	extremely	floor	general
to cycle	to divide	employee	eye	first floor	a general
	to do	employer		flour	gentle
	to do one's best	employment		to flow	gentleman
dad	to do well	empty	face	flower	geography
daily	doctor	end, to end	fact	flu	German
damage	dog	in the end	as a matter of fact	fluent	Germany
to damage	doll	engaged	in fact	fluently	to get
dance	dollar	engine	factory	to fly	to get in
to dance	door	engineer	to fail	a fly	to get out
danger	double	England	fair	fog	to get on
dangerous	doubt	English	fall	foggy	to get off
dark	to doubt	to be English	to fall	to follow	to get away
darling	no doubt	to enjoy	false	fond	to get up
date	down	to enjoy oneself	family	to be fond of	to get used to
daughter	downstairs	enjoyable	family name	food	to get on with
day	dozen	enough	famous	foot	to get to know
dead	drama	to enter	fantastic	football	girl
to deal in	to draw	entrance	far	football ground	girlfriend
to deal with	drawing	to entertain	far away	for	to give
dear	dream	entire	as far as	to forbid	to give back
death	to dream	entirely	so far	force	to give in
December	dress	envelope	fare	to force	to give up
to decide	to dress	equal	farm	to be forced to	glad
to declare	drink	escape, to escape	farmer	foreign	to be glad
deep	to drink	especially	farmhouse	foreigner	glass
definite	to drive	even	farming	forest	a pair of glasses
definitely	driver	not even	fashion	to forget	glove
definition	driving licence	even so	fast	to forgive	to go
degree	to drop	even though	to work fast	fork	to go ahead
delay	drug	evening	fat	form	to go away
to delay	dry, to dry	ever	father	to form	to go on
delicious	to dry up	ever since	fault	fortunately	to go by (bus)

to go for a walk	to have got to	I	keen	life	to manage
to be going to	to have a look	ice	to be keen to	way of life	manager
goal	to have lunch	ice cream	to be keen on	lift	many
goalkeeper	to have … done	ice skating	to keep	to lift	many a
God	had better	icy	key	to give a lift	map
gold	he	idea	to kill	light	March
golf	head	ideal	kilo	a light	market
good	headmaster	if	kind	to light	Common Market
goodbye	head teacher	as if	a kind of	lightning	marmalade
to govern	health	ill	king	like	marriage
government	healthy	to imagine	kiss	to like	to marry
grammar	to hear	immediately	to kiss	what's it like?	to get married
grammar school	heart	import	kitchen	line	marvellous
grandchild	by heart	to import	knee	lip	master
grandfather	heat	important	knife	list	match
grandmother	heating	impossible	to knock	to listen	material
grandparents	heavy	to improve	to know	to listen to	mathematics
grapefruit	height	in	knowledge	little	(maths)
grapes	hello	income		a little	matter
grass	help	incorrect		live	what's the matter?
grateful	to help	indeed	laboratory	to live	it doesn't matter
great	to help oneself (to)	independent	Labour Party	to earn one's living	no matter what
Great Britain	her, herself	independence	lady	living-room	May
greatly	here	industry	lake	lock	may (do it)
green	to hesitate	industrial	lamb	to lock	maybe
greengrocer	hi	to inform	lamp	long	me, myself
to greet	high	information	land	no longer	meal
grey	highly	information office	to land	so long!	to mean
grocer	hill	to injure	landlady	look	meaning
ground	hilly	inner	landlord	to look	a means of
ground-floor	him, himself	insect	language	to look at	by means of
group	to hire	inside	large	to have a look at	in the meantime
to grow	his	to insist	largely	to look after	meanwhile
to grow up	history	to insist on	last	to look for	meat
grown-up	to hit	for instance	at last	to look forward to	to meet
to guess	a hit	instead of	last name	to look like	meeting
guest	to hitchhike	intelligent	last night	to look up	member
guest-house	hobby	intelligence	late	lorry	to mention
to guide	to hold	to intend	to be late	to lose	don't mention it
a guide	holiday	interesting	lately	to lose one's way	menu
guilty	on holiday	interested	later (on)	to get lost	message
guitar	holidays	international	latest	lost property (office)	to take a message
gun	home	to interrupt	the latest news	a lot of	to leave a message
	homework	interview	to laugh	lots of	metal
	at home	to interview	to laugh at/about	loud	metre
habit	honest	into	lavatory	lounge	mid-
hair	honestly	to introduce	law	love	(mid-July)
hairdresser	honey	introduction	lawn	to love	middle
half	hope, to hope	to invent	to lay	to be in love	in the middle of
half, halves	horse	to invite	lazy	to fall in love	might (do it)
half a dozen	hospital	invitation	to lead	lovely	mild
half past two	host, hostess	inwards	leaf, leaves	low	mile
halfway	host family	iron	to learn	luck	milk
hall	hostel	to iron	least	good luck	million
hallo	hot	island	at least	bad luck	mind
ham	hotel	it, its, itself	leather	lucky	to bear in mind
hand	hour		to leave	to be lucky	to change one's mind
to hand	house		left	luggage	to make up one's
handbag	House of Commons	jacket	on the left	lunch	mind
handicapped	House of Lords	jam	leg	to have lunch	to mind
handsome	how	January	lemon		do you mind?
to hang	how are you?	jeans	to lend		I don't mind
to happen	how do you do	job	less	machine	never mind!
to happen to	how about?	to join	less than	mad	my, mine
happy	however	joke	less and less	madam	minus
harbour	humour	to joke	lesson	magazine	minute
hard	hundred	journalist	lessons	mail	mirror
to work hard	hungry	journey	to let	main	Miss
hardly	to be hungry	juice	letter	mainly	to miss
hat	hurry	July	letter-box	to make	to be missing
to hate	in a hurry	to jump	library	to make sure	mistake
to have	to hurry (up)	June	licence	make-up	to mix
to have to	to hurt	just	to lie	man	to mix up
to have got	husband		to lie down	a man, men	model

modern
moment
at the moment
Monday
money
month
monthly
moon
more
more and more
more or less
no more
once more
more than
more famous than
morning
in the morning
this morning
most
most people
most of all
the most famous of
mother
mother tongue
motor
motorbike
motorcycle
motorcar
motorway
mountain
mouse, mice
mouth
to move
movie
Mr, Mrs, Ms
much, not much
how much?
how much is it?
much more
as much as
mum, mummy
museum
music
musical instrument
a musical
must
must not
mutton
my, mine
myself
by myself
all by myself

nail
to nail
name
named
namely
narrow
nation
national
nationality
native
native language
native speaker
nature
near
near London
nearly
necessary
not necessarily
neck
to need

need, need not
negative
Negro, Negroes
neighbour
neighbourhood
neither (of them)
neither ... nor
nephew
nervous
never
never mind!
nevertheless
new
New Year's Day
the news
here is the news
newsagent
at the newsagent's
newspaper, paper
next
next to
nice
niece
night
last night
at night
all night
good-night
nine, ninth
nineteen
ninety
no
no more
no longer
no less
nobody, no-one
noise
noisy
none
none of them
nonsense
nor, neither
nor am I
normal
normally
north
northern
nose
not
not at all
not in the least
not yet
not even
not only
not ... either
not until
notice
to notice
nothing
novel
November
now
nowadays
just now
from now on
nowhere
number
a number of
nurse
nut

object
to be obliged to
obvious
obviously
ocean
o'clock
occupation
October
of
some of you
a cup of tea
made of wood
of course
off
off the table
to offend
to offer
an offer
office
officer
often
oil
okay, O. K.
that's okay
old
old-fashioned
omelette, omelet
on, upon
on business
on holiday
on the whole
once
once again
once more
at once
one
one should ...
one another
one day
one by one
oneself
only
open
to open
in the open (air)
open-air concert
opera
operahouse
opinion
in my opinion
opposite
or
or else
orange
order
an order
to order
in order to
to organise
organisation
other
another
others
each other
the other day
otherwise
ought to
ought not to
our, ours
ourselves
out
outside
out of
out-of-date

out of order
over
over here
over there
over twenty
overcrowded
to oversleep
overtime work
to owe
own
my own bike
a bike of my own
on my own
to own
owner

to pack
packet
page
pain
to have pains
paint
to paint
painter
painting
pair
a pair of shoes
a pair of glasses
pale
paper
paragraph
parcel
pardon?
I beg your pardon?
I do beg your pardon
parents
park
to park
parliament
Houses of Parliament
part
to take part
to play a part
part-time
particularly
party
to pass
passenger
passport
past
to go past
five past one
path
patient
a patient
pavement
to pay
to pay for
payment
peace
pear
pedestrian
pen
penfriend
penny, pence
pencil
people
pepper
perfect
performance
perhaps
period
person

personal
to persuade
pet
petrol
petrol station
phone, to phone
phone booth
photo, photograph
physics
piano
to pick up
picnic
picture
in the picture
at the pictures
piece
a piece of bread
pig
pill
pilot
pink
pint
pipe
pipeline
pity
what a pity!
place
to place
to take place
plan, to plan
plane
to go by plane
plant, to plant
plastic
plate
platform
at platform 3
play
to play
player
playground
pleasant
please
to be pleased
pleasure
it's a pleasure
plenty of
plum
p.m.
pocket
pocket money
poem
poet
poetry
point
police
the police are here
policeman
policewoman
police station
polite
political
politics
pollution
poor
pop music
pop group
popular
population
pork
porridge
port
porter
possible

possibility
postcard
postman
post office
to post
poster
to postpone
pot
a pot of tea
potato
pound
a pound note
a pound of sugar
to pour
powder
power
practical
practice
to practise
to prefer
to prepare
present
a present
president
to press
the press
pretty
pretty bad
price
primary school
to print
a print
prison
prisoner
private
prize
probable
probably
problem
to produce
product
production
profession
professional
to profit
a profit
program(me)
to promise, a promise
to pronounce
pronunciation
to protect
to protect from
to protest, protest
proud
proud of
to prove
pub
public
the public
in public
public opinion
to publish
publisher
publication
pudding
to pull
pullover
puncture
to punish
pupil
purse
to push
to give a push
to put

to put on	to report, a report	sauce	to shine	to smell	state
to put off	reporter	saucer	ship	to smell good	statement
to put out	republican	sausage	shirt	to smile, a smile	station
to put up	to require	to save (people)	shock, to shock	to smoke, smoke	to stay, a stay
puzzle	to rescue	to save (money)	to be shocked	snack	steak
pyjamas	to reserve	to say	shoe	snow, to snow	to steal
	responsible	to say hello to	a pair of shoes	so	to steer
	rest	to say goodbye to	to shoot	and so on	steering wheel
quality	restaurant	scarf	shop	so that	step
quantity	result	scene	to go shopping	so as to	steward
to quarrel, a quarrel	as a result	scenery	shop assistant	soap	stewardess
quarter	to return	school	short	a piece of soap	still
quarter to one	his return	schoolbag	a pair of shorts	so-called	still not
queen	return ticket	schoolboy	shorthand	social	stocking
question	reward	schoolgirl	should	social work	a pair of stockings
to ask/put a question	rewarding	science	I should like to	socialist	stomach
to queue, a queue	rice	scissors	should I go?	a socialist	stone
queueing	rich	a pair of scissors	shoulder	sock	to stop
quick	to ride	Scotland	to shout	a pair of socks	a stop
quiet	to ride a bicycle	Scot, Scotsman	to show	sofa	full stop
quite	right	Scottish	a show	soft	storm
quiz	on the right	scout	shower	soldier	story
	to be right	screen	to have a shower	to solve	straight
	ring	sea	to shut	some	straight on
race	to ring (up)	at the seaside	sick	some butter	straight away
radio	to ring back	season	side	some rolls	strange, stranger
railways	to give a ring	seat	side by side	somebody	street
railway station	to rise	to take a seat	to take sides	someone	to strike
rain, to rain	river	a second	sight	something	to go on strike
raincoat	road	the second day	to be in sight	sometimes	stripe, striped
to raise	to roast	second-hand	at first sight	somewhere	the Stars and Stripes
rare, rarely	roast chicken	secondary school	the sights	son	strong
rather	to rob, robber	secret, a secret	to go sightseeing	song	student
I'd rather	rocket	secretary	sign	soon	to study
to reach	a roll	to see	to sign	as soon as	a study
to react	roof	see you later	signal	sorry	stupid
to read	room	to seem	silent, silence	I'm sorry	suburb
reader	single room	seldom	silk	sort	to succeed
reading	double room	self-control	silly	what sort of…?	to succeed in
ready	rose	self-service	silver	sound	success
to get ready	rough	to sell	simple	to sound good	successful
real	roughly 100	semi-	since	soup	such
really	round	a semi-detached	since 1 o'clock	sour	such a
reality	to show round	house	since it is true	south	such as
to realise	a roundabout	to send	to sing, singer	southern	sudden, suddenly
reason	to row	sense	single	souvenir	to suffer
to receive	a row of houses	sense of humour	to be single	space	to suffer from
recent, recently	royal	sentence	a single room	spaceship	sufficient
recipe	to rub	September	a single to Hull	spare time	sugar
to recognise	to rub off	serious	sir	to speak	to suggest
to recommend	rubber	to serve, service	sister	speaker	suggestion
record	rugby	military service	to sit	special	to suit
record player	ruin, to ruin	social service	to sit down	specialist	a suit
to record	rule	to settle	to be situated	spectator	suitcase
red	as a rule	to settle down	situation	to spell	sum
refrigerator	to run	seven	six	spelling	sun, sunny
to refuse	rush hour	seventeen, seventy	sixteen, sixty	to spend	sunshine
to regard as		several	size	to spend money	Sunday
regards (to)		sex	what size is it?	to spend time	super
regular	sad	to shake	ski, to ski	in spite of	supermarket
relatives	safe	to shake hands	to go skiing	to spoil	supper
to relax	a safe	shall, 'll	skin	spoon	to support
religion	to sail, a sail	I shall go	skirt	sport, sports	to suppose
religious	salad	shall I go?	sky	spot	to be supposed to
to rely on	salary	I shan't go	to sleep, sleepy	to spray	sure
reliable	sale	shape	to be asleep	spring	surname
to remain	to be for sale	what shape is it?	to fall asleep	square	to surprise
to remember	the sale(s)	to share	sleeve	stage	a surprise
to remind (of)	salt	sharp	slice	stairs	sweater
rent, to rent	the same	to shave	slim, to slim	stamp	sweet, a sweet
to repair	sand	she	slow	to stand (up)	to swim
to repeat	sandwich	sheep	to slow down	can't stand	swimming pool
repetition	satellite	sheet	small	star	Swiss
to reply, a reply	Saturday	shelf	smart	start, to start	Switzerland

to switch on, off	therefore	the Tower of London	to understand	Wales	on the whole
	these, those	town	underwear	Welsh	whom
	these days	in town	to undress	a Welshman	whose?
table	they	town hall	unfair	to walk, a walk	whose is it?
tablet	thick	toy	unemployed	to go for a walk	a pupil whose
tailor	thief	tradition	unemployment	wall	why?
to take	thin	traditional	unfortunately	wallet	why!
to take away	thing	traffic	unfriendly	to want	wide
to take care	to think	traffic lights	unhappy	I want something	wife, wives
to take off	third, a third	traffic sign	uniform	I want to go	wild
take-off	thirsty	train	united	war	will, 'll
to take up	thirteen	to train	the United Kingdom	wardrobe	I'll go
it takes … to	thirty	training	the United Nations	warm	won't
to take part	this	tram	the United States	to warn	I won't go
a take place	this morning	to translate	university	to wash	to win
to talk, a talk	this time	translation	unless	to wash up	wind, windy
to have a talk	though	transport	unlucky	to watch	to wind
tall	thousand	to transport	to be unlucky	a watch	window
tape	three	to travel	unnecessary	watchmaker	wine
tape recorder	throat	travel agency	unpleasant	water	winter
taste, to taste	through	to treat	until	way	to wish, a wish
tax	to throw	to treat well	unusual	way in, way out	best wishes (to)
taxi	thumb	tree	up	this way, please	with
tea	thunderstorm	trip	up in Scotland	way of life	without
teapot	Thursday	trouble	upon	by the way	without saying it
to have tea	ticket	in trouble	upper	we	wolf, wolves
to teach, teacher	ticket office	to trouble	up to	weak	woman, women
team	tidy	it's no trouble	up-to-date	to wear	to wonder
to tear	to tidy (up)	trousers	upstairs	weather	wonderful
teenager	a tie	a pair of trousers	us	wedding	wood
a teenage girl	till, not till	truck	to use	Wednesday	wool, woollen
telegram	time	true	use	week	word
telephone	all the time	it's true	used to	weekend	work, to work
to telephone	to have a good time	trumpet	I used to play	at the weekend	to be out of work
telephone booth	three times	to trust	to be used to	to weigh	to be at work
telephone box	timetable	truth	I'm used to playing	welcome	worker
telephone call	tin	to try	it's no use	you're welcome	world
telephone number	a tin of soup	to try on	it's no use going	to welcome	to worry
television	to tip, a tip	to try out	useful, useless	well	don't worry
television set	tired	tube	usual, usually	to be well	worse, worst
to tell	to	the tube	as usual	as well	worth
to tell a story	to London	Tuesday		as well as	it's worth it
temperature	to travel	tunnel		west	it's worth going
ten	toast	turkey	valley	western	worthless
tennis	a piece of toast	to turn	van	West Germany	worthwhile
tent	tobacco	to turn down	various	wet	would
terrible	today	to turn on	vase	what?	would like
test, to test	together	to turn off	vast	what day?	would like to
text	toilet	to turn round	veal	what a day!	would rather
textbook	tolerant	to turn up	vegetable	what else?	wrist-watch
the Thames	tomato	whose turn is it?	vegetables	what about …?	to write
than	tomorrow	it's my turn	vehicle	what's it like?	wrong
greater than	tongue	turning	very	what time …?	to be wrong
to thank (for)	tonight	TV, TV set	very much	whatever	
thank you	too	twelve, twelfth	victory	wheat	
thank you very much	too big	twenty, twentieth	video recorder	wheel	yard
thanks	thank you too	twice	view	when?	year
thanks a lot	tooth, teeth	two	a view of	whenever	yellow
many thanks (for)	toothache	type	village	where?	yes
that	toothbrush	to type, typist	violin	whereas	yesterday
I know that	toothpaste	typewriter	to visit, a visit	wherever	the day before yesterday
I know that you …	top	typical	visitor	whether	yet
a school that …	on top of	tyre, tire	voice	which?	not yet
the	at (in) the top of		volleyball	which of …?	you, your, yours
the … the …	total		voluntary	a school which	yourself, yourselves
theatre	totally blind	ugly	to vote, a vote	while	young
their, theirs	to touch	umbrella	voyage	a while	youth
them, themselves	in touch with	unable		whisky	youth hostel
then	tour	uncle		white	
now and then	tourist	under	wage, wages	Whitsun	
every now and then	towards	underground	to wait	who?	
there	towards the end	the Underground	to wait for	a pupil who	zebra crossing
over there	towel	to underline	waiter, waitress	whoever	zoo
there is, there are	tower	underneath	to wake (up)	whole	